What is life?

It is the flash of a firefly in the night.

It is the breath of a buffalo in the wintertime.

It is the little shadow which runs across the grass
and loses itself in the sunset.

—Crowfoot
Siksika (Blackfoot)

ERS OF THE
GHT

Native Stories and
Nocturnal Activities for Children

KEEPERS OF THE NIGHT

Native Stories and
Nocturnal Activities for Children

Michael J. Caduto
and
Joseph Bruchac

Story illustrations by
David Kanietakeron Fadden

Chapter illustrations by
Jo Levasseur and Carol Wood

Foreword by
Dr. Merlin D. Tuttle
Founder and Executive Director, Bat Conservation International

FIFTH
HOUSE
PUBLISHERS

Copyright © 1994 by Michael J. Caduto and Joseph Bruchac
First Canadian Edition

Published simultaneously in the United States by Fulcrum, Inc., Golden, Colorado

Story illustrations © 1994 by David Kanietakeron Fadden
Chapter illustrations © 1994 by Jo Levasseur and Carol Wood

Cover illustration by John Kahionhes Fadden
Cover design and cover illustration colorization by Karen Groves

The publisher gratefully acknowledges the assistance of The Canada Council, Communications Canada, and the Saskatchewan Arts Board.

Printed and bound in the United States of America
94 95 96 97 98 99 / 6 5 4 3 2 1

Canadian Cataloguing-in-Publication Data

Caduto, Michael J.
      Keepers of the night
      ISBN 1–895618–39–8
1. Night – Juvenile literature. 2. Indians of North America – Folklore – Juvenile literature.
3. Natural history – Outdoor books – Juvenile literature.
I. Bruchac, Joseph, 1942–   II. Title.

E98.F6C32   1994   j398.33   C94–920014–X

Fifth House Publishers
620 Duchess Street
Saskatoon, Saskatchewan
S7K OR1

For Our Elders,

who understand that darkness

does not mean we cannot see

Permissions

Permission to reprint the following is gratefully acknowledged:

The map, "Native North America" on pages xiv–xv, showing the culture regions of the Native North American groups discussed in this book, is printed with permission of Michael J. Caduto (© 1994). Cartography by Stacy Miller, Upper Marlboro, Maryland.

The quote from Chief Luther Standing Bear that appears on page xix, and the quote from The Religion of the Luiseño that appears on page 71 are from Peggy V. Beck, Anna Lee Walters and Nia Francisco's *The Sacred: Ways of Knowledge, Sources of Life* (1992) and are reprinted with permission of the Navajo Community College Press, Tsaile, Arizona.

The quote from Charles Alexander Eastman (*Ohiyesa*) that appears on page xix is from Kent Nerburn and Louise Mengelkoch's (eds.) *Native American Wisdom* (1991) and is reprinted with permission of the New World Library, San Rafael, California.

The quote from Chief Irving Powless Sr. that appears on page xix is from Steve Wall and Harvey Arden's *Wisdomkeepers* (1990) and is reprinted with permission of Beyond Words Publishing, Inc., Hillsboro, Oregon. We are also grateful to the Powless family for permission to use this quote.

The quote from Black Elk that appears on page xxi is from John G. Neihardt's *Black Elk Speaks* and is reprinted with permission of the University of Nebraska Press, Lincoln, Nebraska. Copyright 1932, 1959 and 1972 by John G. Neihardt. Copyright © 1961 by the John G. Neihardt Trust.

The quote from the Shawnee Wampum Belt Message that appears on page xxi is from Frances G. Lombardi and Gerald Scott Lombardi's *Circle Without End* (1982) and is reprinted with permission of Naturegraph Publishers, Happy Camp, California.

The poem "Loon on the Cedar River Flow" on page xxii is from Joseph Bruchac's *Tracking* (1986), published by Ion Books, Inc./Raccoon, Memphis, Tennessee, and is reprinted with permission of the author.

The photograph that appears on page 2 is used with permission of Animals Animals/Earth Scenes, © 1994 Richard Alan Wood.

The section called "Teaching Racial Tolerance, Understanding and Appreciation" that appears on page 18 is adapted with permission from material produced by the Institute for American Indian Studies, 38 Curtis Rd., P.O. Box 1260, Washington, Connecticut, 06793.

The illustration on page 23 was adapted from Karl O. Von Frisch's *Biology: The Science of Life,* © 1964 by Bayerischer Schullbuch-Verlag. Reprinted with permission of HarperCollins Publishers, Inc.

The photograph that appears on page 28 by Dr. Merlin D. Tuttle is reprinted with permission of Dr. Merlin D. Tuttle and Bat Conservation International.

The photograph that appears on page 31 by Steven D. Faccio is reprinted with his permission.

The activity "Scents of Attraction" that appears on page 52 is adapted from an activity found in Jenepher Lingelbach and the Vermont Institute of Natural Science's *Hands-On Nature* (1986) and is used with permission of the Vermont Institute of Natural Science, Woodstock, Vermont.

The poem "Primal Voice" by Michael J. Caduto that appears on page 33 is from *Vermont Natural History* (1983), published by the Vermont Institute of Natural Science, Woodstock, Vermont, and is reprinted with permission of the author.

The photograph of the green frog on page 16 by Alan C. Graham is reprinted with his permission.

The photographs on pages 46, 56 and 59 by David H. Funk are reprinted with his permission.

The illustration on page 48 was adapted from Herbert W. Levi and Lorna R. Levi's *Spiders and Their Kin* (A Golden Guide), ©1987 by Western Publishing Co., Inc., Racine, Wisconsin and is used here with permission. Original illustration by Nicholas Strekalovsky.

The illustration on page 53 was adapted from Robert T. Mitchell and Herbert S. Zim's *Butterflies and Moths* (A Golden Guide), © 1964 by Western Publishing Co., Inc., Racine, Wisconsin and is used here with permission. Original illustration by Andre Durenceau.

The illustrations that appear on page 70 are adapted from Anthony F. Aveni's (ed.) *Archeoastronomy in Pre-Columbian America* (© 1975) and are used with permission of Anthony F. Aveni and the University of Texas Press, Austin.

The photograph of the Pleiades star cluster that appears on page 69 and the photograph of the full moon that appears on page 73 are used with permission, © University of California Regents; UCO/Lick Observatory image.

The illustration on page 77 was adapted from Helen Ross Russell's *Ten Minute Field Trips: A Teacher's Guide to Using the School Grounds for Environmental Studies* (1990), published by the National Science Teachers Association, Washington, D.C., and is used with permission of the author.

The illustration on page 84 was adapted from Anthony Smith's *The Seasons* (1970) and is used here with permission of Weidenfeld and Nicolson Pub. Co., Ltd., London.

The photograph on page 123 is used with permission from the National Museum of the American Indian, Smithsonian Institution, photograph number 14557.

The activities and information throughout this book by Michael J. Caduto are reprinted with his permission.

The stories by Joseph Bruchac throughout this book are reprinted with his permission.

The story illustrations by David Kanietakeron Fadden throughout this book are reprinted with his permission.

The illustrations by Carol Wood that accompany the activities and discussion throughout this book are reprinted with her permission.

The scratchboard illustrations by Jo Levasseur throughout this book, © 1994 by Michael J. Caduto, are reprinted with his permission.

The illustration of the hand used in Chapter 1, in the symbols that precede each activity and at the end of the activities in Chapter 6 is a registered trademark of Michael J. Caduto and P.E.A.C.E.®, Programs for Environmental Awareness and Cultural Exchange. ®1993 by Michael J. Caduto.

Contents

Foreword

Children are naturally curious about the night and its nocturnal inhabitants. Capitalizing on this curiosity, *Keepers of the Night* provides an integrated approach to teaching using the mystery and fascination of an unknown world, combined with Native American stories, to stimulate young people to learn valuable life lessons about our natural world. And, in today's frenzied society of music videos, computer games and short attention spans, the challenge for parents and educators to foster creative thinking in their children has never been greater.

Among the many night animals described, it is appropriate for bats to be featured. Children will be captivated by these fascinating and misunderstood winged mammals. And, because bats are integral components of almost every ecosystem in which they occur, they are excellent tools for teaching children about the delicate balance of nature and the interdependence of life on Earth.

Bats are found on all continents except Antarctica. They have adapted to every environment with the exception of the most extreme polar and desert regions. Nearly a thousand kinds of bats comprise almost a quarter of all mammal species. Bats come in an amazing diversity of appearances, sizes and life styles. Over forty species live in the United States and Canada, where they are the major predators of night-flying insects. A single little brown bat, one of North America's most abundant species, is capable of capturing six hundred mosquitoes in one hour! A colony of 20 million free-tailed bats in central Texas can eat 250 tons of insects in a single night.

Throughout the world's tropics, fruit- and nectar-eating bats are vital to the survival of rainforests, which in turn play an essential role in the stability of world climates. In West Africa bats carry up to 98 percent of the seeds of "pioneer" plants that begin the cycle of forest regrowth on cleared land. In the Sonoran Desert of the southwestern United States and Mexico, long-nosed bats play a key role in the lives of several species of agave and columnar cacti, such as the famous organ pipe and saguaro. In turn, countless other animals, birds and insects rely upon these plants for food and shelter.

Despite their importance, bats are among the world's least appreciated and most endangered animals. Like other wildlife, bats suffer from habitat loss and environmental pollution, but the primary cause of their decline is destruction by humans acting out of fear and ignorance. Whole species have been driven to extinction, and many more are now threatened.

Centuries of myth and superstition have given bats an undeservedly bad reputation. In truth, bats are among the most gentle, beneficial and necessary animals on Earth. Because bats are misunderstood and unjustly feared, they are ideal for teaching about prejudice and fear of the unknown. As children learn to appreciate bats, they may be encouraged to question basic assumptions often made about other unpopular animals and even people.

In human cultures, tradition plays an important role in teaching values and responsibilities. Using the natural world as a classroom, *Keepers of the Night* and its strong use of Native American philosophies will serve well to interpret the sights, sounds and smells of the world around us, and it will encourage children to become responsible stewards of all the inhabitants of our planet, including the long misunderstood masters of the night skies.

—Dr. Merlin D. Tuttle
Founder and Executive Director
Bat Conservation International

Acknowledgments

From the authors: We are grateful to the staff at Fulcrum Publishing for their openness to the idea of *Keepers of the Night,* and for the creative energy they put forth to edit, design and produce this book. Many people have contributed their artistic visions to the pages of this book and, in so doing, have afforded us a rare glimpse into the world of night. The story illustrations by David Kanietakeron Fadden and the scratchboard scenes of nature at night by Jo Levasseur that accompany the text can be identified by their respective signatures. Carol Wood's unsigned illustrations can be found throughout the book, particularly in the "Discussion" and "Activities" sections. The photographers are identified in the captions.

Our thanks to the major reviewers who checked the manuscript for content and accuracy: Charles W. Johnson, Vermont State Naturalist; John Moody, Ethnohistorian and Independent Scholar; and Charles E. Roth, Naturalist/Educator. Other accuracy reviewers include the Arizona Sonora Desert Museum in Tucson, Bat Conservation International in Austin, Texas, and Dr. Robert Fesen, Associate Professor of Physics and Astronomy, Dartmouth College. Our appreciation to Dr. Merlin D. Tuttle, Executive Director of Bat Conservation International, for his willingness to compose the Foreword.

Thank you to the following parents, teachers, naturalists, environmental educators and youth leaders who helped by field testing and evaluating the stories, questions, information and activities: Steven Cleaver; Pete Devine, Education Director, Yosemite Institute; Denise Dumouchel and the staff of the Headlands Institute, Sausalito, California; Mary K. Fitzgerald; Laura K. Hathorn, Educator; Lucy Hanouille; Marijean Legnard, School Program Coordinator, Boston University Sargent Camp; Jenepher Lingelbach, Director of ELF (Environmental Learning for the Future) nationwide, Vermont Institute of Natural Science; Hans Manske, Field Instructor, Yosemite Institute; and Melissa Pangraze, Ecology Specialist, Camp Farnsworth, Thetford, Vermont.

From Michael J. Caduto: My gratitude to all who worked so hard to review and field test the manuscript during their own busy schedules. Thanks to the late Hank Gowdey for providing me with a place to sleep under the stars as I worked at the George Parker Woodland in Coventry, Rhode Island, many years ago. And my heartfelt appreciation to The Woman in the Moon, who has inspired me and lifted my spirits on many a night walk.

From Joseph Bruchac: Thanks to my friends in the Native storytelling community, especially Gayle Ross and Jeanette Armstrong.

ARCTIC
OCEAN

BERING
SEA

PACIFIC
OCEAN

WESTERN ALEUT

EASTERN ALEUT

GENERAL CENTRAL YUPIK (ESKIMO)

CENTRAL ALASKAN YUPIK (ESKIMO)

BERING STRAIT INUIT-INUPIAQ (ESKIMO)

KOTZEBUE INUIT-INUPIAQ (ESKIMO)

NORTH ALASKAN INUIT-INUPIAQ (ESKIMO)

NORTHERN INTERIOR INUIT-INUPIAQ (ESKIMO)

Koyukon

Tanaina

Chugach

Ahtna

Tanana

Han

Eyak

Tlingit

Kutchin

Tutchone

Hare

MACKENZIE INUIT (ESKIMO)

COPPER INUIT (ESKIMO)

CENTRAL I

Yellowknife

CARIBOU INUIT (ESKIMO)

Inland Tlingit

Kaska

Tahltan

Sekani

Beaver

Slavey

Dogrib

Chipewyan

S U B A R

Tsimshian

Haida

Bella Coola

Bella Bella

KWAKIUTL

Nootka

Squamish

Lummi

Nisqually

Quileute

Carrier

Chilcotin

Sarcee

Western Woods Cree

PLATEAU

Okanagan (Colville)

Kalispel

Klickitat

Multnomah

Flathead (Salish)

Nez Perce

SIKSIKA (BLACKFOOT)

Plains Cree

Gros Ventre (Atsina)

Assiniboin (Stoney)

PLAINS ANISHINABE

A R C T

Klamath

Modoc

Yurok

Achumawi

Pomo

Yana

Miwok

NORTHERN PAIUTE (PAVIOTSO)

SHOSHONE

BANNOCK

WIND RIVER SHOSHONE

Absaroke (Crow)

Mandan

LAKOTA (SIOUX)

Teton

Northern Cheyenne

DAKOTA (SIOUX)

GREAT

WESTERN SHOSHONE

Gosiute

BASIN

Utes

Ponca

Pawnee

Yankt

Omaha

Oto

Yokuts

Panamint

PAIUTE

Arapaho

Kansa

Chumash

Serrano

LUISEÑO

Ipal

Southern Cheyenne

Walapai

Havasupai

HOPI

ZUNI

Canyon de Chelly

DINE (NAVAJO)

PUEBLO

Jicarilla Apache

Kiowa

Kiowa-Apache

Yavapai

Western Apache

Comanche

Wichita

Chiricahua Apache

Mescalero Apache

PAPAGO

UPPER PIMA

SOUTHWEST

Lipan

PIMA BAJO

AZTEC (NAHUATL)

PACIFIC NORTHWEST

WEST COAST

LEGEND

BOUNDARIES OF CULTURAL AREAS

YUCHI   NATIVE AMERICAN GROUPS DISCUSSED IN BOOK (CAPITAL LETTERS)

Arapaho OTHER NATIVE AMERICAN GROUPS (INCLINED AND LOWER CASE LETTERS)

- - - - NATIONAL BOUNDARIES

······· STATE AND PROVINCIAL BOUNDARIES

CARTOGRAPHY BY STACY MILLER, UPPER MARLBORO, MD.
COPYRIGHT © 1994 MICHAEL J. CADUTO.

SCALE

0   100   200   400 STATUTE
                          MILES

⟶ ◈ NATIVE ◈ ⟶
NORTH AMERICA
◈

BAFFIN
BAY

IGLULIK

DAVIS STRAIT

BAFFINLAND
INUIT (ESKIMO)

(SKIMO)
GLULINGMIUT

C   T   I   C

SATLIRMIUT
(SOUTHAMPTON INUIT)
(ESKIMO)

LABRADOR
SEA

LABRADOR INUIT
(ESKIMO)

HUDSON
BAY

Montagnais

Naskapi

West
Main
Cree

East
Cree

GULF OF
ST. LAWRENCE

ANISHINABE
BWAY or CHIPPEWA)

MICMAC

Algonquin
Nipissing   HAUDENOSAUNEE
(IROQUOIS)

MALISEET
PASSAMAQUODDY

ABENAKI

PENOBSCOT

WABANAKI PEOPLES

ASTERN

MENOMINEE

Huron
(Wyandot)

Potawatomi
Sauk
Neutral
Fox
Kickapoo

MOHAWK

PENNACOOK

Mahican

Massachuset

squakie
Winnebago

ONEIDA
ONONDAGA
CAYUGA
SENECA
TUSCARORA

Erie

Susqu

WAMPANOAG
NARRAGANSETT
Mohegan, Pequot

Munsee

WOOD-

Miami

DELAWARE
(LENNI
LENAPE)

Illinois

SHAWNEE

Nanticoke

LAND

Powhatan

East Coast Algonquians

apaw   Chickasaw

YUCHI   ANI YUNWIYA
(CHEROKEE)

TUSCARORA

Catawba

MUSKOGEE (CREEK)

SOUTHEAST

Choctaw

atchez

LF OF MEXICO

Seminole

Miccosukee

ATLANTIC

OCEAN

Cultural areas and tribal locations of Native North Americans. This map shows tribal locations as they appeared around 1600, except for the Seminole culture in the southeast and the Tuscaroras in the northeast. The Seminoles formed from a group which withdrew from the Muskogee (Creek) and joined with several other groups on the Georgia/Florida border to form the Seminoles, a name which has been used since about 1775. In the eastern woodlands the Haudenosaunee (Iroquois) consist of six nations, the Cayuga, Mohawk, Oneida, Onondaga, Seneca and Tuscarora. The Tuscaroras were admitted to the Iroquois League in 1722 after many refugees from the Tuscarora Wars (1711–1713) in the southeast fled northward. The Wabanaki Peoples include the Abenaki, Maliseet, Micmac, Passamaquoddy, Pennacook and Penobscot. The southern tip of this map shows the northern boundary of the Aztec (Nahuatl), whose traditional range continues well to the south of the map's range.

Where Great Buzzard's wings beat downward, the valleys appeared.
Where his wings beat upward, the hills and mountains rose.

Native North Americans and the World of Night

The Birth of Light

(Yuchi—Southeast)

In the time before light, the world was covered with water. There was darkness everywhere. Only Wind moved across Earth back then.

"Who will make land?" Wind asked.

Then Crayfish came up out of the dark waters of night. "I will make land," Crayfish said.

Crayfish went down below the water and stirred up the mud with his tail. He piled the mud with his claws until land began to appear above the water.

But as Crayfish did this, the Old Ones who were the keepers of the land beneath the water saw what was happening.

"Who is making land appear above the water?" said the Old Ones. They watched and saw it was Crayfish.

"We must stop this," the Old Ones said. But when they came after Crayfish he stirred up the waters with his tail so that the waters were dark with mud and the Old Ones could not find him as he worked.

At last he had done enough. The land rose up above the water.

Then Wind blew over the land, but Wind was not satisfied.

"This land is not dry," Wind said. "Who will dry this land?"

Then Great Buzzard appeared. Great Buzzard flew above the land, fanning the earth and drying it with his wings. Where his wings beat downward, the valleys appeared. Where his wings beat upward, the hills and mountains rose.

Now the land was dry, but there was still darkness everywhere. Everywhere there was night.

"Who will make light appear?" said Wind.

"I will do so," said Star. Then Star shone in the sky, but the light of Star was so weak that it did not go far. More of Star's sisters and brothers appeared in the night sky. But even though they were beyond counting, their light was not enough. It still remained night on the new earth.

"Who will make more light?" Wind asked.

"I will do so," said Moon. Then Moon shone down, but his light was not enough. There was more light on the new earth, but it was still night.

T'cho the Sun spoke then. "I will make enough light for everyone," she said.

Then Sun went to the east and began to shine down upon the earth. As she moved across the sky, daylight came to the world for the first time. Sun tried so hard that some of her sweat fell upon the earth. Where that sweat fell, the first people sprang up. They were the Yuchi, the children of the Sun.

Night is more than a period of time between sunset and sunrise. It is another world—the nearest frontier to our doorstep. When the first stars grow visible overhead the darkness rises up from the valleys, inspiring fear, wonder and awe. As this Yuchi story of "The Birth of Light" reveals, nothing in nature but fire and the light of the stars and moon stands between us and total blackness. Some anthropologists believe it is the use of language or mastery of tools that distinguishes human beings from the animals, but animals can do both of these things. Only people can create and control fire at will—drive back the world of the night.

Perhaps it is because, in this story, people formed from the sweat of T'cho, the sun, that we are at home when she is overhead beaming down on us. Fears of the dark are as old as humankind. Many Native North American stories tell of terrible beasts that roam the night. *Haudenosaunee* (Iroquois) tales speak of a fearsome vampire skeleton and a terrible monster, as tall as a tree, with eyes that blaze like fire pits, razor-sharp teeth and claws like the tips of spears. Tales of people being caught and eaten or escaping by clever trickery animate the time passed around campfires during long, cold winter nights.

It is understandable that such tales arise from darkness. We are often taught to fear what we cannot see and do not understand. Centuries ago, long before the bears, wild cats and other large mammals were wiped out from most of their former ranges, a walk away from the protective circle of light around the campfire was rightfully a time for caution and heightened awareness. While today we may have better cause to fear the beast that walks on two legs rather than four, the reflex is the same when caught unexpectedly in an unfamiliar place at night. Tiny muscles try to raise the fur that we no longer have, producing goose flesh as a shiver runs down our spine.

Owls, bats and many other symbols of the night evoke strong feelings. Nighttime is often associated with death and dying. The soft silent wings of an owl carry it to a roost from which its calls echo in the valley. Among some Native North Americans an owl's call presages the death of someone close. This Kwakiutl belief was a defining theme in Margaret Craven's *I Heard the Owl Call My Name* (New York: Dell, 1973). Among the *Aniyunwiya* (Cherokee) when a person dies his or her spirit travels to the "darkening land." *Lenni Lenape* (Delaware) mourners would traditionally blacken their faces for up to a year. The souls of the dead among the Lenni Lenape travel to the spirit world in the sky, leaving spirit footprints in the form of stars along the *Milky Way*, the "path of the souls." When consoling the relatives of the deceased at the Council Fire near the place of burial, the Haudenosaunee tell the family that a time will come when "the black clouds shall leave and the bright blue sky can be seen once more. They shall be at peace in the sunshine again."[1]

NIGHT AND THE GREAT CIRCLE

For countless generations children have wondered at the vastness overhead, full of questions while peering up at a starry sky. From an early age Native North American children are taught that night is part of the Great Circle. The night sky is a dome that enshrouds Earth and all life upon it.

Lakota children, like all others, asked questions and were answered to the best ability of our elders. We wondered, as do all young, inquisitive minds, about the stars, moon, sky, rainbow, darkness and all other phenomena of nature. I can recall lying on the earth and wondering what it was all about. The stars were a beautiful mystery and so was the place where the eagle went when he soared out of sight. Many of these questions were answered in story form by the older people. How we got our pipestone, where corn came from and why lightning flashed in the sky, were all answered in stories.[2]

—Chief Luther Standing Bear
Oglala Lakota (Sioux)

Children are taught not to fear and avoid the time of darkness. Frequently the night is shared as a time to be close to the Creator.

If the child should chance to be fretful, the mother raises her hand. "Hush! Hush!" she cautions tenderly. "The spirits may be disturbed!" She bids it be still and listen—listen to the silver voice of the aspen, or the clashing cymbals of the birch; and at night she points to the heavenly blazed trail through nature's galaxy of splendor to nature's God.[3]

—Charles Alexander Eastman (Ohiyesa)
Santee Dakota (Sioux)

Each of the roughly 550 cultures of Native North America explains the world of night in a certain way within a particular world view. Everything on the Great Circle has a place and a purpose. All is connected on the Circle in a way that makes sense and has meaning.

The Creator said we will have daylight and we will have darkness. The darkness will be for sleep and rest. But you will also have a night-sun which you will call the moon. The moon will be your Grandmother. And she will have special duties also. She will give moisture to dampen the land at night. She will also move the tides. Along with the moon there will be stars. The stars help give us directions when we travel and, along with Grandmother Moon, tell us when we should begin our ceremonies. The moon and the stars were put there for these purposes. And we see, last night, that the moon and the stars are still here doing their duties. And for this we are very grateful. So, in our appreciation, let us all put our minds together as one and give thanks to the stars and the moon. And let our minds be that way ...[4]

—Chief Irving Powless, Sr.
Onondaga

The world of the night is part of the order of the Great Circle; it is an occasion for ceremonies that give thanks for the gifts of life, as well as a time for continuing the dance of life itself. Among the Haudenosaunee the *Moon Dance* is performed twice in the yearly cycle. This dance expresses gratitude and respect to Grandmother Moon who works with the People and helps with crops. The Moon Dance helps to ensure that life continues through women and serves "to keep everything in order, such as the female life, the plant life, the animal life, the water life and many others."[5]

Lenni Lenape thanksgivings are celebrated with dances that go on well into the night. As

in many Native North American cultures, a Lenni Lenape youth courts in the traditional way by playing love songs on his flute at dusk. He may arise in the middle of the night when sleep eludes him because he cannot get his beloved out of mind. He will walk toward her dwelling, stand outside under the stars and serenade her with flute music that expresses his love and heart's desire.

In traditional Native cultures night is not seen as a time that disturbs the order of things in our lives on the Great Circle; it is considered a crucial part of the balance established by the Creator. *Balance* in Native North American cultures is the root of the harmonious workings of the universe. The dualities all around us—night and day, sun and moon, winter and summer, male and female—complement one another and maintain the natural balance. A person strives to live in balance with himself or herself, with other people, with the natural world and with the land of spirits and ancestors.[6] Health and well-being depend on our conduct in these important relationships in our lives. When someone is living out of balance with one or more of these relationships he or she can be ill. Good and evil, and health and sickness are different ways of referring to states of balance and imbalance, respectively. Healing comes when an individual is restored to balance. The complement of night and day is an essential part of the balance of the universe.

The growing power is rooted in mystery like the night, and reaches lightward. Seeds sprout in the darkness of the ground before they know the summer and the day. In the night of the womb the spirit quickens into flesh.[7]

—Black Elk
Oglala Lakota

I have made a fire out of the dry elm—this fire is for all the different tribes to see by. ...This fire is not to be extinguished so long as time lasts. I shall stick up a stick close by this fire, in order that it may frequently be stirred, and raise a light for the rising generation to see by; if anyone should turn in the dark, you must catch him by the hand, and lead him to the light, so that he can see that he was wrong.[8]

—Wampum Belt Message
Shawnee

To the Shawnee, as to many other Native North American cultures, dreams and visions are an insight into a person's state of balance or imbalance. Those people gifted in the ability to see and understand things in our lives that many people do not perceive are sometimes referred to by nonnatives as "shamans." These far-seeing individuals search for the sacred root of a person's level of balance and use this information to maintain health and well-being and to restore balance when necessary.[9] The word *shaman* is not of Native North American origin. It comes from the word "saman" from the Tungus people of Siberia. Each Native North American culture has its own word for those people who fulfill this important role. Children among the Baffin Island Inuit who are thought to have the gift of far-seeing are called *Tarak'ut inilgit,* "those who have eyes in the dark." Among the Abenaki of the East one word is *Medawlinno* or "scholar."

Through dreams the night becomes a time of revelation. *Dreams* are considered to be an important connection with the spirit world. The Netsilik Inuit believe that dreams help the far-seeing person to discover things within herself or himself that are hidden to others. Dreams are an important window by which the deep wisdom of our selves comes to light in the darkness. In the Haudenosaunee tradition, if a person receives instructions in a dream he or she is encouraged to follow those instructions, either literally or symbolically.

Dream guessing is an important part of the Mid-Winter ceremonies among the Haudenosaunee.[10] During dream guessing a person tells a dream to others in an obscure way. Listeners must guess what the dream is and do something to satisfy the dreamer's wishes. It is believed that dreams uncover disorders of the mind that are causing a person to be out of balance. Once the dreamer's wants, as revealed in the dream, are fulfilled, she or he is made whole again—restored to balance. This harmony benefits the community as well as the individual.

❖ ❖ ❖

Overhead, on any night when the moon is nearly full, you may wake from a dream and look at the sky to see cottony cumulus clouds drifting across the face of cool light beaming down. Over the millennia Native peoples of North America have been moved by this vision, framed by a sky spangled with stars and planets. There is something about the night sky that touches a place deep inside, connecting us to all who have stood in the darkness and gazed at the sky dome. Perhaps it is a feeling of awe—one that humbles and puts us in our place—that brings us closer to those who have been similarly touched by a reverence for nature's vastness. Here is a reminder of our place on the Circle of Life, or our roots in the cosmos, of being a part of something far beyond understanding. The Great Mystery.

Loon on the Cedar River Flow

On a night when the sky
is one cloud
and the Moon's light silvers
from horizon to horizon

look out across the water
where the mountain and line of trees
at its base reflect
in the mirror
of the Cedar River Flow

the wings of bats
small fans
snap open and shut
embracing wind
and the lives it carries

silence enough
to hear the glow
of the firefly
bouncing off still water

time enough
to read the shape
made by its slow circle
of quiet fire

as the loon
calls from the south
where flow narrows
into mist between islands . . .[11]

—Joseph Bruchac
Tracking

NOTES

1. Barbara Barnes (Kawenehe), Mike (Kanentakeron) Mitchell, Joyce (Konwahwihon) Thompson, et. al. *Traditional Teachings.* Cornwall Island, Ontario: North American Indian Traveling College, 1984, p. 60.

2. Peggy V. Beck, Anna Lee Walters and Nia Francisco. *The Sacred: Ways of Knowledge, Sources of Life.* Tsaile, Ariz.: Navajo Community College Press, 1992, p. 59.

3. Kent Nerburn and Louise Mengelkoch, eds. *Native American Wisdom.* San Rafael, Calif.: New World Library, 1991, p. 17.

4. Harvey Arden and Steve Wall. *Wisdomkeepers: Meetings with Native American Spiritual Elders.* Hillsboro, Ore.: Beyond Words Publishing, 1990, p. 114.

5. *Traditional Teachings,* p. 10.

6. *The Sacred,* p. 102.

7. John G. Neihardt. *Black Elk Speaks.* Lincoln: University of Nebraska Press, 1972, p. 209.

8. Frances G. Lombardi and Gerald Scott Lombardi. *Circle Without End.* Happy Camp, Calif.: Naturegraph Publishers, 1982, pp. 48–49.

9. *The Sacred,* pp. 100–101.

10. Barbara Graymount. *The Iroquois.* New York: Chelsea House Publishers, 1988, pp. 37–38.

11. Joseph Bruchac. *Tracking.* Memphis: Ion Books/Raccoon, 1986, p. 17.

CHAPTER 1

Tips and Techniques for Bringing This Book to Life

INTRODUCTION TO *KEEPERS OF THE NIGHT*

Keepers of the Night is a book like no other. Through stories, information and activities the world of night is rediscovered. Share these stories with children and seven dancing boys rise into the sky to become stars, Chipmunk is tricked by the Owl Sister, Grizzly Bear is redeemed as he journeys along the Milky Way to become the Great Bear in Sky Land and a small brown squirrel who makes a sacrifice to help Sun rise into the sky is given the gift of flight as the first bat. In another story, Sun is created from rock crystal, turquoise, red rain, lightning and feathers; Moon is then made from mica, white shells, sheet lightning and water from the four directions.

Keepers of the Night continues the tradition begun by its predecessors in the *Keepers* series, *Keepers of the Earth* and *Keepers of the Animals*. Here each parent, camp counselor, teacher, naturalist and storyteller is given the tools to bring the wonder and magic of the stories and lessons into the lives of children by empowering them with the knowledge, skills and enjoyment found in the activities. There is adventure in the unknown. Even the familiar looks different when it is visited with the intent of discovering what has been looked at and not yet seen, heard yet seldom listened to. Whether in the backyard, the school grounds, a vacant lot, nature-center lands or a wilderness area there are discoveries awaiting in the mysterious world of night.

This is a book about learning to understand, live with and care for nature at night: a gathering of carefully selected Native North American stories and hands-on activities that promote an understanding and appreciation of, empathy for and responsible stewardship toward Earth,* including human beings. *Keepers of the Night* is a valuable aid for those who want children to be excited by and connected with nocturnal environments and associated plants and animals as well as the night sky. When the stories and activities in Chapters 2 through 4 of this book are followed carefully, they provide a complete program of study in the important concepts and topics of astronomy, nighttime weather and other aspects of the night sky as well as nocturnal plants and animals from habitats throughout North America, from seashore to desert. Chapter 5 presents stories and activities for around the campfire, including storytelling, dancing, Native foods and games. Environmental issues and stewardship are explored in Chapter 6.

Tell children a story and they listen with the deepest levels of their beings. Lead children to touch and understand a cricket, listen to an owl's song and see the streak of a bat's wings as it darts by, taste and smell a flower's nectar and discover the tracks of a raccoon and you begin to establish connections between children and their nocturnal surroundings (Figure 1-1). Have them watch and listen to a cricket—feel it, study the way it lives, how it creates its song and what that song communicates to other crickets. Help them to

---

*As used here, Earth *refers to all of our surroundings: plants, animals and the physical environment, which includes air, water, soil, rocks and sky. Although, by convention, people are often referred to separately in the text, here they are considered to be a* part *of Earth, as Native North Americans believe them to be.*

Figure 1-1. Flying squirrels are beloved by children. These common mammals often live in close proximity to people, yet they are rarely seen because of their nocturnal habit. Their nests are made in the crowns of trees in the deciduous forest or mixed deciduous-evergreen woodlands. Nests are often constructed in city parks and even in attics. Although flying squirrels do not actually fly, they can glide over 150 feet (46 meters) using flaps of skin stretched between the legs. The northern flying squirrel is shown here. Size: body, 6 inches (15.2 centimeters); tail, 5 inches (12.7 centimeters). (Photo by Animals Animals/ Earth Scenes, © 1994 Richard Alan Wood.)

understand how a bat is part of a natural community of plants, animals, rocks, soil and water—all fueled by the plant-growing energy of the sun. Explain that the bat eats thousands of insects each night and is essential to maintaining the balance of nature. Visit places where people have affected the homes of nocturnal plants and animals to help children appreciate their stewardship role in the world, how all things are intertwined. Keep the children at the center of their learning encounters. Build on these experiences with activities that help them to care for, and take care of, the natural world and other human beings—to develop an environmental ethic. The Shoshone story of "How

Grizzly Bear Climbed the Mountain" tells us that we can correct our mistakes, do good things and be a positive symbol for others.

As the stories unfold and you help the children to bring the activities to life, a *holistic, interdisciplinary, multicultural* approach to teaching about nocturnal plants and animals and Native North American cultures begins. With their close ties to Earth, Native North Americans are a crucial link between human society and the world of night. The story characters are voices through which the wisdom of Native North Americans speaks in today's language, fostering listening and reading skills and an understanding of how traditional Native people relate to the night. Each story is a natural teaching tool which becomes a springboard as you dive into the activities designed to provoke curiosity among children and facilitate discovery of the plants, animals and their nocturnal environments and the influence that people have on those surroundings. In addition, the chapters on the night sky and campfire adventures are opportunities for hours of fun, exciting educational experiences. These activities are pedagogically sound and extensively field-tested. They involve the children in creative arts, theater, reading, writing, science, social studies, mathematics, sensory awareness and more. The activities engage a child's whole self: emotions, senses, thoughts and actions. They emphasize creative thinking and synthesis of knowledge and experiences. Because of the active and involving nature of the experiences found in this book, children who have special needs physically, mentally and emotionally respond well with proper care and skilled instruction.

These stories and activities have been used and enjoyed by families and children at home, in camp settings, nature centers, environmental education programs, public and private schools, library story hours and in both rural and urban settings. Churches and other spiritual groups have found Native North American traditions to be an inspiration for developing environmental steward-ship and deeper ties with Earth as part of Creation. While the stories and activities arise from North America, with some adaptations for local conditions, they are relevant and useful to people and places in other lands as well.

Native North Americans see themselves as *a part* of nature, not apart from it. Their stories use natural images to teach about relationships between people and between people and Earth. Native North Americans emphasize a close relationship with nature rather than control over the natural world. To the Native peoples of North America, what is done to an evening primrose, a bat or an owl, to a tree, a rock or a river, is done to a brother or sister. This perspective has important im-plications throughout this book where it deals with stewardship toward the world of night.

In many stories the lessons are taught both directly and through metaphors. Two good examples of this are the Paiute story "Moth, The Fire Dancer" in Chapter 3, and the Onondaga story "Oot-Kwah-Tah, The Seven Star Dancers" in Chapter 4. Moth does not heed his father's warnings to not fly too close to the fire. He dances closer and closer to impress the young women and finally plunges into the flames. Just when he is thought to have been killed, Moth astounds the people by appearing transformed into the Fire Dancer with wings red as flames. Similarly, the boys in the story of the Seven Star Dancers do not heed the admonition of the old man who tells them to stop holding their own ceremonies. One evening they dance up into the sky and become stars in the constellation known to the Onondaga as The Dancers, which is today often called the Pleiades. Even though the parents of these boys did not listen to them a long time ago, Onondaga parents of today watch them closely and begin the Midwinter Ceremony when The Dancers reach the top of the sky during January or February. These two stories tell us that children, too, have

something to teach parents. There may be a purpose to their actions that even parents cannot see. *Keepers of the Night* provides a path for our journeys together, young and old, and the means for sharing these insights and this knowledge with children so they may learn to live in a healing relationship with Earth and each other.

STEPS FOR USING THIS BOOK EFFECTIVELY

The Preface provides insight into how some traditional Native North American cul-tures perceive and relate to the world of night. This chapter provides an overview of *Keepers of the Night*. It offers thoughts and suggestions for facilitating the use of stories, guided fantasies, puppet shows and activi-ties, as well as tips for conducting outdoor activities with children at night. Additional sections discuss "Plants and Animals in the Wild: To Collect or Not to Collect" and "Teaching Racial Tolerance, Understanding and Appreciation." If you would like to deepen your background in certain areas before beginning Chapters 2 through 6, refer to the Teacher's Guides to the other *Keepers* books, which discuss the nature of Native North American stories and cultures. They also describe Earth stewardship and *ecologi-cal education*—the philosophy and approach upon which the *Keepers* books are based.

In Chapters 2 through 6—the heart of the book—we use stories as an introduction to the subjects explored in the activities. In some cases the activities follow directly from the story, while in others the story is a stepping-stone that leads into the activities in a more general way. Stories and activities are arranged under broad topical headings in the table of contents.

Each story is followed by a "Discussion" section that provides background informa-tion on the topics it introduces. These discus-sion sections in themselves constitute a unique collection of essays that enhance understand-ing of the Native North American context of the stories, as well as examine the natural history and environmental issues related to nocturnal plants and animals, Native North American night habitats, the night sky and a Native campfire. Relevant "Questions" offer additional help with bridging the stories and activities. Chapters end with suggestions for "Extending the Experience."

Following the title of each activity are several symbols that provide a quick reference to both the setting(s) and the topic(s) of that activity.

These two symbols identify activities that occur

 outdoors, or

 indoors (many of these activities can also be done outdoors, although it is not necessary to do so)

When an activity is marked with both the indoor *and* outdoor symbols, it means that parts of the activity are better conducted outdoors while other parts are better when conducted indoors.

In addition, the activities focus on one or more of the following four subject areas, each of which is represented by a corresponding symbol:

 sensory awareness of the night world

 understanding of the night world

caring for nocturnal plants, animals and environments

caring for people

Begin by sharing a story and illustrations with the children or by having them present the story. Lead a discussion using the background information from the "Discussion" section and the "Questions." Some leaders prefer to conduct some or all of the activities before sharing the story to give the children some prior background in that subject. It is a matter of approach.

Each "Activity" begins with a title and a brief description of what the children will do during the activity. Broad educational "Goals" are also included. Conduct the activities that are at the appropriate "Age" as indicated in the text. Activities are marked as being appropriate for younger children (roughly ages five to eight) and older children (roughly ages nine to twelve). Some activities are appropriate for both age groups and are so marked. Many of the activities can be adapted to work well with different ages, and this book has been widely adapted for use with children from thirteen to fifteen years of age. All of the "Materials" you will need to conduct the activity are also listed. Virtually all of the materials needed for the stories and activities can be found outdoors, at home and in the learning center: they are simple, common and inexpensive.

A detailed "Procedure" is provided for each activity. These sections use a simple, cookbooklike approach that has been found to work very well with leaders from all backgrounds working in every kind of learning situation. Use the activities described under "Extending the Experience" at the end of each chapter to reinforce and supplement the lessons of the stories and activities. A valuable tool to consult is the "Glossary and Pronunciation Key to Native North American Words, Names and Cultures" found at the end of *Keepers of the Night*.

Explore, with the children, the Native North American cultures from which the stories come. The map on pages xiv–xv shows the cultural areas and tribal locations of Native North American groups discussed in this book. These specific cultures are described briefly in the Glossary. Their larger cultural groupings are described in detail in the Teacher's Guides for the *Keepers* series.

We encourage you to be creative and use this book as a complement to your family experiences, campfire activities or your educational program for elementary age children.

TELLING THE STORIES

The natural curiosity with which children regard Native North Americans is a window to educational opportunities. Chapters 2 through 6 in *Keepers of the Night* begin with one or two Native North American stories that are the key to unlocking a child's imagination while evoking useful images and exciting interest in the subjects that are then explored in the activities. Several chapters contain supplemental stories that introduce or enhance the lessons of the activities.

Although none of the Native stories appears in the original language in which it was first told, we have tried in our retellings to capture the motion and the imagery of the original tales and to make sure that the central message of each story is kept intact, for stories are powerful tools used to teach and discipline in Native North American cultures. If you decide to retell these stories, to memorize them rather than read them from the book, or to develop them into puppet shows, plays or skits, we urge you to pay close attention to the way these stories work. They are, however, meant to be *told*, rather than read silently.

Among many Native North American cultures there were certain stories that were usually told at specific times of the year. Northeastern peoples told stories during the long cold season between the first and last frosts. Although you may not be able to restrict your use of these stories to this period of time, it is good to point out to children the traditional storytelling seasons.

Seeing the Story

To begin with, read each story aloud to yourself several times before you read it to children or tell it from memory. This was the method of the old-time Native North American storytellers, who listened again and again to each tale, rehearsing the story alone before

trying to share it with an audience. You may find yourself "seeing" the story as you tell it. At that point you might wish to bring your telling to life with descriptions of those things you see as you tell the tales aloud. Once the story becomes a part of you and you are sharing it effectively with the listeners—creating the "reality" of that story—the characters and events will live and move in their mind's eye.

Be careful as you do this and do not try changing the endings or combining these stories together. The elements of a story create a whole, a living being unto itself. Stories, to many Native North Americans, are *life*; they help to maintain the cultural integrity of the people and to keep the world in balance. When you "see" a story, it is like seeing an animal after having only heard about it before. It comes alive for you. But one animal is different from another and so, too, is each story. Some stories may be wolves. Some may be turtles. But to combine the two does not work.

Be sure to look up the meaning of any unfamiliar Native North American words or names that appear in the story before you share it with the children. These terms are identified and explained in the Glossary at the end of this book. In this way, when the children ask "What is a Medicine Society?" or "What is the Fifth World?," you will be ready with an informed response.

Once you "see" a story and feel comfortable with its telling, you may find it helpful to have a way of recalling the story at the proper time. The *Haudenosaunee* (Iroquois) storyteller or *Hage'ota* carried a bag full of items that acted as mnemonic devices—each item represented a story. The Hageota, or perhaps a child in the audience, would pull an item out of the bag, the item would be shown to the people and the story would begin. This process transforms the storytelling into a shared experience by bringing the children into the act of choosing the stories to be told.

Making a storyteller's bag is an easy project. You and your children can gather things from the natural world or make things to add to the bag. Feathers, stones, nuts, small carvings, anything that can be jostled around in a bag without breaking can be part of your collection. Read the stories in this book carefully and then use your imagination.

The Setting of the Story

In many Native North American cultures, everyone was allowed to have a say and people listened with patience. People would sit in a circle during the time of storytelling because in a circle no person is at the head. All are "the same height." Remembering this may help you, and it is good to remind your listeners—who are not just an audience but part of the story—of that.

Pay close attention to the setting in which you read or tell a story. If it is in a quiet place where people can sit comfortably in a circle—whether around the campfire, in chairs, on the ground or on the floor—you are already one step ahead. But if other things are going on around you, if some people are seated outside the group or where they cannot hear well, your story will lose some of its power. We have often waited until we have brought a child into the circle before beginning a story. It is amazing how quiet and involved someone who was standing outside a group and acting uninterested or hostile will become when "brought in." Be sure that you are comfortable as you do your storytelling. Pay attention to how you feel as you speak from a standing position or while seated in a chair. There is no *one* right way for everyone. Some people do best while sitting in a chair or on the floor, others feel more assured while standing or even walking around. Find *your* way.

Speaking the Story

Breathing is one of the most important things for a storyteller. Too many people try to speak while breathing from high in the chest. This tightens your chest and can strain your voice. Your breath—and your voice—

should come from your diaphragm, that part of your body which is just below your ribs and above your stomach. Place the tips of your fingers there and breath in. If your diaphragm does not move out, then your breathing is wrong. Native North American people see that area as the center of power for the body, and it is certainly the source of power for oral presentations. Your voice will be stronger, project farther and sound better when it comes from the diaphragm.

Resonance is a vital part of a good speaking voice. Try humming as an exercise to develop that natural resonance. One common method of voice training is to hum the vowel sounds, first with the letter "M" before them and then with the letter "B." Clarity is as important as resonance, so when you read or tell your stories, be sure you do not let your voice trail away, especially on significant words. Remember that you are the *carrier* of the story. You must bring it to everyone in the room with you. Lift your chin up as you speak and look to the very back of the room. Imagine your voice as beginning in front of your mouth and reaching to the farthest wall. You do not have to shout to be heard.

Pace is also important in telling a story. Many people tend to either speak too fast or too slow. If the story has truly become a part of you, then you should be able to sense its pace and follow it in your reading or telling. You may wish to check yourself by tape-recording a story as you read or retell it from memory. See if there are places where you speak too quickly, if there are words that are not well enunciated and if you have placed emphasis on the points in the story that should be emphasized.

You may want to make use of any one of a number of formulaic beginnings and endings traditionally used by Native North American people when telling stories. One way the Abenaki people begin a story is with the words, "Here my story camps." They then close the story with such phrases as "That is the end" or "Then I left." The Haudenosaunee often begin by saying, "Would you like to hear a story?" as do many other Native North American people. They then end with the words, *"Da neho!"* which mean, "That is all." Such simple beginnings and endings may help you as a storyteller because they give you a clear way into and out of the tale.

Involving the Listeners

A good story cannot exist without a good listener. There are certain things which you, as a reader or teller, can do to help your listeners be more effective and more involved. We have already mentioned the setting in which the story is told, but there are other ways to bring the listeners into the tale. One device is the use of "response words." Tell the listeners that whenever you say "Ho?" they are to respond with "Hey!" That will let you know that they are still awake and listening. The "Ho?" and "Hey!" can also be used as pacing elements in the story or to make the listeners feel themselves entering the tale. For example:

"The closer the squirrel came, the hotter Sun became … "

"Ho?"

"HEY!"

"My fur is burning, said the squirrel … "

"Ho?"

"HEY!"

"Sun grew so hot … "

"Ho?"

"HEY!"

"That the squirrel's tail burned away … "

"Ho?"

"HEY!"

As you tell your story, do not look at the same person in your audience all the time. If you are telling stories to a large group of children, make eye contact with different people and see them as individuals, not just as a faceless mass. Ask questions that can be answered by someone who has been listening to the story. For example:

"And so that bright red suit of feathers went to whom?"

"Cardinal!"

"Yes! Then Buzzard tried on another suit of feathers. It was blue with a black-streaked crest. But that suit was not fine enough, either, for the messenger of all the birds. So that blue suit went to whom?"

"Bluejay!"

If there is singing, chanting, movement or hand-clapping in your story, teach it to the children before the story begins. Then, at the appropriate time in the story, have everyone join in.

As you tell a story, be aware of how you use your hands, your facial expressions, the motions of your body. Some storytellers or readers prefer to sit quite still and let their voices do all of the work. Others become theatrical. Again, you should find the way you are most comfortable. Flailing your arms about aimlessly can be distracting or overly dramatic. One way to make your hand gestures more meaningful and to give the eyes of your listeners something really significant to focus upon is to incorporate Native North American sign language in your tellings. Many of the signs are the same as those used by the deaf, and the *lingua franca* sign language that Native North Americans developed because of widespread trade across pre-Columbian America is both effective and beautiful to watch. Two inexpensive and easy-to-use books that teach Native American sign language through photographs and simple drawings are *Indian Sign Language* by William Tomkins (New York: Dover Publications, 1969) and *Indian Talk: Hand Signals of the North American Indians* by Iron Eyes Cody (Happy Camp, Calif.: Naturegraph Publishers, 1970).

We find that, when sharing longer stories with very young children, it sometimes helps to take a brief break halfway through. Use this interlude to share and discuss the story illustration(s) as they relate to events that are unfolding. This technique prolongs the childrens' attention span.

LEADING THE
GUIDED FANTASIES

Guided fantasies create firsthand learning experiences that would not otherwise be possible. Some examples are *"The Spider and the Firefly"* (Chapter 3) and *"Journey to the Star Bear"* (Chapter 6). In all cases the guided fantasies build upon subjects introduced by Native North American stories that open the chapters.

While reading the fantasies, have the children

• assume a comfortable position (we often have them lie on their backs);

• close their eyes;

• relax;

• take a few slow deep breaths; and

• clear their minds to make them more receptive to the images conjured up.

Have them visualize that they are in a safe, quiet place, or one they love best, to help them relax. Ask everyone to remain quiet throughout so those who are into the journey will not be disturbed. Reassure children who have difficulty sitting still and imagining the fantasy—not every kind of activity works well with everyone. Incorporate sounds into the fantasy, such as music, a drumbeat or sound effects to enhance the experience. Use different voices and be dramatic!

PERFORMING PUPPET SHOWS

Prepare the children for puppeteering by having them make stick puppets or finger puppets of animals with which to practice puppet motions (Figure 1-2). For *finger puppets,* sculpt the puppet out of clay or salt dough. Each child will press a thumb up about the length of a finger into the bottom of the puppet to leave a hole just larger than a finger needs to fit into. Paint the puppet when it hardens. The finger will be hidden by a simple, tube-shaped piece of cloth (an infant's sock works well), with the closed end pressed up and glued into the hole in the bottom of the puppet.

The puppets to be used in the shows could also be simple, one-sided or two-sided crayon-colored cardboard *stick puppets* (Figure 1-2), or elaborate three-dimensional puppets such

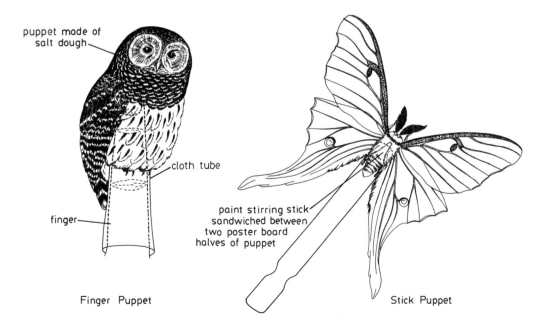

puppet made of
salt dough

cloth tube

finger

Finger Puppet

paint stirring stick
sandwiched between
two poster board
halves of puppet

Stick Puppet

Figure 1-2. Two kinds of puppets that are easy to make: a finger puppet (left) and a double-sided stick puppet (right).

as a bullfrog that hops or a bat and owl that can flap their wings. Larger puppets are more visible to the audience. Have the children take turns acting out different animal movements in front of the group while those watching work their puppets to mimic those actions, such as flying, hopping, crawling, walking, climbing and jumping. Have the puppets talk to each other and express being sad, surprised, happy, shy and other emotional states.

As the children practice working their puppets behind a stage, have them imagine that they *are* that puppet—doing, thinking and feeling all that it does, thinks and feels. Have them look up at their puppets as they bring them to life. Encourage them to develop a puppet's character and voice and to try and be consistent. Energy and movement make the puppet expressive. Puppets should enter the stage from an appropriate place: A luna moth will fly in from overhead, a katydid will call from up in a tree, a crayfish will enter from down below, a bat may fly in from above and a rattlesnake could be curled up on a rock at the side of the stage.

Special effects enhance the performance. Spray a little perfume out into the audience to represent the scent of the luna moth's male attractor. Use a rattle to imitate a rattlesnake shaking its tail. Play a recording of a bullfrog's or katydid's call. Make your own original sound effects!

A number of useful books are available on puppeteering, including *Puppets: Methods and Materials* by Cedric Flower and Alan Jon Fortney (Worcester Mass.: Davis Publications, 1983); *Introducing Puppetry* by Peter Fraser (New York: Watson-Guptill Publications, 1968); and both *Puppet Shows Made Easy!* and *Puppetry and the Art of Story Creation* by Nancy Renfro (Austin Tex.: Nancy Renfro Studios, 1979).

TAKING CHILDREN OUTDOORS AT NIGHT

Clouds blow over the face of the moon; a screech owl calls in the distance; flowers scent the breeze over a garden; a pungent smell wafts from the pavement near a vacant lot after a rain. After sunset the world is transformed into a feast of sensory delights. Air temperature drops and the atmosphere becomes still and moist. Not only are all of our senses heightened because we cannot see as well, it is actually easier to hear and smell because scents and sounds travel better through the cool, damp night air. Our pupils open wide in less than fifteen minutes after being away from artificial lights but it takes forty-five minutes for the retina to fully adjust to the darkness. In nature at night the stars and moon shine the way. Snow-covered, moonlit nights are so bright that snow crystals sparkle and sharp shadows dance atop the rolling whiteness.

Begin the night walk with a brief discussion outdoors or in a darkened room so the children's eyes can begin to adjust to the darkness. Ask the children, "Are you excited about going outdoors in the dark? What kinds of things do you expect to see? How well are your eyes going to work in the dark? How long will it take them to get used to the dark? What are the other senses that we can use to increase our awareness? Why is it so important to be quiet while outdoors at night? Is there anything to be afraid of? How can we conduct this night experience safely?" Use the information from the "Discussion" in Chapter 2 to answer any sensory questions you may not be sure of, and to describe the meanings of the words "nocturnal," "diurnal" and "crepuscular."

The beginning of a night excursion is a good time to discuss *peripheral vision,* what we see off to the sides along the extreme limits of our field of vision. Have the children explore their peripheral vision by moving a finger from directly in front of the face around to the side while keeping the eyes looking straight ahead. How far back can they move the finger before it disappears entirely? That is the limit of their field of vision.

It is extremely important to allow children to recognize their fears while informing them of the relative safety of the nocturnal adventure that lies before them. Talk about each fear that arises and explain how the object of that fear can be dealt with so that it no longer needs to be an obstacle to enjoying the excursion. Tell the children, "No matter what happens, concentrate on overcoming your fears and enjoying the world of night. If something scares you do not panic. Slow down, take a deep breath and, if you do not sense any real danger, continue with what you are doing. If you *do* think there is something dangerous at hand, bring it to the attention of one of the leaders in your group."

Familiarity dispels fear. Introduce the group to the area a bit at a time. Start off with a short journey that does not last very long and gradually increase the length of the visit and distance ventured forth into the night-time environment. This approach helps to alleviate fears and the possibility that some-one will get lost.

Here are some additional guidelines for preparing and conducting safe, fun and informative nighttime experiences.

Preparation

Prepare thoroughly and well ahead of time. Choose the area you will visit and obtain permission from the owners of the site beforehand. As a matter of courtesy, check in with the owners when you arrive and check out as you depart. If possible, plan to begin the walk where there is a restroom available. Choose a site that is away from roads, bright lights and other sources of noise and visual distraction. Instruct everyone who will take part in the night excursion to wear the appropriate clothing as described below.

Conduct the whole program in your mind's eye beforehand and plan for all contingencies such as transportation and proper attire for seasonal weather conditions, especially rain, snow, cold and extreme heat. If you are planning a program at a nature center, send a letter home beforehand to parents or to the visiting classroom teacher so

the children come prepared with proper clothing. Parents, teachers, seniors, older students and other community volunteers are excellent resources for helping with the excursion.

Choose activities that fulfill your goals and objectives. Think of a theme for the entire program; something broad like "survival" allows for focus and flexibility. Children love to play games en route to a site. You can use the "deer walk" to create suspense and interest. First have the children cup their hands behind their ears to create "deer ears." Listen carefully and compare the intensity of sounds heard with and without the deer ears. Ask the children why deer can usually hear people coming before the people notice the deer.

"Because they listen quietly?"

"Right, and that's how we'll walk, with our deer ears alert and as quiet as can be," you reply. "Deer will signal danger by raising their tails and showing the white patch underneath. Whenever you see a white flag (hold up a sample flag), quietly gather around and we'll look at whatever our fellow deer thinks is interesting to see." (Pass out white flags to everyone.) In this way the walk becomes part of the experience. Puppets, stuffed animals, stories or other fun props keep the children's interest.

Once you have arranged for your site and chosen the activities, gather name tags and all necessary materials, then make a brief outline of the evening's activities and other important reminders on note cards that fit into a pocket. Scout out the area during the day that you intend to take your children to at night and become familiar with the site. Note the plants, animals and physical aspects of that place and include them in your activities. If a nature trail is present, use it. If not, plan a route that will do minimal damage to plant and animal communities. When multiple trips are planned into a wild area, establish a path to reduce widespread trampling of the plants, or vary the route in and out to disperse the traffic. Consider the access carefully if your group includes children in wheelchairs or with other special needs: No one wants to be left behind.

Safety

Safety is the primary concern. Scout out the trail and make sure it is relatively flat and free of dangerous obstacles such as holes, fallen logs and branches that might poke someone in the eye. Be certain there is no poison ivy, oak or sumac so close to the trail that the children could come in contact with these plants (Figure 1-3). *Do not venture into areas known for poisonous snakes and other dangerous animals, or where crime is a problem.* Know the dates of the hunting season in your area and *never conduct a night experience outdoors during the hunting season.*

Arrange for small groups of no more than ten children per group. There should be at least three adults for a group of this size for adequate supervision at night: the more adults, the better. Tell two helpers, who are going to remain home and available for the duration of the night experience, exactly where your group is going. Inform them of the exact departure time and plan a time to check in when the excursion is over.

Bring along a complete portable first-aid kit. Include anti-bee-sting serum and a snake-bite kit and know how to use them. You or a coleader should be certified in first aid as well as CPR for both children and adults.

Include the following items in your trail kit:
- small, sharp knife;
- matches packed in a waterproof container;
- compass;
- map of the area, preferably a topographic map;
- insect repellant;
- water, especially for long walks;
- an extra flashlight or two for emergencies;
- spare flashlight batteries; and
- trash bags.

Tell the children that if someone gets lost, she or he is not to look around for others. Tell them to "find a dry, sheltered spot close by where you got separated from the others, call out to let the group know where you are and *stay put.* If no one finds you right away, do not move until morning when you can see to find a way out."

Have the leaders of each group take a head count at the beginning of the excursion, again after each activity along the way and one last time when everyone has returned to the point of departure. Walk slowly, carefully and in single file along the trail. Have young children hold onto a guide rope when traveling between trailside stations. Position one adult at the head of the rope or group, one in the middle and one as a trailer at the end.

Here are some precautions to take to avoid encounters with dangerous animals:
- Do not hike where dangerous animals live, or where there are signs of them.
- Do not carry food, especially greasy or sweet-smelling food.
- Do not use perfumes and deodorants.
- If you inadvertently enter the territory of a dangerous animal, calmly turn around and leave the area. Sing, whistle or talk loudly to make your presence known.

If you encounter a dangerous animal:
- Stay calm.
- Do not startle the animal with sudden moves or noises.

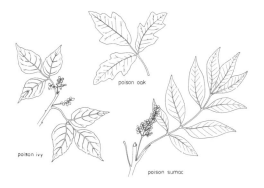

Figure 1-3. Be certain to choose a trail for the night excursion along which the children will not contact these and other poisonous plants.

- Do not run. Animals will instinctively chase and most can outrun a human being.
- Move slowly away, stay *upwind* and give the animal a wide berth.

If you encounter a mountain lion or other wild cat, stand tall and appear as big as possible. If a grizzly bear charges, climb at least 12 feet (4 meters) up a stout tree. If this is not possible:

- Turn sideways and assume a non-threatening posture.
- Avoid eye contact.
- *If all else fails,* drop to the ground, curl up and cover your head with your arms.
- Remain motionless until the bear has left the area.

Comfort

Comfort is important for a successful nighttime experience. Have the children and aides wear warm, dry clothing that is dark to provide good camouflage. Clothing that has been rubbed with the leaves from a strong-smelling local plant (one that is not poisonous), such as sagebrush, sassafras, bayberry or sweetfern, helps to mask the human smell. Dark, high-top, waterproof boots keep feet dry and protect from poisonous plants and snakebites. A light, waterproof mat or pad is a must if you plan to stop, sit on the ground and observe. If necessary, bring earth-friendly insect repellant. Have the children visit the restroom, if they need to, before embarking.

Since most kinds of weather can be enjoyed if you are prepared for them, it is a good policy to go outside under all but the worst conditions. Heavy rains, winds, lightning or other severe weather, however, can come unexpectedly depending upon the weather patterns in your region. Be ready with a full complement of "rainy night" activities just in case.

Lighting

Use natural lighting whenever possible. As a basic rule, there is no need to use a flashlight to get around during the night excursion. Plan to conduct the night visit during a part of the month when the moon is at least one-quarter full. Since your eyes will adjust to the dark, and you will be familiar with the trail, there will be plenty of light by which to navigate. Cover the lens on one of your flashlights with red cellophane (See "*Night by Light*" in Chapter 2 for instructions. Also see the "Discussion" in Chapter 2 for an explanation of why red light does not seem to affect many kinds of animals.) Children do not need flashlights unless they are required for an activity. Collect all flashlights from children before embarking and pass them out when, and if, needed for an activity later on. If possible, use rechargeable batteries: Used conventional batteries are a form of hazardous waste.

Binoculars enhance night vision and can be used to magnify the details of the moon, planets and other objects in the sky.

Conduct

Go calmly and gently into the night. Silence is very important for a rewarding nighttime experience. The night world comes alive when we are quiet and still because our senses are attuned and the animals are more apt to reveal themselves and be active nearby (Figure 1-4). Have the children walk softly and in silence. Ask them to talk only as part of a planned activity, when they have a question or when they want to point out something interesting and exciting. Remind them that "since there are so many of us, we need to respect each other when someone is talking. Please raise your hand if you want to say something and listen whenever someone is speaking. If you see me raise my hand, that is the signal to raise your hand too and listen because there's something to see, do or discuss."

Involve attention-seeking children in the discussion or activity by asking them for help.

Figure 1-4. Opposite. A northern spotted owl roosts in a Douglas fir on a moonlit winter night in the temperate rainforest of the Pacific northwest. Size: body, 16 inches (41 centimeters); wingspread, 3.5 feet (1.1 meters).

Stand near an overly active child and put your arm around her or his shoulders. These techniques comfort and give attention to the attention-seekers in a positive way while avoiding a confrontation. Send clear messages, not mixed ones. Establish the rules and the consequences of excessively disruptive behavior early in the lesson and be consistent in applying both. If a rule is questioned, explain the meaning behind it and turn the experience into a constructive dialogue. This approach fosters the development of positive personal moral standards. Do not use power plays or demeaning methods of punishment. A child who is a severe problem and a continual distraction may have to leave the group so the learning can continue. Ask the child to reflect on what has happened, why and how he or she could learn from the experience.

Make sure the children leave gum, candy and other foods behind. Chewing gum and sucking on sweets not only diverts the attention of the one who is eating but the noise that the wrappers and chewing creates makes it harder for everyone to hear. These foods also promote tooth decay. Discarded chewing gum that is eaten by moles and other small animals can be deadly. Plan a snack break with healthy foods and drinks if you are going on a long field trip.

Tell the children, "We are here to enjoy ourselves and have a positive experience and we need all of your help to do this. You need to be respectful of each other and the plants and animals that live here. Do not scare anybody or shine a light in someone's eyes. Stay with the group at all times—do not go off on your own."

Now it's time to go! The children are anxious to begin and energy is high.

"There are a few things that I want to say before we go outside," you begin. "We're visiting the plants and animals in *their* homes, so how do you think we should act?"

"On our good behavior," someone says.

"Right, if you pull a leaf off a plant you're tearing off part of a living thing. When you take a rock off the path or turn a log over, you're removing the roof of an animal's home. Do you think you'd like it if someone walked by and ripped a piece off of *you,* like your arm, or visited your home and tore the roof off?"

"No!" they respond.

"Okay, then what should you do if you see a beautiful flower or a colorful leaf that you want to pick?"

"We should look at it where it is growing and leave it there."

"Exactly—you can always come back and visit it later on. And what should you do if you look under a rock or log?"

"Put it back the way we found it!"

The tone of empathy and caring is set for the whole walk during the crucial first minutes. This is also a good time to orient the children, in a general way, to the theme of the field trip and to what they can expect. Don't forget to keep plenty of surprises up your sleeve!

You are on the trail now and there is something you want to point out. Walk past that spot far enough so that roughly one-half of the group has passed it. Then backtrack to the spot, and you will be standing in the middle of the group to make it easier for the children to hear. If the sun has not quite set, stand facing it so the light will not glare in their eyes. Ask questions to help them discover what you want them to see. Draw the children in and include everyone. These are great times to tell stories or to listen to one of the children's stories. But be careful! You will need to limit their storytelling. Children love to share *long* stories. Handle this tricky issue by allowing special times for their stories toward the end of the field trip.

Approach the excursion with structured flexibility, being open to the unexpected find or event. Dusk is a magical time to take an excursion. An exciting prelude to or part of a nocturnal excursion is "Disappearing Trees" in the activity called *"Night Walk"* (Chapter 2). One of our favorite activities along the trail is the camouflage game. First hold a brief discussion-and-answer period about what camouflage is and how animals use camouflage, such as cryptic coloration, hiding behind things and under leaves or being shaped like a natural object. Be sure to have pictures of some well-camouflaged animals to hold up as you talk. Tell the children you want them to camouflage themselves whenever you yell "Camouflage!" Give them ten seconds to hide and tell them not to go more than 20 feet (6 meters) away. Close your eyes as you count. Call out the names or locations of children that you can see when you open your eyes.

After you have played the game once, tell the children that the counting time will be shortened by one second during each round of the game, which can come at any time along the trail when you suddenly yell "Camouflage!" This adds an undertone of anticipation to the excursion.

When children are quiet and listening, they often see special things. Suppose a child comes up to you after the *"Night by Light"* activity (Chapter 2) and says, "I saw a moth and it had two huge eyes on its wings! It's over there on that tree." Postpone the next planned activity and use the occasion as a time to marvel at the moth's "eyes" while letting the children generate their own questions about why a moth would have colors that look like eyespots on its wings. Use some creative questioning to tie the sighting in with your lesson. Quell some fears about insects and, at the same time, increase the children's understanding of the fascinating interrelationships between different kinds of animals.

Snack breaks are good times to share special moments. They are also opportune for reading or telling one of the stories in this book that relates to the theme of your walk.

During these discussions and while sharing stories, spiritual beliefs are bound to surface because children are often quite open about deep-seated convictions. Encourage the children to listen to, acknowledge, respect and appreciate the beliefs of others. A child may say, "This story says that Moon was created out of mica, shells, lightning and water, but that's not what I was taught to believe." We have found a good response to be: "Yes, people believe in different accounts of creation. This story tells about the beliefs of a particular Native North American culture." Spirituality is an important part of environmental activities in appropriate settings. Spiritual beliefs and religious practices are major factors in determining a child's orientation and conscience toward Earth and other people.[1]

Keeping a Field Journal

Include quiet time. Children enjoy keeping a journal in which they make entries immediately following the night excursion. Have them record outdoor experiences as a log of natural events, an accurate learning tool that reveals patterns in nature as well as unusual sightings. Ask them to write down a simple observation, illustrate something seen, make leaf or bark rubbings, create a poem, photograph special places and paste the photographs in the journal or record a tune that comes to mind while hiking. Tailor the format to the children's age level.

Have them build on the journal over time. They should include, if possible:
• date, time, place and conditions;
• observations, answering the questions of who, what, when, where, how and why;
• thoughts and interpretations of what is seen;
• sketches, illustrations or photographs to accompany the written observations; and
• connections between natural life in the field: a bird eating a certain insect or the remains of a particular animal in another's droppings.

Enhance the experience by having them research and record the natural history and ecology of the plants, animals and other aspects of nature observed.

CONDUCTING THE ACTIVITIES

The following checklist provides specific ideas for creating experiences that are meaningful, informative and fun. A detailed discussion of each item in this checklist is found in Chapter 2 in all of the main books in the *Keepers* series. *Ecological Education*—the educational foundation for the *Keepers* books—is discussed in Chapter 1 of the Teacher's Guides to *Keepers of the Animals* and *Keepers of Life*.

• Plan in detail and use the available time wisely.

• Choose and adapt activities for the children's level of understanding.

• Involve the children in planning the excursion and make them coleaders.

• Allow time for discussion and questions.

• Set the stage with a few preactivities.

• Link the activities in a meaningful way with questions and discussion.

• Put the children into the center of the experience.

• Teach by example; model positive behaviors.

• Use firsthand, sensory experiences whenever possible.

• Use creative questions and answers to encourage discovery.

• Emphasize positive, caring feelings as well as knowledge.

• Provide a supportive atmosphere, a trusting and respectful experience.

• Foster aesthetic appreciation, quiet moments, stories, poems, music... .

• Emphasize group work and positive social interaction to build self-esteem.

• Foster problem solving/research skills; find solutions to problems together.

• Use long-term projects that involve individuals and groups over time.

• Include connections with other cultures, communities and countries.

• Avoid bias; identify and discuss bias, prejudice, stereotyping and ideology.

• Include moral issues; environmental and social empathy, ethics and behavior.

• Consider the children's level of moral development during values education. [2]

• Deal with problems and controversy constructively and positively.

Figure 1-5. Most frogs court and mate during the evening and nighttime hours. This green frog makes a call that sounds like a loose banjo string being plucked. The sight of a frog compels many children to want to take the amphibian home. A frog encounter is an excellent opportunity to discuss the reasons why plants and animals should be observed in their natural habitats. Size: body, 3 inches (7.6 centimeters). (Photo by Alan C. Graham.)

• Respect and appreciate differences in spiritual and religious beliefs.

• Respect the right to privacy regarding personal beliefs and feelings.

• Discipline compassionately, positively, decisively and consistently.

• Keep a sense of humor, joy and appreciation.

• Be yourself; use whatever works best for your personality.

• Provide a culminating activity or experience to create a sense of closure.

PLANTS AND ANIMALS IN THE WILD: TO COLLECT OR NOT TO COLLECT

We strongly recommend that children be discouraged from collecting animals (including insects) and from picking parts of plants or uprooting plants of any kind. Children can "capture" a plant or animal with a photograph or illustration instead. Our philosophy is to protect, enjoy and observe plants and animals in their own habitats, which is where we learn the most about them (Figure 1-5). Animals may carry diseases and it is illegal to collect, pick or dig up certain species of rare or endangered plants and animals, including many wildflowers.

At night it can be difficult or impossible to identify a plant or animal and distinguish it as being harmless or poisonous. *Be sure of the identity of the plants you are picking to avoid poisonous plants that cause painful skin irritations. Also, do not allow the children to eat any plant parts unless you have picked them ahead of time and are absolutely certain they are edible.*

It takes an adult's patience and determination to instill respect for the natural world. As a simple nervous habit, for instance, some children and adults will tear up and destroy the grass and other plants all around where they are sitting. *Gathering* plant parts that have *naturally* died or fallen off, such as seeds, autumn leaves or beautiful winter weed stalks is okay as long as the children treat even these plant parts with respect and take only what they need.

In those cases where you, the educational facilitator, *must* collect plant parts to be used by you and the children during activities, we offer the following suggestions.

• Obtain permission to collect on private or public land.

• Pick only what you *need.*

• Only pick from common species of plants and where there is a healthy population.

• Thin out, lightly, from several different patches of plants you are picking from.

• *Never collect any rare, threatened or endangered species or parts of them.* Become acquainted with all laws governing the collection of wild plants, particularly rare species. Keep rare plant sightings a secret and report them to the appropriate conservation group.

• Refrain from conducting experiments involving wild plants.

• Never take the largest plant, leaf, berry, flower or other plant part found amid those you are gathering. This is the "Grandmother" and should be left out of respect.

• Gather plant parts that you need ahead of time. It is better to not have children watch you do the picking, which sets the example that it is all right for them to pick, too. If *you* must pick plants when the children are present as part of an activity, use the occasion to teach them the ideas and practices for good stewardship that follow.

• Always use sharp pruning shears to collect plant parts. Cut back to the nearest living part of the stem to allow the plant to grow over and heal the wound. Openings left in a plant's protective outer tissues allow insects and diseases to enter and damage the plant.

• Bring along a small cooler with a bit of water and ice in the bottom to keep the plants fresh and cool until you are either ready to use them or can get them to a refrigerator.

• Do not collect wild plants or plant parts that someone is selling. You can never be sure of how they were obtained.

Whether gathering live plant parts yourself, picking live berries or accompanying children as they gather dead leaves or weeds, we offer a way of relating to the plants. Forms of these simple practices are used by a number of Native North American peoples to keep strong the circle of giving and receiving with the "plant people."

• Ask permission of the plants in order to show respect.

• Say "thank you" to the plants. Take the first of your gift from the plants, such as the first handful of berries or colorful leaves gathered, place it on the ground near the plants that created that gift and express your appreciation. Leave your gift there and gather what you need. You might bring a special gift of seeds, for example, to leave for the plants. Many Native North American cultures show their appreciation to the plants in this way.

• Take only what you need: Thin out but never take all from any given patch. This is sharing with other animals or humans who may come along later looking for the same thing you now need. Thinning allows a healthy growth of plants to maintain the population.

• Complete the circle of giving and receiving. Use only what you *need* and return unused plant parts to the soil where they were found, beneath the plants that produced them.

TEACHING RACIAL TOLERANCE, UNDERSTANDING AND APPRECIATION

It is easy, in the course of an activity that incorporates Native North American stories and ideas, to unintentionally fall into the common practice of using language and conduct that show disrespect for Native cultures. This is more likely to occur during the excitement around a campfire. The best approach is to involve local Native peoples when planning and conducting activities. Teach tolerance and appreciation for cultural differences that can enrich and expand all of our lives. A few simple dos and don'ts help to avoid this common problem.[3]

•**Don't** say "dress like Indians." This is offensive to Native peoples, just as putting dark makeup on for Martin Luther King Day would be to African Americans. Costumes prompt children to make war cries and to do other things that mock Native peoples.

•**Do** study and try to understand the unique and valuable customs of Native peoples and learn from them while maintaining the context of your own culture, habits and dress. Have the children speak to local Native people around the campfire. Explain that, like many other people who live in North America, many Native people are of mixed ancestry and there is no way to tell if someone is Native simply by looking at him or her.

•**Don't** refer to Native North Americans with words like "savages," "war-loving" and "primitive." This reinforces the fallacy that Native cultures are somehow backward, warlike and less advanced and civilized than people of European and other ancestry.

•**Do** discuss the particular language and customs of local Native people and those from whom the stories come. Help the children to understand these peoples as unique cultures. Ask the children if they can think of other cultures.

•**Don't** instruct the children to "sit Indian style," "walk Indian file" or to stop acting like a "bunch of wild Indians." Refrain from having the children refer to each other with words such as "squaw" and "brave." These words are offensive to Native peoples, and they imply that Native languages and cultures all use the same forms of speech. Many words are completely misunderstood. To be called a "squaw" has become an insult and implies that women are beasts of burden and public property.

•**Do** use simple, direct language like "walk single file," "sit on your bottoms and cross your legs" and refer to "boys" and "girls."

•**Don't** speak of Native North American cultures as if they only existed in the past. They have a history *and* are here among us today. Contemporary Native peoples often dress and look much like the general culture in which they live. They do not wear loin cloths, headdresses and other Native attire except at museums and during ceremonial occasions.

•**Do** discuss that Native North Americans live in the modern world. They work at jobs, go to school, play sports, drive cars and have family lives in our contemporary world. Some live close to the traditional ways and others are more immersed in modern culture.

•**Don't** speak as if Native North Americans are of one large culture. Not every Native culture traditionally lived in tepees and rode around on horses hunting buffalo as many plains peoples did historically. There are over 550 distinct nations in Native North America, each with its own language, customs, beliefs and ways of living in the world.

• **Do** refer to each Native person by his or her tribal name. Discuss the language, beliefs and customs of each culture as the distinct, unique people that they are, closely connected to their local environment.

• **Don't** belittle sacred ceremonies and beliefs by trying to imitate them or adapt them to an activity. Stay away from them entirely. These are the heart and soul of Native cultures and are easily trivialized by misunderstood mimicry. They are meant to be conducted by members of a particular culture only. Would you, for the fun of it, conduct part of a Catholic communion service or a Buddhist meditation rite around a fire with the children?

• **Do** invite local Native people to visit with the children to discuss their beliefs and ceremonies. Study Native ways objectively and as a lesson to be understood without being imitated and practiced. Encourage children to learn more about their own spiritual tradition and how their beliefs support our being close to, and caring toward, Earth and other people—for example Judaism, Islam, Christianity, Hinduism, Buddhism or Baha'ism.

AUTHORS' NOTES
Use of Gender Language

The use of gender varies among individuals and cultures. In order to maintain the accuracy and spirit of word usage and meaning among the writings contributed to this book by other authors, we have included them in their unedited forms. The balance of the text has been written to avoid any gender bias.

Use of Terms for Referring to Native North Americans

In this book, we use the term *Native North American* to refer to Native peoples of the United States, Canada and Mexico. These peoples are often, by convention, called "Native American" and "American Indian." Not all Native North Americans are American Indians. The *Inuit* (Eskimo) peoples of the far north comprise cultures that are distinct from the North American Indians who inhabit this continent.

In the United States, *American Indian* and *Native American* are terms used interchangeably to refer to the Native aboriginal inhabitants of North, Central and South America. In Canada, the terms *Native Indian, Métis* or *Aboriginal* are commonly used rather than *Native American*. In all cases, it is best to refer first to the person with regard to her or his individual nation, for example, "Lakota," "Yuchi," "Diné" or "Shoshone."

❖ ❖ ❖

This chapter has provided both ideas and practical suggestions for effectively using and integrating the Native North American stories and nocturnal Earth activities found in Chapters 2 through 6. Now it's time to begin! We hope that you and your children enjoy these stories and activities as much as we enjoy sharing them.

NOTES

1. Robert Coles, *The Spiritual Life of Children*. Boston, Mass.: Houghton Mifflin, 1990, 119–120.

2. See Michael J. Caduto, *A Guide on Environmental Values Education*. Paris, France: United National Educational, Scientific and Cultural Organization (UNESCO), 1985. General reference.

3. This list is adapted with permission from material produced by the Institute for American Indian Studies, 38 Curtis Rd., P.O. Box 1260, Washington, Conn., 06793, as found in *Native American Sourcebook: A Teacher's Resource on New England Native Peoples,* by Barbara Robinson, Concord, Mass.: Concord Museum, 1988, p. 167. For ordering information contact Concord Museum, 200 Lexington Road, P.O. Box 146, Concord, MA 01742.

The small brown squirrel came close and began to chew at the branches in which Sun was caught.

CHAPTER 2

How the Bat Came to Be

(Anishinabe—Eastern Woodland)

Long ago, as the sun began to rise one morning, he came too close to Earth and became tangled in the top branches of a tall tree. The harder Sun tried to escape, the more he became caught. So, the dawn did not come.

At first, the birds and animals did not notice. Some woke, then went back to sleep thinking that they had been mistaken and it was not yet time for morning. Other animals which love the night, like the panther and the owl, were happy that it remained dark and continued to hunt. But after a while, so much time had passed that all the birds and animals knew something was wrong. They gathered together in the dark to hold a council.

"Sun has become lost," the eagle said.

"We must search for him," said the bear.

So all of the birds and animals began to look for Sun. They looked in caves and in the deep forest and on the mountains and in the swampy lands. But Sun was not there. None of the birds or animals were able to find Sun.

Then one of the animals, a small brown squirrel, had an idea.

"Perhaps Sun is caught in a tall tree," he said.

Then the small brown squirrel began to go from tree to tree, going further and further toward the east. At last, in the top of a very tall tree, he saw a glow of light. He climbed up and saw that it was Sun. Sun's light was pale and he looked weak.

"Help me, Little Brother," Sun said.

The small brown squirrel came close and began to chew at the branches in which Sun was caught. The closer he came to Sun, the hotter it became. The more branches he chewed free, the brighter Sun's light grew.

"I must stop now," said the small brown squirrel. "My fur is burning. It is all turning black."

"Help me," said Sun. "Do not stop now."

The small squirrel continued to work, but the heat of the sun was very great now and it was even brighter.

"My tail is burning away," said the small squirrel. "I can do no more."

"Help me," said Sun. "Soon I will be free."

So the small brown squirrel continued to chew. But the light of the sun was very bright now.

"I am growing blind," said the small squirrel. "I must stop."

"Just a little more," said Sun. "I am almost free."

Finally the squirrel chewed free the last of the branches. As soon as he did so, Sun broke free and rose up into the sky. Dawn spread across the land and it was day again. All over the world the birds and animals were happy.

But the small squirrel was not happy. He was blinded by the brightness of the sun. His long tail had been burned away and what fur he had left was now all black. His skin had stretched from the heat and he clung there to the top branches of that tree which had held the sun, unable to move.

Up in the sky, Sun looked down and saw the small squirrel. It had suffered so much to save him. Sun felt great pity and he spoke.

"Little brother," Sun said, "you have helped me. Now I will give you something. Is there anything that you have always wanted?"

"I have always wanted to fly," said the small squirrel. "But I am blind now and my tail has been burned away."

Sun smiled. "Little Brother," he said, "from now on you will be an even better flyer than the birds. Because you came so close to me, my light will always be too bright for you, but you will see in the dark and you will hear everything around you as you fly. From this time on, you will sleep when I rise into the sky and when I say goodbye to the world each evening you will wake."

Then the small animal which had been a squirrel dropped from the branch, spread its leathery wings and began to fly. He no longer missed his tail and his brown fur and he knew that when the night came again it would be his time. He could not look at the sun, but he held the joy of the sun in his heart.

And so it was, long ago, that Sun showed his thanks to the small brown squirrel who was a squirrel no longer, but the first of the bats.

DISCUSSION

It is ironic that the small brown squirrel in this Anishinabe story, "How the Bat Came to Be," is turned into a bat as a reward for making a great sacrifice to save Sun from being tangled in a treetop. Many people are afraid of bats: They harbor unfounded fears of having a bat fly in and get tangled in their hair. While it is true that bats may carry rabies, the same as raccoons, foxes and many other mammals, and that a bat bite should be avoided, the bat has not earned the loathsome regard with which people hold it. Indeed, certain bats are capable of devouring their own weight in mosquitoes and other insects in a single night! When the squirrel receives the gift of flight and is transformed into a bat, it flies off holding "the joy of the sun in his heart." As is the case with many things in nature, bats could just as well be celebrated if we chose to see them in a different light.

While most people are familiar with *diurnal* animals—those that are active during the day—bats afford a glimpse into a world of darkness that is, to most people, an unexplored frontier. *Nocturnal* animals are those that are active at night. From bats to ghost crabs, from deer to insects (Chapter 3) and from snowshoe hares to cottontail rabbits— many *crepuscular* animals are active at dawn and at dusk in the deepening twilight.

The Sensory Night

Many people are afraid of the night because they think they cannot see in the dark. However, with the exception of the few moonless, heavily overcast nights that we experience each year, it may be of some comfort to know that human eyes are capable of seeing as well as, or better than, many animals that are active at night.

NIGHT VISION. As night sets in, the eyes gradually adjust to decreasing light. Since the *rod cells* of the eye's light-catching *retina* are sensitive to even dim light, the eyes of many nocturnal animals are packed with rod cells (Figure 2-1). Most animals, therefore, can see well enough at night to find and catch food, flee from predators and navigate around objects. Few wild animals go bump in the night.

Many nocturnal animals, however, have only a few color-sensing *cone cells* because there is usually not enough light present for color to be detected at night. As a result, and because their cone cells are insensitive to the long wavelengths of red, few animals can see a red light, which affects cone cells but not rod

cells. A bright red light, such as a flashlight covered with red acetate or cellophane, cannot be detected by many vertebrate animals. Since human beings *can* detect the red end of the spectrum, we can see animals at night by using a red beam of a light that they, apparently, cannot perceive. Interestingly, the lighter colors by day, such as reds and yellows, appear as darker grays at night, whereas blue, which is not as bright during the day, appears as a brighter shade of gray after dark.[1] Human eyes are especially sensitive to blue at night.

While it sometimes appears that the eyes of certain animals "glow in the dark" when we shine a flashlight into them, we are really seeing *eyeshine* as the light of the beam is reflected. These animals have a reflective layer of tissue called the *tapetum* at the back of the eye, behind the light-sensitive cells of the retina, which sends light back over these cells to increase the eye's efficiency in low light levels. Extreme light from a bright source that animals can detect, such as a flashlight or car headlights, reflects out of the cornea and the animal's eyes seem to "glow." Each kind of animal has eyeshine of a particular color, ranging from the bright yellow of a raccoon

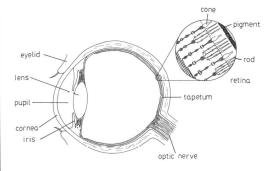

Figure 2-1. Cross-section of a nocturnal mammalian eye. The retina contains many rod cells that are sensitive to dim light. The tapetum reflects light back over the light-sensitive cells of the retina to increase the eye's efficiency at low light levels. This reflected light appears as eyeshine which varies in color among nocturnal animals. (Close-up view of retina adapted with permission from Karl O. Von Frisch, Biology. *New York: Harper Collins, Pub., 1964, p. 176.)*

to the iridescent green of a bullfrog to a bear's orange and an alligator's deep red. Coyotes have greenish-gold eyeshine while that of the gray wolf is greenish-orange.

Some animals, such as mice, lack this reflective layer. Humans exhibit eyeshine to a certain degree, which sometimes shows up as "red eye" in photographs taken using a flash. People have night vision that exceeds that of a rabbit or whip-poor-will, and is about as good as that of an owl or lynx in low light.[2] We cannot, however, simply step out of our brightly lit houses and see well in the darkness outside; our eyes must first adjust. After about fifteen minutes in the dark our pupils are completely open, but it takes the pigments in our retinas about forty-five minutes to become entirely sensitized to the night. The stars alone provide enough light by which to orient if we move about carefully, and we can even make out faint shades of color on bright moonlit nights. The rest of the time we see no colors at night.

OTHER SENSES AT NIGHT. Darkness creates a different world in which hearing, smelling and, on the darkest of nights, even touching take over where sight falls short. These senses, which tend to be obscured during the day when we orient mostly by sight, are enhanced at night. Sounds seem to be louder and more acute: water dripping, leaves brushing against one another in a breeze, surf crashing, a brook gurgling or animals calling, perhaps a frog, toad, nighthawk, owl, cricket, cicada or coyote. Besides owls, many other birds call at night, especially when the moon is bright: mockingbirds, song sparrows, American robins and other thrushes, ovenbirds, red-winged blackbirds, marsh wrens, white-throated sparrows and migrating geese. Certain animal sounds, like most of the high-pitched calls of bats and rats, are above the pitch audible to the human ear. Some people, though, can hear the lower-pitched clicking sounds of hunting bats.

Night is a good time to exercise our intuition or sense of presence beyond the five physical senses; what some people call a *sixth sense*. It may alert us to the presence of an animal or person, only to be confirmed by a sound nearby—a deer snorting in alarm, leaves rustling or footsteps approaching.

TEMPERATURE CHANGES AT NIGHT. Nature by night is a sensual experience. As we walk along the air feels more cool and damp than it does during the day. Pockets of warm, soft air lie next to cold in even the smallest dip or valley. Odors are enhanced in the high humidity of night air and sound travels more easily through the cool moisture. A rock or a sandy beach may still be radiating heat stored during the daylight hours, although these surfaces lose their heat quickly. Water, however, is among the most efficient heat sinks whose effects are heightened at night by a stroll along a lakeside or seashore. On cool summer nights the water feels warm; on warm nights it feels cool. The water vapor in clouds traps the radiant heat of Earth like the panes of a greenhouse on overcast nights. This heat radiates out into space on clear nights so temperatures drop lower.

Nocturnal Animals: Adaptations and Habits

As twilight deepens, the activity of daytime animals gradually subsides while their counterparts on the night shift come alive. Spring peepers may fill the night air with piercing, sleighbell-like songs while green frogs (Figure 1-5) and bullfrogs punctuate the summer evenings with their calls which sound, respectively, like a loose banjo string being plucked and a deep-throated "jug-o-rum." A loon's haunting call rises from a lake. Swallows are often still feeding on insects over the pond when the bats join them, eating mosquitoes by the hundreds as the hunter becomes the hunted. While cardinals have long since become silent for the night, an earnest thrush or vociferous crow may let loose its last notes before retiring. Whip-poor-wills begin calling out their names, or perhaps it is a chuck-will's-widow in the southeast or poor-will in the west.

Some animal activities, like the woodcock's intricate spring mating display, are particular to the twilight hours. One early spring, from some shrubs at the edge of a field, we heard a familiar, ventriloquistlike "peent" being repeated methodically several seconds apart. At first the sound seemed close, then far away, then close again. For years this perceived change in distance from the source puzzled us, until we once got close enough to see that the male woodcock, as it calls from the ground, turns roughly 90 degrees between each peent, projecting its voice in different directions in the hope that a potential mate might be listening. At the end of this sequence of peents, the mating urge drives the male to perform one of the most elaborate avian courtship displays in North America.

After about five minutes of calling we saw a fleeting, brown, chunky bird with a prominent beak dart out of the brush, wings whistling as it etched broad spirals higher and higher into the dusky sky. When the bird reached the top of its spiral, out of sight, we sprinted half the distance to its calling post where we hid again, waiting for its return. Soon the woodcock descended on twittering wingbeats that created a warbling sound, until it glided in to land in exactly the same place it had left. The peenting began anew.

All animals that are active and others that rest quietly once the sun has set, are superbly adapted to life after dark. Birds are able to perch while sleeping by virtue of strong tendons that enable their feet to grip a branch tightly when at rest. The weight of the bird pulls the tendon in tight around the branch. Even if the bird dies, its feet hold fast. Animals commonly return to the same or a similar place to perch or rest each night. Birds, for instance, often return to the same tree, shrub or place on the ground. Frogs, toads and salamanders, which are susceptible to drying in the heat of the day, prefer the humid, cool night air. They often cross roads in numbers on rainy nights. A copperhead, rattlesnake or water moccasin (cottonmouth) may lie in the shadows, depending on whether they occur

in your area. These *pit vipers* pinpoint the body heat of *warm-blooded* prey, such as rodents, using tiny depressions or *pits* located between each eye and nostril. Even in total darkness the pits can detect minute temperature differences up to several feet away.

Most small birds take advantage of the cover of darkness as a time to *migrate,* including thrushes, shore birds, wood warblers, flycatchers, wrens, most sparrows, vireos, rails and orioles. Not only are these birds safer at night from predators, they use the daytime when they can see to find and eat their food as well as to rest, to conserve and replenish their stores of energy. Birds that feed at night, such as the nighthawk, migrate by day.

It is safer for many animals, such as squirrels, grasshoppers, cardinals and groundhogs, to find and eat their plant food during the day because nighttime tends to be a time to either stalk or be stalked. Depending on the species, this food may consist of nuts, berries, leaves, nectar and other sources from plants. Those herbivores that do come out mostly at night—mice, flying squirrels, rabbits and deer—must constantly be on the alert for an owl or some other predator, such as a fox, coyote, bobcat or lynx, weasel, fisher or mink.

Flying squirrels are common and lively nocturnal rodents that have reddish-orange eyeshine and soft, thick fur that is a shiny olive-brown above and whitish along the undersides. Rarely seen because they sleep during the day, flying squirrels come out just before the deep dusk to play and forage for such foods as nuts, seeds, birds eggs and insects. Food is often cached in tree crotches and nests. Sometimes they live in abandoned woodpecker holes or attics but they also construct nests out of leaves, twigs and bark. Squeaky "chuck chuck" sounds or musical chirping notes can sometimes be heard coming from the nests. Measuring about 11 inches (28 centimeters) from the tip of the nose to the end of the tail, the northern flying squirrel is the larger of the two species found north of Mexico, while the southern flying squirrel matures at about 9.5 inches (24.1 centimeters). In good habitat there are usually one to two flying squirrels per acre (2 to 5 per hectare) during the summer, but they may overwinter in dens of more than twenty. From a height of 60 feet (18 meters), flying squirrels can glide over 150 feet (46 meters) on flaps of skin that stretch between the extended front and hind legs on each side of the body (Figure 1-1).

Flying squirrels are among the many prey caught and consumed by the larger species of owl such as the great horned and barred owls. Owls hunt primarily by sound. The large "facial disks" formed by feathers funnel sound to the ears located just behind and below the eyes (Figure 2-4). Owls' ears are asymmetrical so that sound is perceived differently by each ear. This allows the owl to use triangulation to pinpoint the prey's location. In one experiment, barn owls were as successful at hunting as usual even when they were placed in completely darkened rooms or blindfolded.

An owl's eyes do gather light better than a person's, causing an object to appear two and one-half times brighter to their eyes. In practice on a dimly lit night, however, owls do not see appreciably better than we do because there is so little light available. Owls cannot turn their heads all the way around, but they can turn them three-quarters of the way around in each direction from facing forward. So if an owl were spotted with its head turned full left, it could conceivably be seen spinning its head around a dizzying one and one-half full turns to where it was turned all the way to the right! Like all birds, an owl's eyes are very large relative to their skull size so they have a limited ability to move in their sockets—birds must often turn their heads to look around. Some owls have eyes that are so large they nearly touch in the middle of the skull!

Bats are another group of night stalkers. These amazing animals—the only true flying mammals—are classified in their own order as the *Chiroptera,* meaning "hand wing." Bats

are *not* rodents—they are, in fact, more closely related to primates. The *Abenaki,* "People of the Dawn" of the northeastern United States and southeastern Canada, call the bat *madagenilhas,* which means "fur-hide bird." Bats use a form of sonar to navigate and to locate their prey on the wing (Figure 2-2). The ultrasonic pulses of sound that bats emit bounce back from an object to tell the bat of its whereabouts. A bat's sonar is a more effective navigational tool than the sight of many animals. We do not need to worry about bats flying into us.

Certain bats of temperate climes undergo a partial dormancy called *diurnation* during their restful daytime periods, which are spent in caves, hollow trees, attics, barns and other shadowy nooks and crannies. Their drop in body temperature during these periods helps to conserve energy. When they emerge in the twilight hours after sunset most bats pursue insect prey, which are caught and eaten in flight. In two hours the little brown bat (*Myotis*) can eat one-fifth of its own weight in insects. Pipistrelles of eastern North America are capable of consuming one-fourth their body weight in insects in one-half hour: This is roughly equivalent to five thousand gnats or sixty-six moths in one hour.[3] Bats also can drink from a pond while on the wing.

Not all bats are insectivorous. Many species, such as the longnose bat of southwestern North America, feed on flower nectar. When flying from flower to flower the longnose bat pollinates the blooms that it visits, such as those of the saguaro cactus and

Figure 2-2. Opposite. A little brown bat (Myotis) *chases a mosquito over the mixed prairie speckled with fireflies. This bat ranges throughout North America and can eat one insect every three and one-half seconds on the wing! Insects are frequently caught with a wing, or in the tail, then transferred to the mouth. Size: body (not including tail), 1.6 to 2.2 inches (4.1 to 5.6 centimeters); length of forearm, 1.5 inches (3.8 centimeters); wt., .25 to .33 ounce (7.1 to 9.4 grams).*

Figure 2-3. A lesser longnose bat approaches a saguaro cactus flower. Its nectar-feeding tongue can extend up to a third of the bat's body length. Nectar-feeding bats are indispensable for the pollination of many night-blooming flowers. Size: body (not including tail), 2.8 to 3.7 inches (7.0 to 9.5 centimeters); length of forearm, 1.8 to 2.2 inches (4.6 to 5.7 centimeters); wt., .6 to 1.0 ounce (18 to 30 grams). (Photo by Dr. Merlin D. Tuttle, Bat Conservation International.)

agave (Figure 2-3). Nectar- and fruit-eating bats of the tropical rainforest and other environments play a crucial role in pollination and seed dispersal.

Baby bats are born after the females come out of hibernation in the springtime. Each mother usually gives birth to one young. At first, among some species such as tree bats, the batlet or *pup* is carried by its mother on hunting flights while attached to her nipple. When the offspring becomes too heavy, the female leaves it behind at a roosting site while she hunts. Female *Myotis* bats begin foraging within a few hours of giving birth. The young cluster in groups called *creches*. A mother can recognize the high-pitched squeaks of her own offspring from among the many young hanging on the ceiling or wall of the roost. Young are also identified by scent and by their location. Females will accept and nurse young other than their own. Some bat species migrate south when fall arrives. Many

other North American bats migrate to caves and hibernate. They use their stored fat to survive as body temperatures drop to a few degrees above that of the cave.

Maturing male bats gradually leave the colony over the course of the summer. By fall there are only females left to hibernate en masse, while males overwinter alone or in all-male groups. Much mating occurs in autumn among cave species as they arrive at the *hibernacula*. During warm winter spells males seek out hibernating females and copulate with them while they are still dormant. At some point during the winter the females become pregnant. They are able to store the sperm until their eggs are ready to be fertilized in the spring, so all of the young in a particular cave are born no more than one week apart.

Bats may be one of the classic nocturnal animals, but an amazing number and diversity of animals are active from dusk to dawn. Toads, frogs and salamanders hop, swim and wriggle about on the forest floor and in the wet places. A porcupine may be nearby munching on leaves or needles or stripping off the outer bark of a tree to get at a meal of the tender, nutritious inner bark. Mice, shrews, voles and lemmings scamper in the darkness, but they could easily fall prey to a red or gray fox, skunk or weasel. Raccoons and opossums are out scavenging while snowshoe hares, cottontail rabbits and deer nibble on tender shoots and buds under the cover of darkness. Earthworms are busy feeding and leaving their droppings or *castings* at the burrow's entrance.

A Sampling of Nocturnal North American Habitats

Few places are more alive at night than *freshwater environments —ponds, lakes, streams, rivers* and *wetlands*. Trout snap at the water's surface in the moonlight to catch the aquatic nymphs of stoneflies, mayflies and caddisflies as they shed their skins and take to the air as adults. Ducks feed in the shallows while a heron stalks its prey nearby. Crayfish scavenge for food along the bottom. A barred owl calls from the edge of a swamp while a huge old bullfrog attacks and devours a younger, smaller male that wanders into its territory. Glowworms creep amid the wet moss and plants as fireflies flicker overhead. A decaying fish along the shore glows eerily with its covering of luminescent bacteria. An orb-weaving spider creates its miraculous web by starlight. There, in the shadow, a night heron stands statuelike in wait for a fish, frog or crayfish to ambush. A muskrat munches on aquatic greens along the shore.

Mammals come to the wet places in search of food. Bears forage on blueberries while beavers gnaw at the bark of an aspen or birch. When something spooks a beaver and causes it to submerge, it closes the valves on its nostrils and ears to keep the water out. A raccoon reaches for crayfish beneath a submerged rock, an otter cruises for fish, a mink slips fluidly by on the bank while a muskrat flees to its burrow. A telltale pile of crayfish skeletons on a rock or log along the shore reveals the raccoon's voracious appetite.

Every aquatic environment has a night life that often rivals or exceeds that of the daylight hours. *Oceans* are alive with crustaceans and other animals that live in the dark zone, swimming upward at night and returning to the shadowy depths by day. Squid, fish and other predators come to feed on these crustaceans at night. Many jellyfish migrate close to the surface at dusk and during cloudy daytime periods. Eels are night-active, as are flounder, crabs and fish larvae, many of which feed on crustaceans. Sardines can often be located by the glowing, *bioluminescent* plankton they stir up in the surface waters. As many as half of all deep sea fish are luminescent; their surreal glowing lights form patterns along their sides or hang like lanterns held upon fleshy appendages protruding from the head. These lights help them to find food, locate a mate and sense danger. Some shrimp have extremely long antennae that they use to sense their surroundings in the lightless depths.

A nighttime walk along the *edge of the sea* is high drama, especially at lowest ebb just as the tide begins to rise, bringing food along with it. From a whisper to a roar, the sound of waves breaking over a sandy beach or rocky shore engulfs and mesmerizes the tide walker. The sand, seaweed, tide pools and rocks are alive with mussels, barnacles, small fish, sea stars, anemones, snails, sea urchins, beach fleas and other leaping, crawling and swimming crustaceans. Ghost crabs emerge from their burrows to eat and wet their gills. Hermit crabs scuttle about scavenging for a dead animal or some other detritus, well-protected in their adopted shell homes that do not seem to hinder their agility. Horseshoe crabs crawl about in the shallows. Many animals use the darkness to cloak their activity of laying eggs in the sand—sea turtles and some fish such as the capelin of the North Atlantic and their relatives the grunion of coastal southern California. In the light of early dawn the mysteries of the night shore can be seen, recorded in the fascinating scrapings and trails etched in the sand by crabs, worms, mice, skunks, raccoons, plovers and others.

North America's *terrestrial environments* range from arctic tundra to tropical rainforest. In the north country, the silence of an *arctic night* is broken by the calls of the gray wolf. During the long "night" of midwinter the moon stays constantly above the horizon. At this time of year polar bears become dormant and overwinter in their dens dug into deep snowbanks. By the bright of the stars, moon and northern lights or *aurora borealis* hunts the wolf, the largest wild North American dog. Although it is usually gray, its fur can vary from blackish to almost white in the far north. Wolves hunt mostly at night in packs of a dozen or more and may cover a hunting territory that is 60 miles (97 kilometers) in diameter. The wolf's diet ranges from small rodents and birds to caribou and deer. As an effective means of camouflage, the arctic fox, weasel, snowshoe hare and ptarmigan don a winter coat of white. Large eyes are an advantage in the long winter nights of the polar regions. The fiery yellow stare of the snowy owl looks out over open fields, prairies, beaches, marshes and dunes throughout Canada and it nests in the arctic tundra when summer arrives. Snowy owls overwinter as far south as the northern United States and beyond in severe winters.

North America's diverse forests harbor an array of nocturnal creatures. The *coniferous forests* of the north country reach south along the spines of the mountain ranges. This is the realm of spruce, fir, pine, hemlock and larch; home of the moose, woodland caribou, beaver and boreal owl. Here, during the mating season, moose are most active at dawn and dusk. Weighing up to 1,400 pounds (635 kilograms), standing as tall as 6.5 feet (2 meters) and having a rack of antlers that can reach over 6 feet (1.8 meters) across, the moose is the largest member of the deer family. Moose habitat includes conifer forests, swamps, brushy areas and

lakeshores. During the summer they eat mostly aquatic plants, but winter food consists largely of the twigs, buds, bark and saplings of woody plants. With their long legs, moose can run up to 35 miles (56.3 kilometers) per hour. The loud slap of a beaver's tail as it dives is often heard in moose country as a warning signal to other beavers that danger is near. Beavers emerge from the lodges after sunset to feed on the bark and small twigs of such trees as aspen, poplar, birch, alder, willow and maple. Beavers seem to work constantly at building lodges, making and repairing dams and maintaining canals and burrows. Another resident of the conifer forests and muskegs is the 9.5-inch (24.1-centimeter) boreal owl. This brownish owl is speckled with white and is extremely tame. Its beautiful call has been likened to the sound of dripping water or the tinkling of a bell.

Fascinating communities of plants and animals are found in the *temperate rainforests* of Pacific northwestern U.S. and Canada. In the Cascade Mountains of the northwestern U.S. 70 to 80 inches (177.8 to 203.2 centimeters) of rain falls each year, mostly during the autumn, winter and spring months. Western hemlock and western red cedar are dominant trees in this forest. One ancient tree may harbor fifteen hundred species of insects and other invertebrate animals. Martens emerge from their tree cavities to stalk the streambanks for their prey, which can range from frogs to beetles and birds to squirrels. These swift, agile, secretive members of the weasel family have been known to travel for miles amid the tree crowns. Generations of red tree voles live their entire lives in the crown of a Douglas fir, giant trees that can survive over one thousand years and grow to over 250 feet (76 meters) tall. Red tree voles often fall prey to the threatened northern spotted owl, another predator that also feeds on the northern flying squirrel among other prey. The rare Pacific giant salamander—the largest land salamander—grows to nearly 1 foot (30.5 centimeters) long and eats animals as large as mice and frogs.

Figure 2-4. The tiny saw-whet owl hunts using both its eyesight and a keen sense of hearing. Ears are hidden under feathers just behind each eye. This diminutive owl roosts in forests, dense thickets and conifers. When encountered during the day it is extremely tame. Its call is a long, rapidly repeated series of whistlelike notes that sound like it is saying "too, too, too, too, too. . ." Size: body, 7 inches (17.8 centimeters); wingspread, 17 inches (43.2 centimeters). (Photo by Steven D. Faccio.)

Deciduous forests are found in the temperate climates of North America where there are large, unbroken expanses in the east. The deciduous trees found in these forests vary greatly depending on the regional climate and they are mixed in many places with hemlock and pine and, in colder areas, patches of spruce and fir. Birch, beech, maple and ash are common in the northern hardwood forest. Oak and hickory are found in mid-temperate areas down toward the Great Smoky Mountains where a diversity of trees grows, including yellow birch, buckeye, hemlock, sugar maple, basswood and yellow poplar (tulip). South of here the forest includes pecan, hickory, magnolia, cypress, persimmon, live oak, longleafed pine and palmetto. Other southern deciduous trees are sycamore, walnut and cottonwood. White-tailed deer search for food after sunset in the forests, brushy areas, swamps and fields: twigs, buds, grass, acorns, fungi and herbs. At night, listen for their loud snort which alerts others to the presence of danger. Flying squirrels are also common in the nocturnal deciduous forest, ever alert for the presence of a hunting great horned owl or barred owl. A saw-whet owl can sometimes be heard calling from a thick stand of young evergreens (Figure 2-4). The little brown bat, big brown bat and eastern pipistrel can be seen at dusk feeding on insects throughout much of the eastern deciduous forest. Black bears, which are widespread in the northern coniferous forest, are most active at dusk and night in many wild regions of the deciduous forest where they forage for berries, nuts, roots, honey, insects and many other foods, including carrion and refuse.

Far to the south, near-night conditions prevail in the dense, mature *tropical rainforests* of Central America. Even during the day the forest floor is dark and heavily shaded. Nighttime is virtually black and the sky is masked by dense foliage overhead. Hummingbirds have one last burst of activity at dusk as they buzz from bloom to bloom. Nectar-sipping bats unfurl their wings. A cacophony of calls from owls, tree frogs, toads and katydids drifts down from leaves and branches. Many animals now begin to stir including porcupines, opossums, sloths, lizards, deer, tapirs, anteaters, collared peccaries and honeybears (kinkajous). These, and their young, are potential prey for a puma, jaguar or boa constrictor, which can exceed 6 feet (1.8 meters) in length.

Prairies and other grasslands have their own distinct night life. Standing under the moonlight in waving grass whipped by the wind you can imagine moving over a great grassy sea. In the mixed grasslands of central North America, myriad insects sing at dusk. The rough chirp of the mormon cricket may be heard or the sweeter song of the field cricket. A swift fox stalks a prairie vole while the "coo-coooo, coo-coooo" of a burrowing owl sounds gently in the darkness. The eerie howl of a coyote rolls over the land. Hunger drives this best runner among North America's members of the dog family from its den in search of prey, perhaps a black-tailed jack rabbit.

Nighttime offers great advantages to animals of the *desert,* allowing them to venture forth when the air is cooler and more humid than during the intense heat of day. A rattlesnake senses the body heat of its prey and zeros in for a strike. The prey could be a kangaroo rat, which is also eaten by the kit fox, coyote, badger and spotted skunk. An elf owl looks on from its nest in an old gila woodpecker's or flicker's hole chiseled out of a saguaro cactus. On the ground there may be a jack rabbit, gecko, scorpion or gila monster. Although the coyote is often associated with the deserts and grasslands, coyotes have one of the most widespread ranges of all North American animals. They also frequent woodlands and brushy areas. These scavengers occasionally hunt in pairs and often cache leftover food. Highly intelligent and adaptable, coyotes are most active at night and are found from extreme northern Alaska south into Mexico. Coyotes have spread farther east in recent times.

Cave-dwelling animals display extremes of sensory adaptation to a world that is permanently enveloped by total darkness. Many cave animals have no eyes at all or are sightless, such as blind cave salamanders and fish. Often cave animals have white skin without pigment because they are never exposed to the potentially harmful ultraviolet rays of the sun. Cave crayfish have extremely long antennae and sensory hairs on their legs as powerful detectors of chemical scents. The Texas blind salamander, which is only known to exist in one subterranean pool, senses vibrations in the water to locate shrimp and other prey. Cave scuds—small crustaceans that have no color—search the bottom of dark pools for bacterial

slime and bits of decaying plants. Some cave scuds are so rare that they can only be found in a particular pool in one cave, nowhere else. Many above-ground animals take temporary refuge in caves as well, including bears, foxes, snakes and bobcats.

Unlike the eternal darkness of caves, *cities* present environments where a brightly lit night follows each day. When pigeons, gray squirrels, house sparrows and starlings rest the wildlife of the night take over. Nighthawks call out with a nasal "peent" as they trace their erratic flight patterns in the glow of bright lights that attract their insect food. Night herons stalk the waters of many city parks and suburban wetlands. Frogs and toads, crickets and cicadas are calling. Earthworms and moles tunnel through garden soil while snails and slugs graze on greens overhead. A fox or mink hunts a park on the city fringe while a coyote prowls deeper into the concrete urban wilds. Raccoons and opossums scavenge for scraps of food. Flying squirrels forage for nuts and berries in the treetops. They retire at dawn to an attic or cavity in a hollow tree where they sleep away the day while curled up with as many as four or five others of their kind.

One tragic outcome of city lighting is its attractiveness to the hatchlings of threatened and endangered sea turtles along the coast. Hatchling sea turtles normally orient toward the bright horizon of the sea as they make a perilous journey from the sandy nest down to the water where they swim in relative safety. The lights of nearby hotels and condominiums, however, are often brighter than the night sky on the horizon. In this situation, many hatchling turtles turn away from the ocean toward the artificial lighting, only to be crushed under the wheels of a vehicle or die from exposure in the hot sun the next day.

Even in the city a number of night-migrating birds pass through while most people sleep. A majority of the songbirds migrate at night because it cloaks them from predators and because they can find food more easily during the day to sustain them for their night flights. However, great numbers of certain birds that migrate at night, such as swifts, perish when they fly into lighthouse beams, television and radio antennae and guy wires.

❖ ❖ ❖

With the first pink glow on the eastern horizon the call of a loon foretells the coming of dawn. As the animals of the dark hours gradually take cover, their daytime "alter-egos" begin to stir. You awake to the cool, lingering dampness of night and the breezes of the warmer morning air. A ballooning spider lets out a silk thread that catches the rising breeze and wafts it up on a journey homeward, wherever that may be. Out on a walk you notice the tracks of a raccoon in the mud as a spider's funnel-shaped web is highlighted by dew in a grassy field—proof that events as fantastic and intriguing as the stuff of our dreams have come to pass out-doors while we slept.

Primal Voice
Dawn mist dew
stirring in soft breezes
on sleepy pond.

Lace-leaf wand
conducting a toad chorus.

Ancient voice from age of
cave bone tools
call to daybreak
life in murky pool.

Know you secrets deep
wise Earth spirit,
this morning cool?[4]
—Michael J. Caduto
Vermont Natural History

QUESTIONS

1. Why do you think the small brown squirrel travels east to look for Sun? Why not travel north, south or west?

2. Why does the small brown squirrel climb the tree and get so close to Sun? Would you have made such a great sacrifice to free Sun from being tangled in the branches of the tall tree?

3. What happens to the small brown squirrel when he gets too close to Sun? How does Sun reward the squirrel for this brave sacrifice?

4. What causes night and day? How would you define "night"?

5. What are the advantages of having the cycle of day and night? Do you think it would be better to have daylight or night all of the time? Why or why not?

6. What are the advantages for animals that come out at night? What are the disadvantages?

7. What is the word that describes an animal that is active at night? What is the word that describes an animal active in the evening or in the morning?

8. Name a nocturnal animal that lives near you. What are some of the adaptations that help it to survive in the dark? How does it get around, find and catch its food and sense its environment?

9. What is the function of the retina in our eyes? Which of the cells in our retinas help us to see in dim light? How long does it take for our eyes to fully adjust to the darkness?

10. Do animal's eyes really glow in the dark? What really happens when an animal's eyes shine in the beam of a flashlight or car headlights? Why do animals have eyes that reflect light?

11. Which of your senses become stronger and more important as you walk around at night when your vision is not very good?

12. Why does sound carry better at night? Why do sounds seem louder?

13. Name one nocturnal animal from each of these environments: field, forest, pond, stream, ocean, seashore, desert, cave, arctic. What are some conditions in these different environments to which these animals must adapt to survive?

14. Why do most birds migrate at night?

ACTIVITIES
Night by Light

ACTIVITY: Sit quietly in one place to observe the crepuscular and nocturnal animals by (A) using a red light that few vertebrate animals can detect in order to view animals going about their natural activities, and (B) using a blue or white light to attract insects and other animals for viewing.

GOALS: Observe and experience the activities of crepuscular and nocturnal animals during their natural behavior and when they are drawn toward a light that attracts them.

AGE: Younger children and older children

MATERIALS: (A) "Discussion" section; one flashlight for each viewing area where children are stationed, with the beam covered with transparent red cellophane, red acetate or some other red filter taped or otherwise attached (Figure 2-5); fresh batteries for the flashlights; masking tape; insect repellant; hats to keep biting insects out of the hair; warm clothing; mats to sit on to keep dry and warm; Figure 1-1; Figure 2-2; Figure 2-3. (B) Flashlights with fully exposed white beams or with the beams covered with blue acetate or other blue-tinted lens.

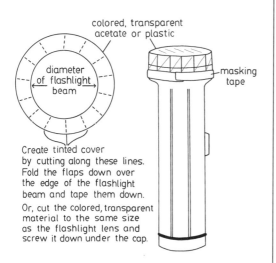

Figure 2-5. Creating a colored flashlight beam for "Night by Light" and other activities.

PROCEDURE A: *Night Watch.* Beforehand, choose a local environment that night animals are likely to frequent, such as the edge of a field and forest, pond, grassland, scrub/shrub chaparral, desert, rainforest, lakeshore, riverbank, beaver pond or the seashore. Collect flashlights, one for each viewing area. Be sure they shine brightly; add fresh batteries if necessary, and bring new batteries with you. Cover the lenses with red cellophane, red acetate or some other red covering through which light can pass (Figure 2-5). Acetate, which can be purchased at art supply stores, is preferable because it is made of cellulose from trees (plastic is made from oil). Another approach is to unscrew the lens cap from the flashlight and use the clear lens as a pattern to cut out a piece of tinted material of the same size. Either cover or replace the lens with the tinted material, place over the lightbulb and screw the cap back onto the flashlight.

Note: Some sporting goods catalogs sell spotlights with a snap-on red filter.

This is a simple observational activity. Go with the children to your chosen environment. Visit the site by day to search for signs of nocturnal animals, such as a deer trail, fox den, rabbit warren or a beaver pond. Decide which is the most likely location of animal activity. Choose an inconspicuous viewing area nearby, such as behind a hedgerow, shrub or tree, where you will all be able to sit and watch what happens. You may need several such blinds to accommodate the group. Discuss the meaning of "crepuscular" and "nocturnal" and have the children think of some animals they might expect to see. Share the illustration and photograph of the bat (Figures 2-2 and 2-3) as well as the photograph of the flying squirrel (Figure 1-1) with the children to pique their curiosity.

Discuss with the children how different kinds of light affect wildlife, as described in the "Discussion." For example, red light cannot be detected by the eyes of many animals so we can use it to observe without disturbing them. Blue or white light, however, *attracts* many insects and other animals. Tell the children that they are to use their senses of seeing, hearing and smelling especially. Encourage them to use their sixth sense to detect animals nearby.

Go back to the site just after sunset and position each child comfortably on a dry cushion or other seat behind one of the natural blinds you chose earlier. Have the children wait, watch, smell and listen *quietly*. When they need to turn to look at something, have them turn *very* slowly until their heads face that direction. Demonstrate how to do this. They are to turn the red beam of the flashlight onto any animal that happens by so they can watch it closely. Have them ask themselves what the animal is doing and why. Relax and enjoy the wildlife of night.

Leave the site quietly, like the animals. Once you have all left the site, hold a sharing circle to recall the events and sightings of the evening. Return the next morning to look for tracks and other signs that the animals you saw at night may have left.

Note: A variation on this activity and the following one, "Light Catch," can be done from the porch of a house. Turn off all the lights in the home and yard and use the porch as your blind while conducting these activities as they are described.

PROCEDURE B: *Light Catch.* Follow the procedure for *"Night by Light"* and add the following twist. At some point after darkness has set in, place a flashlight with an uncovered beam, or, preferably, a beam covered with a material that gives a blue tint, in the observational area near your blind. Do this quietly and have the beam facing away from your eyes at the blind but positioned so that you can see what kinds of insects and other animals are attracted to it. Return to the blind and observe the animals that are lured in by the light. Turn this beam off after about ten minutes, then resume your *"Night by Light"* watch.

Night Walk

ACTIVITY: Go on a nighttime excursion that is a feast of sensory delights.

GOALS: Experience the heightened sensory awareness that comes from being outdoors at night, including sight (night vision), hearing, touch, taste, smell and intuition or the sixth sense.

AGE: Younger children and older children

MATERIALS: Light rope at least 20 feet (6 meters) long; water bottle; first aid kit; insect repellant; extra warm clothing for the children; flashlight concealed in a backpack; blindfolds; bag or cooler containing food to sniff such as mint leaves, banana, popcorn, orange slices (prepeeled and sectioned), strawberries, lemon (cut in half), apple slices; mats or pads to sit on at stop 4.

PROCEDURE: Beforehand, read this activity over carefully and scout out an appropriate trail through forest and field and a *safe* location for a silent watch at the end of it. Note that stop 1 requires forest and that stop 2, "Sound Stalkers," requires an open, level area, such as a field, dirt parking lot or lawn. Safety is the key when considering this trail. Choose a trail that is relatively flat and easy to walk and in an area where crime is not a problem. Be certain there is no poison ivy, oak or sumac near the trail or at the site for "Watchers in the Night." Inform a friend, who will not be coming, of your whereabouts and expected time of return. Make sure you have permission to use the property you will visit and that the owners are expecting you at a certain time. Check in when you arrive and check out when you depart.

This walk consists of a wide variety of brief sensory activities to be conducted in the dark. No flashlights are involved and we do not allow children to bring them along because a person's night vision can be undone for forty-five minutes by the brief flash of a beam. Bring along a first-aid kit and one flashlight concealed in a backpack in case of an emergency. A ratio of no less than one adult per three children is advised. Take a head count at the beginning of the walk, after each activity and at the end before departing. The maximum group size should be ten people. Have all children use the restroom *before* you begin! Take one final check to see that everyone has on warm, dry clothing, insect repellant and dry shoes such as boots.

Begin by going outside into the darkness and discussing how our eyes need time to adjust to the dark (see the "Discussion"), and how our other senses become heightened to compensate for a reduced sense of vision. Tell the children that this is a walk to be done in silence since sound will frighten away any animals that might be encountered along the trail. For the duration of this special walk they are to talk only in response to the leader's questions. There *will* be a sharing time at the end of the walk. Walk single file between activities. With younger children we advise using a rope that they can all hold onto as they walk along for safety and to alleviate fears of being separated from the rest of the group. Adults can be interspersed along this rope, with one at the beginning to lead, one in the middle and one at the end as a trailer. Encourage the children to step high over bumps and to use both sight and the feel of the ground beneath their feet to navigate without tripping.

Once you have arranged everyone in position, have the group stand still and listen quietly for a minute or two to the sounds around them. Say nothing, then take the front of the rope and lead on into the night.

Stop 1: *Disappearing Trees.* Stand along the trail and have each child find a small tree to look at that is about 20 feet (6 meters) away in the shade of the forest. Have them stare at their tree *without looking away* and *without blinking.* The tree will slowly disappear! Ask the children what they think causes this to happen. (Rod cells are located along the periphery of the retina, and cone cells are concentrated toward the center. Since cone cells, which detect color, are not sensitive to low light levels, objects seem to disappear on dark nights when we stare directly at them. If we look using our peripheral vision then the light-sensitive rod cells are involved and we are better able to see in dim light.)

Stop 2: *Sound Stalkers.* In this activity, children will follow the sounds you make. Have the group hold onto the rope, single file, with a designated leader at the front. You may want to blindfold every child (younger children) or allow them to blindfold themselves (older children). Some leaders prefer an honor system in which everyone is asked to keep eyes closed. This helps in case children have to suddenly stop and look where they are going. Also, blindfolds irritate some children's skin or eyes. Never insist that a child wear a blindfold when he or she seems afraid or uncomfortable doing so.

Tell the children they are to follow the leader at the head of the line as she or he moves toward each sound that you will be making. There can be *no talking* or they will not hear well enough to participate. Explain that they will have to stop and listen frequently to determine the direction of each new sound. Designate and demonstrate a special sound that will signal for them to take off their blindfolds and search for you. Make sure they recognize this sound well and do not use other similar sounds during this activity or they may remove their blindfolds prematurely.

Start by walking off quietly and whistling from one place. The group will come toward you. Move swiftly and quietly to a new location *while the group is moving* so the children do not hear where you are going. When the group pauses to listen again, make a new noise to draw them over. Keep repeating this sequence with different noises (owl calls, dog barks, etc.), each time moving off quietly in another direction as the group shuffles toward your last sound. After about six to eight rounds of this game, run behind a bush or other object and make the agreed upon sound as a signal for them to remove their blindfolds and search for you.

Stop 3: *Feel, Sniff and Munch.* Have the group line up shoulder to shoulder with blindfolds on. Tell them you will be placing an object under their noses, and then letting them feel it as you go down the line. They are to guess what it is, but *keep silent* about it until all have had a chance to experience it. When you get to the end of the line and all have smelled and touched the object, have them raise their hands and call on someone to tell the group what she or he thinks it is until someone gets it right. Have the children use the water bottle to wet their noses around the nostrils to heighten their sense of smell.

Use aromatic foods that are strange to the touch for this activity: partly crushed mint leaves, a peeled banana, popcorn, orange slices, strawberries, a lemon cut in half or a sliced apple, for instance. Use about six different smells—any more and the activity starts to drag. Once they have guessed all of the foods, have the group sit down and eat the foods in the dark.

Do the flavors seem any stronger than usual? Why or why not? How does our tongue taste foods? Does smell have anything to do with flavor? Hold your nose and try eating a strawberry. Do you taste it? Why would flavors seem stronger if we ate some food outdoors in the dark? Is our sense of smell stronger at night? Why?

Stop 4: *Watchers in the Night.* Assemble in a special meeting place. Explain to the children that this is a time for them to be alone with the night, yet safely near their friends and the adults in the group. Tell them approximately how long their night watch will be and explain that the time may *seem* longer than it actually is. Ask them why this is so. Say, "The night is a friend if we know how to live within it. There is no need to be afraid, and, if you are, don't worry because we are right here nearby."

Tell them they will be assigned a spot to be "Watchers in the Night." They are to sit quietly while they watch, listen to and smell their surroundings. No talking, gesturing to their neighbors or moving around is allowed.

While there, the children may watch the stars, listen to the wind through the trees and the sounds of insects and other animals, smell the air and the earth around them. Ask them not to pick any plants while at their spot, not even grass. (Children have a way of tearing off great quantities of plant material while "sitting still.") The object is to clear their minds of other thoughts, to help them become a part of the night world, to blend and fade into it, to use their "sixth sense" to notice the presence of animals around them. Demonstrate a call that you will use to signal the end of the activity when they will all return to that same meeting place.

Pass out one mat or pad for each child to sit on since the ground will be damp. Walk along and place the children so that they cannot see each other but where they are all in sight of at least one of the adults. Allow them to sit for ten to twenty minutes, depending upon their age, level of maturity and the group's frame of mind. Then call them in with the signal and allow time for them to share their experiences.

Why Animals Don't Go Bump in the Night

ACTIVITY: Put on a fun puppet show in which nocturnal animals reveal a number of their adaptations for surviving in the night environment.

GOALS: Understand many forms of nighttime sensory awareness and other adaptations found among nocturnal animals, and how these help to ensure each animal's survival.

AGE: Younger children and older children

MATERIALS: One stick to mount each puppet onto; outline sketches of an owl, bullfrog, crayfish, katydid (Figure 2-6), bat, luna moth and rattlesnake; crayons or colored pencils to color in the puppets; pencils; paper; cardboard backing for the puppets; scissors; glue or paste; tape; script for *"Why Animals Don't Go Bump in the Night."*

PROCEDURE: Beforehand, have the children prepare puppets-on-a-stick of an owl, bullfrog, crayfish, katydid (Figure 2-6), bat, luna moth and rattlesnake. Make a few props suggesting a pond with lily pads, a grassy shoreline with a large rock and a big tree growing next to the pond. Set up a stage using the props and a blue blanket, bedspread or construction paper for the water.

Have the children think of means by which different nocturnal animals find their way around, locate and catch their prey, find a mate and generally sense their environment at night. Then have them perform the following puppet show. Encourage the puppeteers to adopt voices they think their animals would sound like.

Note: This puppet show can also be performed in costumes as group theater.

Why Animals Don't
Go Bump in the Night

Mr. Barred Owl: (whispers from up in the tree) Psst-psssstt. Hey, Mr. Bullfrog,

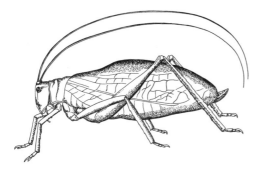

Figure 2-6. The true katydid, which is a kind of long-horned grasshopper, is aptly named for the repetitive mating call made by the male from a perch in a tree or tall shrub. It sounds remarkably like it is saying "katy-did" or "katy-didn't." The katydid creates its "song" by rubbing its wings together. Size: 1.6 inches (4.1 centimeters). (Adapted with permission from Donald J. Borror and Richard E. White, A Field Guide to the Insects. Boston, Massachusetts: Houghton Mifflin Co., 1970, p. 81.)

is that yooou swimming around down there in the lily pads?

Mr. Bullfrog: Why, yes ... who ... what ... where are you ... where is your voice coming from?

Mr. Barred Owl: Up here, it's me, Mr. Barred Owl. (*loudly*) Who cooks for YOU, who cooks for YOOOU all?

Mr. Bullfrog: Mr. Barred Owl, you know I eat my food raw. Why do you ask such a silly question?

Mr. Barred Owl: It's not a silly question. It's my mating call. I'm calling my mate because she flew over to the far hill.

Mr. Bullfrog: Hey, listen to this. (*deeply*) Jug-o-rum, jug-o-rum, jug-o-rum. That's how I call my mate. But Mr. Barred Owl, how will she ever hear you way over there on that distant hillside?

Mr. Barred Owl: We owls have great hearing yooou know. This dish-shaped arrangement of feathers around our eyes catches sound like a satellite dish and funnels it to our ears. Heck, I can hear better than yooou can, Mr. Bullfrog!

Mr. Bullfrog: Ears? I don't see any ears. Mine are big flat patches behind my eyes. Where are yours?

Mr. Barred Owl: They are just below and behind my eyes. When I point my head so that the sound reaches my ears in a certain way I'm looking right at the animal making the sound. And I can turn my head three-quarters of the way around in either direction. My hearing even helps me to find food in the dark. When I swoop down and get close enough I can also see my prey because my eyesight works well even by the dim light of the stars and moon.

Ms. Crayfish: (*from the pond*) What's all the racket around here! Can't a crayfish sleep? Who woke me up with all that noise?

Mr. Barred Owl: We were the ones—me and Mr. Bullfrog that is. Our mating calls woke you up.

Mr. Bullfrog: Yes. We didn't mean to wake *you* up though.

Mr. Katydid: (*from up in the tree*) Have you heard *my* mating call yet? Here goes. Katy-did-it, katy-did-it, katy-did-it.

Ms. Crayfish: Hey! Keep it down! What's with you guys? Don't you have anything better to do than hang around making a racket all night? Goodnight! (*leaves*)

Mr. Katydid: (*screams loudly*) Aaaahh! (*Ms. Bat comes swooping in near Mr. Katydid*)

Ms. Bat: (*flies in*) Whoosh—Don't worry, Mr. Katydid, I'm not going to eat you. (*flying around while talking*) I've already eaten one hundred, no two hundred, no three hundred—oh well, I forget how many mosquitoes and other insects I've eaten tonight.

Mr. Barred Owl: How do you ever find insects in the dark, Ms. Bat?

Ms. Bat: (*still flying around*) Don't you know? I make very high-pitched sounds and they echo off of things, like trees and insects, and then come back to my ears to tell me what and where those things are. I'm very good at it. I never bump into anyone and I almost always catch the meal I'm chasing. Hey, got to go, the sun will be coming up soon! (*flies away and disappears*)

Mr. Katydid: Katy-did-it, katy-did-it. Hey, who's that brushing up against me?

Ms. Luna Moth: (*from up in the tree*) It's me, Ms. Luna Moth. I'm up here trying to attract a mate too.

Mr. Katydid: What? I didn't hear you calling him.

Ms. Luna Moth: Oh no, I don't have to. I create a special odor with my scent glands and it travels downwind. If there is any potential mate of my kind for miles away he will sense my scent with his feathery antennae and come right to me.

Mr. Katydid: Wow, I've got to hand it to you, Ms. Luna Moth, that's some powerful perfume! (*Mr. Katydid and Ms. Luna Moth exit*)

Mr. Bullfrog: Oh my … oh no … it's, it's a snake! I'm going underwater to hide! (*disappears*)

Ms. Rattlesnake: (*from the grassy shore*) Sssoo, I've come across a gathering of great sssircumstansss, it would ssseem.

Mr. Barred Owl: How did you ever sneak up so quietly, Ms. Rattlesnake?

Ms. Rattlesnake: Why, I just ssslithered along sssilently. I'm looking for a place to digest my meal of a moussse.

Mr. Barred Owl: How did you ever catch a mouse in the dark?

Ms. Rattlesnake: Well, Mr. Barred Owl, I have two *pits,* tiny openings between each eye and nostril on my head. They are very sssensitive to heat. When a mouse comes within a few feet of me I ssstrike at its body heat! I rarely miss, and I don't need my eyes to catch it. You might say that when a mouse sees or hears me coming it's the *pits!*

Mr. Barred Owl: Very funny, Ms. Rattlesnake! (*yawns*) Oh, oh—the sky is getting brighter and brighter, it's almost morning, my bedtime.

Ms. Rattlesnake: Yesss, I must ssslither up to my rock so I can bask in the ssssun and digest my meal. Goodbye! (*crawls over to the rock*)

Mr. Barred Owl: Well, I'm going to sleep now. Goodnight, I mean, goodday everyone.

Dark Detectives

ACTIVITY: Set up and map a route along which to observe animals at night. Travel this route for several nights. Stop, observe and listen at stations along the way. Record your observations, then learn about and report on the animals that you saw and heard.

GOALS: Realize that familiarity with a particular path is an important part of being able to move about at night. Discover what some local animals are doing at night and learn about those animals. Understand that observing animals in the wild takes patience and that keeping records is an important tool for gathering information.

AGE: Older children

MATERIALS: Paper; pencils; clipboards or cardboard backings to write against in the field; compass; flashlights with red light (see *"Night by Light"* on page 34 for instructions on making red flashlights); "Extending the Experience" from Chapter 5; leaves of a strong-smelling local native plant that is nontoxic and nonirritating; blindfolds; large sheet of paper and crayons or markers for making the map; references to the natural history of animals and (optional) branches; green or brown tarpaulin and other materials with which to build a lean-to or tepee-shaped blind (see "Extending the Experience" in Chapter 5).

PROCEDURE: During the day, take the children into a local environment where animals are likely to be active at night. Look for signs of animals and find several places near these signs from which to make nighttime observations. For example, search for an animal trail, droppings, twigs that have been browsed, a den such as a hollow tree or burrow. Locate several good observation posts downwind (use the prevailing winds) from the animal signs to hide the children from the animals: large trees or rocks, dense shrubs or overhanging branches or a stone wall. Sketch out a map showing the landmarks in this area, such as prominent stones, trees, holes, walls, etc. Use the compass to draw magnetic north on the map so that it is oriented. Make sure the route avoids dangers such as poisonous plants, obstacles, holes and dropoffs.

Walk this trail in daylight several days in a row to become familiar with it. Have the children practice by each leading a blindfolded partner. Concentrate on making a mental map that will guide you at night. Look and take notes of fresh signs of animals during each day visit. You may want to build a lean-to (see "Extending the Experience" in Chapter 5) or a tepeelike blind to hide in at one of the most active observation posts. Plan every precaution to safely go out into the local environment. For example, in the desert, have the children move slowly, use red flashlights to see where they are stepping and wear heavy boots up to their knees to avoid poisonous animals such as scorpions, rattlesnakes and the gila monster.

Before going out on the trail as *"Dark Detectives,"* have the children take a few precautions to keep the animals from seeing or smelling them. Make sure they wear dark clothes that have been left outside in a dry location for several days to air out the human scent. Prior to leaving, have the children rub themselves with a strong-smelling native plant to mask their smell. Know the identity of the nontoxic, nonirritating plant from which the leaves come that the children are rubbing on themselves. *Be absolutely certain you know the identity of local poisonous plants, such as poison sumac, ivy or oak and do not use leaves from these plants.*

Walk the *"Dark Detectives"* trail several nights over the course of a few weeks. Bring some red flashlights to use for observing animals without disturbing their natural behaviors. Stay at least five minutes at each observation post and write down everything you see, hear and smell of the animals around each post. Once a good record of field notes has been gathered, have the children use this information to make complete record logs describing what was observed at each site over time. Plot the sightings of animals on the map and look for patterns of movement. Now have the children use references to learn the natural history of the animals they have experienced. Finally, instruct the children to use the information from their observations and research to write and present reports about the animals they saw.

With proper preparation and dress this activity can be conducted any time of year. *"Dark Detectives"* is a magical experience when reading the signs of animals in the snow and walking in the winter whiteness under a bright, moonlit night.

Note: Use the activities called *"Stalking"* and *"Tracking"* from Chapter 15 of *Keepers of the Animals* for more tips to deepen the experience of *"Dark Detectives."*

EXTENDING THE EXPERIENCE

• Visit a natural area at dusk and make some owl calls, then wait for a response. Calls recorded on commercially available bird song tapes work well. The great horned owl is found in woodlands, deserts, scrub/shrub lands, canyons and bottomlands throughout North America. The male's call is a deep "hoo, hoo-oo, hoo-hoo," while the female's call, which is a lower pitch, has more hoots: "hoo, hoo-hoo-hoo, hoo-oo, hoo-oo." Another common North American owl is the barred owl, which responds very well to calls made by humans. The barred owl's "Who cooks for YOU? Who cooks for YOU all?" is commonly heard in woodlands, wooded swamps and along floodplains. Wear a hat just in case the owl is really convinced and flies in thinking you are invading its territory.

• Visit your nearest zoo and observe the animals there that are normally nocturnal. Some zoos have a special exhibit in which the animals live in a light-controlled environment that has them thinking it is nighttime when it is really day. This way you can see them going about their nocturnal activities.

• Go out after nightfall and use red cellophane-tinted flashlights to search for frogs, newts, salamanders, toads and other amphibians. Amphibians move about their habitats after warm rains, especially near ponds and streams. These animals often travel at night when the air is cool and moist. Early spring is a good time to search for amphibians, right after the first rainfall of the season when the temperature reaches above freezing. Some, such as the spotted salamander, come out in numbers just once each year. Spotted salamanders deposit fertile eggs in vernal ponds and pools, then return to their dark home in the soil and leaf litter. Amphibians, such as the spadefoot toad, come out in great numbers after a desert rain.

• In places where you hear "birds" chirping at night well after dark, move into an opening and look up into the trees. You may see that flying squirrels are the real source of the chirping (birds seldom chirp at night). It is fun to see them gliding from tree to tree and chasing each other about.

• *Color the Night.* Hand out one index card and crayon to each child after deep night has set in. Have the children use the crayon to write their name on the card as well as the color they believe their crayon to be. Have them hang onto the crayon as you collect the cards. Later, at a time when light is available, give the cards back. How many guessed the correct color? Were any groups of colors more often correctly guessed? Which ones? (Thanks to Charles E. Roth, naturalist/educator, for the idea for this activity and for the previous suggestion for observing flying squirrels.)

• Search for reptiles at night in warm places. As the cool evening air settles in, warm pavement, rocks and other places that retain the heat of the day attract many snakes and lizards. *Consider safety first: Watch for cars along roadways.*

• Take a daytime field trip to a southwestern desert where cacti are blooming and scout out a safe trail into the area. Return at night (you will need to dress warmly because desert nights can be quite cold) and use the red flashlight beam to observe bat and insect activity at cactus blooms. Flower nectar in the blooms of the saguaro cactus in the Sonoran Desert, for example, attracts the longnose bat. Moths visit yucca flowers for a source of pollen. Elf owls, screech owls and pygmy

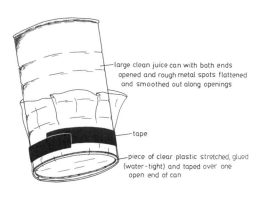

large clean juice can with both ends
opened and rough metal spots flattened
and smoothed out along openings

tape

piece of clear plastic stretched, glued
(water-tight) and taped over one
open end of can

Figure 2.7—Making a pond scope.

owls can be found nesting in abandoned holes that were chiseled into saguaro stems by gila woodpeckers.

• If you live within the breeding range of the American woodcock (southeastern Canada and roughly east of the Mississippi in the United States), look and listen for the male's courtship displays at dusk in the late winter/early spring. Woodcocks prefer shrub swamps, moist woodlands and wet hedgerows near old fields or pastures above which they display. (See the "Discussion" for a description of this display.) Be careful not to get too close: Disturbing the bird's mating ritual can cause them to abandon the breeding ground.

• Use a flashlight beam tinted red (Figure 2-5) to explore the nocturnal aquatic life of streams, lakes, ponds, marshes (fresh- and saltwater) and tide pools. Many insects and other animals in these environments are nocturnal. They can be seen actively feeding and moving about at night. You might also try a white flashlight to see which insects and other animals are attracted to it. Make and use a simple pond scope (Figure 2-7) to get a clear view underwater.

• Set up a telescope or use binoculars to watch for spring and fall birds migrating as they pass in front of the face of a bright moon.

• Make a bat box to provide shelter for local bats. (For information on how to become involved with bat conservation, contact Bat Conservation International, P.O. Box 162603, Austin, TX 78716, [512] 327-9721.)

• If you work at a nature center or other environmental center with a budget for equipment purchases, you may want to purchase an ultrasonic sound detector for bat sounds, available from Bat Conservation International (see above).

• Read *America's Neighborhood Bats* by Dr. Merlin D. Tuttle (Austin, Texas: University of Texas Press, 1988).

• Put some rolled oats out on a second floor window ledge or in window bird feeder to attract flying squirrels. The food has to be high enough, such as outside a second-story window, for the squirrels to be able to glide in to and out from. Flying squirrels inhabit trees in suburban and urban neighborhoods as well as rural woodlands.

• Two books that will enhance and deepen your understanding of the natural world after dark are *Reading the Outdoors at Night* by Vinson Brown (Harrisburg, Penn.: Stackpole Books [United States] and Scarborough, Ontario: Thomas Nelson & Sons, Ltd. [Canada], 1972) and *Nature's Night Life* by Robert Burton (London: Blandford Press, 1982 [distributed in the United States by: Sterling Publishers, 387 Park Ave. South, Fifth Floor, New York, NY 10016-8810]).

• Read the *Muskogee* (Creek) story "How Grandmother Spider Stole the Sun" in Chapter 7 of *Keepers of the Earth*. Compare what happens to Buzzard in that story when he carries the sun to the top of the sky, with the fate of the small brown squirrel in "How the Bat Came to Be."

NOTES

1. Loris J. Milne and Margery J. Milne. *The World of Night*. New York: Harper Colophon Books, 1956, pp. 99–100.

2. Ibid., pp. 8–9.

3. Ibid., pp. 123–124.

4. Michael J. Caduto. "Journeys Between." In *Vermont Natural History*. Woodstock, Vt.: Vermont Institute of Natural Science, Autumn 1983, pp. 22–23.

CHAPTER 3

Moth, The Fire Dancer

(Paiute—Great Basin)

Long ago, Moth had black wings. He was a great dancer as he flew and he loved to dance around the people's fires. The people would watch him as he danced and the young women would laugh as he dove and fluttered and circled. They would try to catch him and dance with him, but he would always escape them.

"Be careful," his father told him, "do not dance too close to the fire." But Moth did not listen to his father. He liked to dance and flirt with the young women while the fires burned bright. He danced this way all through the spring and the summer.

One night, near the end of summer, Moth came to dance around the fire. The young women laughed as he danced and he danced even harder, coming closer and closer to the flames. He dove down wildly and flapped up again and the young women tried to dance with him.

"You cannot catch me," he said. "I am Moth. I am the greatest dancer of all!" But as he bragged he flew too close to the flame. The fire caught him and he spun down onto the coals with burned wings. It seemed as if he was dead.

His father had been watching from the shadows. He flew down and carried his son away into the forest. He put medicine on his son's burned wings and wrapped him up in a gray blanket and hid him in the bushes.

Throughout the winter, the people talked in their lodges about Moth, the dancer. The young women were sad as they thought of how he had been killed by the flames. They would miss his dancing around their fires at night. They would miss playing with him as he dove and circled. At last the winter was gone and the days began to grow longer. One night, not long after the Moon of New Grass, the people sat around a fire late at night. All was quiet when suddenly, out of the night, came the flash of wings. Then, with wings as bright as the red of flames, someone was dancing around the fire, dancing as Moth had danced.

"Who is it?" the people said.

"He dances the way Moth danced," said the young women. "Moth has come back, but his wings now are filled with flame!"

The young women laughed as Moth danced and he danced even
harder, coming closer and closer to the flames.

And so it was. Wrapped in his gray blanket, Moth's burns had healed and he had come back to dance once more with the people. But now his wings were no longer black. They were gray as a blanket above and as red as sparkling flames below.

"We can no longer just call him Moth," the people said. "He must have a new name. We will call him The Fire Dancer." And that has been his name to this day.

DISCUSSION

A moth spirals and darts around a lantern or the light of a candle. It flutters out of the darkness and into the rings of light with which we keep the night at bay. A soft, downy moth's wing brushes an arm, eliciting a squeamish reaction as the harmless insect is brushed away. Most likely, the moth is in the *Noctuid* family, the most common moths that fly around lights at night. Their name comes from the Latin word *noctua* meaning "a night owl."

In this Paiute story of "Moth, The Fire Dancer," Moth is drawn irresistibly to the light of a fire, compelled to circle closer and closer to the flames. In the wild, *moths* forage flowers and other sources of sweetness and nectar at night. Because they navigate by keeping their wings at a constant angle relative to the moon they are also drawn to bright artificial lights, around which they fly in confused circles. Moths will flutter around a campfire or into almost any open window where they are attracted by a lamp or other light. Moths and other insects are especially attracted to blue light. Red light is hard for them to detect and is least likely to draw them in. A yellow light is not very attractive to insects yet it gives off sufficient light for people to see by. If, in a circle of light, you catch a glimpse of a moth's golden-red eyeshine, keep watching for a time and these tiny reflections will slowly disappear as the moth's eyes adjust to the light.

A moth's antennae, which are highly sensitive to odors, help it to find a mate in the darkness. The females of some species emit a scent that can draw a male in from over 6 miles (9.7 kilometers) away! Males respond to this powerful perfume by traveling purposefully upwind to the waiting female. Although scent is the lure used to find a mate, many moths, such as the polyphemus, promethia and cecropia, exhibit beautiful artistry on their wings. The luna moth, with its pale green wings bearing eyespots, is among the most exquisite creatures astir at night.

The bolas spider of the southeastern United States uses the male moth's extreme sensitivity to the female's mating perfume to its own advantage. Weaving no web, the spider lets down a small dewy drop on the end of a piece of silk. The drop gives off an imitation of the mating scent of a female moth, drawing the unsuspecting males in to be eaten. Amazingly the bolas spider can even mimic the scent of female moths from a number of species.

It is no surprise that moths orient at night using sight and scent, but some are capable of using sound in an ingenious way to survive. Certain moths can confuse predatory bats and avoid being found by creating ultrasonic clicks of their own that jam the bat's echolocation radar. The longeared bat has responded to this challenge by turning off its radar when approaching a moth to avoid being detected. It then zeroes in on the moth by listening to the moth's wingbeats.

Insects and Spiders at Night

The drone of cicadas and chatter of grasshoppers gradually give way at dusk to the calling of katydids from trees and shrubs and the chirping of crickets from bushes and tufts of grass. Golden-eyed lacewings fly overhead. Junebugs crash into screen doors while fireflies flicker in a nearby meadow, protected from human intrusion by hungry female mosquitoes on reconnaissance for a blood meal (Figure 3-1). Some wasps hang still and upside-down from the bottom of their paper nests. Bumblebees and butterflies often spend the night on the last flower they visited before nightfall. Bumblebees are partial to resting on thistle.

From the wilderness to the heart of the city, many insects congregate wherever there is a bright light: moths, Junebugs and even the giant water bug, which is aptly nick-named "toe biter." Ants move about searching for food by following scent trails that, to their senses, are as well marked as highways. In the Lilliputian world of the ant, the stillness of night is often broken by violent ant wars as battle is waged over food and territory.

Down in the wet places, when whirligig beetles cease their wild gyrating in the open water and seek refuge in quiet bays, and when water striders no longer hunt the surface film but have sheltered up in the wet leaves and branches until morning, the night air comes alive. Delicate, newly hatched mayflies, stoneflies and caddisflies speckle the air near ponds, streams and rivers.

Some insects have even become adapted to live in the eternal darkness of caves. Cave-dwelling camel crickets, for example, are able to compensate for visual deprivation; they use long antennae and sensory leg bristles to detect chemical scents. Bat guano is food for many cave insects, which are in turn eaten by cave spiders and centipedes.

Crickets and cicadas are familiar insects that are poorly understood by many people. Cricket calls are made by the males to attract a mate, to warn other crickets of danger and to defend their own territory, such as a clump of grass, from other males. You can often return to a certain clump of grass to find the same male calling on different occasions. Crickets make these calls by rubbing a scraper on one wing against ridges on the other. The male and female use their antennae to find each other because it is thought that they mate mostly at night. The females of some species of cricket also make calls. Among these species both male and female sing back and forth to one another as they move closer together.

Under protection of an early summer night, the mature nymphs of *cicadas* burrow up from where they have been feeding on the

Figure 3-1. Left: Firefly displays etch patterns in light over a meadow at dusk. Right: The hard shell of these Photinus *fireflies reveals that they are a kind of beetle. This mating pair are members of the same species of firefly shown displaying in the field (left). Size: about .4-inch (1 centimeter). (Photographs by David H. Funk.)*

sap of tree roots and crawl onto the bark of a tree or other surface. Adults then emerge from a split in the exoskeleton that runs up the middle of the back. The nascent adults then pump their wings up with blood in preparation for a morning liftoff to a singing perch from which to start the life cycle again. Among some common cicadas this life cycle is repeated every one to three years. Nymphs of the seventeen-year cicada, however, spend seventeen years underground before emerging. Cicada songs drift dreamily amid the heat and rustle of a midsummer day. Unlike crickets, cicadas create their songs by vibrating two drumlike membranes located on the sides of their thorax. A cicada's large abdomen is mostly hollow to amplify the sounds.

Beetles fly about or creep over the ground at night looking for a meal. The black, 1-inch (2.5-centimeter) sexton beetle, *Nicrophorus,* has beautiful orange markings on its wing covers. Its antennae are alert for the scent of death as it searches for food on the wing. When it has discovered a potential meal it spirals down to the carcass, such as that of a mouse, and gradually buries it a few inches below the surface of the soil. Eggs are laid in the dead animal which serves as food for the growing larvae when they hatch. Adults do not abandon the eggs, however; they feed the grubs regurgitated food and even create a tunnel in which the larvae can pupate.

With eyes to the ground you may also see a *glowworm,* which is either an immature *firefly* of some species or the wingless adult female of one genus of fireflies, *Phengodes.* No one knows for certain why fireflies glow in the immature stage. Fireflies or *lightning bugs,* which are found the world over, are really beetles. It is known that fireflies create light in their abdomens virtually without heat through a process called *bioluminescence.* A protein called *luciferin* is combined with an enzyme, *luciferase,* and, in the presence of oxygen, the resulting reaction causes luciferin to produce a cool light. About 90 percent of the energy is converted into light

in this reaction, with the remaining 10 percent given off as heat. Crepuscular fireflies, those that are active at dusk, generally emit a yellow glow, while the true fireflies of nighttime give off a green light. It is thought that, at dusk, there is much green light reflecting off foliage, so the yellow glow helps the fireflies to stand out against the leaves.

There are several techniques that the different species of firefly use to attract a partner. Timing is everything during the most common displays that are seen in the northern temperate regions. Patterns of light reveal both the sex and species of the sender. In some species, wingless females first send up a light signal from the ground. Males of the same species that see the female's signal wait a certain amount of time, then respond with their own sequence of flashes. Finally the female answers with a display that tells the male she is a willing mate of the same species. The pattern created by the flashes and the periods of time in between are important cues. Each species has its own unique form of this language of light.

Fireflies have many variations on this theme of displaying. Some females glow continuously and attract nonluminescent males who are flying overhead. Other females flash to elicit a male response, while some only flash in response to a male's signal. In some species, the males gather and flash in synchrony as females fly to them. The adults of different species mature and begin displaying at various times, so we see a number of beautiful patterns throughout the firefly season each summer.

Both larval and adult fireflies are carnivorous. Once the female of one species of firefly, *Photuris versicolor,* has performed her own light display and successfully mated with a male of her own kind, she switches over to mimic the light display of the female of a different species. When an unsuspecting male of that species lands and crawls over to the female expecting to find a mate, he becomes her meal instead.

Fireflies also use their lights as an alarm or defense signal, or to demonstrate aggres-

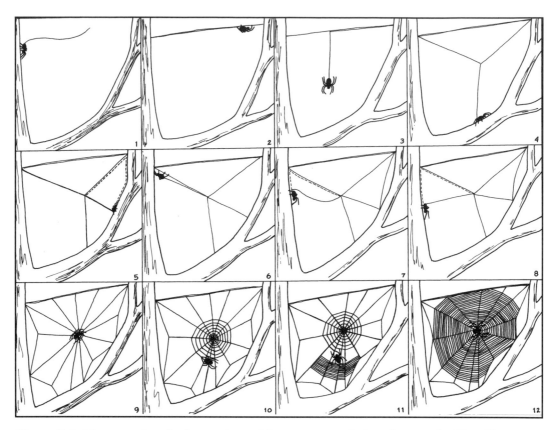

Figure 3-2. Many species of orb-weaving spiders construct their webs at night. This illustration shows one of many different techniques used for creating the orb web. First, the spider either walks and carries a line from one place to another to create a silken bridge, or, more often, it lets out a silk thread into the wind (1) until the thread touches a surface, sticks and creates a bridge (2) which is often reinforced with more thread. The spider then attaches a thread to a strand in the center of the bridge (3) and drops down to anchor that vertical thread (4). A radius thread is attached at the hub of the web-to-be, carried up to the end of the bridge and down to where the new thread is snugged and anchored (5). Other radius threads are created in this same way (6–9). The hub may be reinforced with more silk threads. The spider then creates a temporary spiral (10) and uses its legs to measure distances between each round. Once the temporary spiral is completed, the spider reverses direction, rolls up the silk of the temporary spiral and circles inward as it creates the closer strands in the new spiral of sticky silk (11). As it does this it retraces the path back to the center of the web (12).

Webs are rebuilt both day and night. Some spiders incorporate a particular decoration in the center and some take the web down during the day. A hideaway of silk in rolled-up leaves is created at the edge of some webs where the spider waits in contact with a line that connects with the hub and senses vibration of insects caught in the web. (Adapted with permission from Hebert W. Levi and Lorna R. Levi, Spiders and Their Kin. Racine, Wisconsin: Western Pub. Co., *1987, pages 54–55. Original illustration by Nicholas Strekalovsky)*

sion. Some even appear to use landing lights. The *Photuris* fireflies flash ever more quickly as they approach the ground, until the flash becomes a constant glow, which they turn off upon landing.

Spiders are fascinating denizens of the night world. Wolf spiders, trapdoor spiders and others have eyeshine that appears like tiny speckles in the beam of a flashlight because most spiders have eight eyes. Orb weavers and doily spiders create an intricate, lacy web that, among many species, is woven at night (Figure 3-2). Other groups of spiders make webs in the shapes of sheets and funnels. All of these webs are spun of *silk* made by special glands on the rear of the spider. The glands spin silk of different thicknesses that serves for a number of daytime and nighttime uses besides weaving webs, such as to cover and protect eggs, to wrap food and as a *lifeline* by which the spider lowers itself down. Some young spiderlings practice *ballooning* during which they climb to a high point, release a long mesh of silk threads into the wind and are often carried off for great distances. Thick spider silk could support 60,000 pounds per square inch (4,218 kilograms per square centimeter). This is about the same tensile strength as the highest quality steel wire of a comparable thickness.[1]

Plants at Night

A white-lined sphinx moth, hovering like a hummingbird, feeds on nectar from a night-blooming cereus with its fragrant water-lily-like flowers that measure up to 4 inches (10.2 centimeters) across (Figure 3-3). Another species, *Pronuba,* the yucca moth, gathers pollen from yucca blooms whose sweet scent of whitish petals fills the desert night air. The female moth lays eggs at the bottom of the flower's ovaries and purposefully smears the male pollen onto the female stigmas, thus fertilizing the flowers. When *Pronuba* larvae hatch they have a ready-made food supply in the developing yucca seeds. Yucca flowers bloom throughout the nights of April and May from late afternoon until mid-morning the next day. These flowers are finely adapted to the yucca moth's life cycle: The yucca needs the moth to produce seeds each year. Elf owls, poor-wills and other desert animals prey on these nectar feeders.

Many plants of the desert and other environments open at dusk when nocturnal insects become active. Yucca flowers spread their petals in late afternoon and remain open all night until mid-morning. Flowers of the Joshua tree, which is really a large species of yucca, also bloom at night, and the night-blooming cereus is true to its name. Some flowers even produce a stronger fragrance at dusk than at other times of day. Numerous flowers that bloom after dark appear white to humans but may have ultraviolet markings—rings, spots, stripes and other forms—that are invisible to people but can be detected by nocturnal moths, butterflies and other insects. Once the insects fly in close to a bloom, these markings, called *pollen guides* and *nectar guides,* point the way to the flower's sources of pollen and nectar.

For over 150 million years flowers and insects have been evolving in tandem. Flowering plants are pollinated by insects, while insects use leaves, flowers, sap, bark, branches, roots, hollows and holes in plants for shelter, food and drink. Assassin bugs, as well as the small (.1- to .2-inch [2.5- to 5.1-millimeter]) flower spiders, which are species of crab spiders, take advantage of the flowers' attractiveness by using them as a perch from which to ambush prey at night. The perfectly camouflaged spiders slowly change color from white to deep yellow to green, matching the hues of the flowers they wait in ambush upon. When a hapless insect comes along looking for a meal of nectar and pollen, the spider, instead, catches the forager, holds it overhead and sucks out its body fluids. The toxin used by flower spiders affects bees, beetles, flies and other insects considerably larger than the spiders.

When focusing on the activities of animals at night, it is easy to take plants for granted. But nocturnal animals could not survive without the food, shelter and other necessities they derive from plants. Flying squirrels and birds, for example, seek safety in hollow trees and thick shrubs. Insects are protected under leaves, in the hollows of branches and beneath tree bark. Plant foods eaten at night include berries, nuts, bark, buds, pollen and nectar. Plants are as essen-

tial to the lives of nocturnal animals as they are to animals that are active during the day.

Plants also affect how you experience the night. As the moon glows through the tree-tops myriad shadow shapes dance about your feet. Looking up, you might see the dark spire of a pine, hemlock or fir as the wind breathes through the needles. Perhaps the soft, powerful sound of wind through the full crown of a maple is overhead, or the lacy, angular branches and light whisper of the black locust. One Native story from the east says that flowers on black locust are really pieces of the moon. Moon Woman hangs them from the branches as she changes the moon's shape by trimming off or adding pieces at different times in the lunar cycle. The crowns of black locust are a veil over the face of the rising moon. Perhaps the wind plays the hard, leathery sound of windblown oak leaves, the light rustling of aspen or willow. In the desert Southwest, the saguaro cactus stands, arms reaching upward—a sentinel against the starry desert sky. On the prairie, wind moves tall grasses in great waves that create an undulating, rushing sound.

You do not have to visit distant lands: A strange enticing night world of plants is all around you. For water lilies, the end of the day begins when their blossoms close around noon, having opened at the break of day. As dusk approaches the petals of other flowers close tight—poppy, dandelion, daisy, pansy and tulip. The leaves of many plants droop at night, including wood sorrel or *Oxalis, Wisteria,* clover, beans and other plants in the pea family. This leaf movement is actually part of a gradual twenty-four-hour cycle, with the leaves being fully open and erect at midday, then closed and drooping around midnight. When placed in total darkness plants continue to follow this cycle for three to five days. In continuous light, however, the leaves remain continuously erect.[2] The leaves of rhododendron and grape turn up at night and show their lighter undersides.

A nighttime walk with senses attuned is all you need to discover the plants that are most active when the sun sets. Many of the plants seen each day show a different face at night. Evening primrose blooms when the sun sets, as does honeysuckle, its sweet perfume lingering in the night air. The blooms of many desert plants unfold their petals in the dark when the risk of losing precious water is less than during the heat of the day.

Sometimes the world of plants and plant-like organisms at night can leave us breathless. Walking the deciduous woodlands some evening, you may encounter the jack-o'-lantern mushroom with its glowing, pale green gills under the cap. One autumn, when we got caught coming down a mountain slope after sunset, we spotted an eerie, moonlike light hovering a few feet above the ground. We paused at first and tried to figure out what it was. As we rushed over to take a closer look, we stirred up hundreds of newly fallen leaves and the ground beneath our feet began to glow with a thousand pale stars. When we reached the hovering light we could see that it was, in fact, attached to the side of a rotting tree. To the touch, this luminescent mass felt cool and damp. At last, we realized that it was the glowing fungus *foxfire*, which has undoubtedly inspired many stories about encounters with otherworldly creatures of the night. Foxfire is but one of countless discoveries that await anyone who goes about alert and with senses attuned after sunset.

Figure 3-3. Opposite. A white-lined sphinx moth hovers as it feeds on nectar from the sweet-scented flowers of night-blooming cereus in the desert southwest. The gray, angular stems of this small bush of desert flats and washes produce beautiful white blossoms during or around the month of June. The pollinated flowers, which open after sunset and close soon after sunrise, will form bright red fruit. Size of moth: body, 1.6 inches (4.1 centimeters); wingspread, 3 inches (7.6 centimeters).

QUESTIONS

1. Why is Moth in the Paiute story "Moth, The Fire Dancer" drawn toward the flames of the fire?

2. What eventually happens to Moth? How is Moth changed when he returns to the people after his burns are healed?

3. Why do moths come out at night? Why do you think moths circle and dance around flames and bright lights?

4. How do moths, other insects and spiders find their way around at night? Which senses do they use?

5. Which insects are active at night? Which insects are not active at night?

6. To what kinds of habitats near your home would you go to find insects and spiders after dark?

7. Do you like searching for and looking at insects at night? Why, or why not?

8. Why do crickets call? What do they sound like? How do they make their sounds?

9. Do you like crickets? Why or why not?

10. Have you ever seen fireflies creating their lights at night? What does it make you think of as you watch their lights flickering?

11. What do fireflies use their lights for? How do they make their lights?

12. Why is night a good time for some spiders to spin their webs? What do spiders catch in those webs? How do they spin silk?

13. How are plants important to insects at night? How are insects important to plants at night?

14. Do you know of any plants that bloom at night? Why do you think they do this?

15. What else are plants doing at night? How is this different than what they are doing during the day? Why would a plant be active at night instead of during the day?

16. Do you know of any fungi that glow in the dark? What are they? Have you ever seen them glowing? Where?

17. What do you see, hear and smell when you stand in a forest or field after dark? What is your favorite place to be outdoors when it is dark?

18. How can you tell the wind is blowing at night? What tells you the wind is there? What does the wind sound like in a pine grove? In a forest of broad-leaved trees? In a prairie or desert?

19. Have you ever visited the seashore at night? Did you like it there? What did it smell and sound like?

20. How do you think most people feel about being out in the night? Why?

ACTIVITIES
The Scents of Attraction [3]

ACTIVITY: Play a game during which children pretend to be different species of moths that pair up by means of the male's attraction to the female's scent.

GOALS: Understand that female moths give off a scent that is particular to that species, and by which they attract a mate. Understand why scent is a good attractant for moths and why night might be an advantageous time to find and fly to a mate. Discover that the sense of smell is also important to nonhuman animals.

AGE: Younger children and older children

MATERIALS: Enough pleasant liquid scents (floral perfumes, spice oils, etc.) to have one scent per pair of children in the group; enough small empty bottles (such as those that pills, vitamins or rolls of photographic film come in) for half of the group (male moths) to each get a bottle; one piece of cotton to put in each bottle; "Discussion"; one blindfold for each child; Figure 3-4.

PROCEDURE: Beforehand, gather enough different kinds of liquid scents so that each pair of children in the group will have its own distinct scent. Find scents that are pleasant, such as those of different flowers and spice oils: floral perfumes, vanilla, mint, almond, anisette, etc. Now collect one small bottle, such as an old pill or vitamin bottle, for each child who is going to play the role of a male moth in the activity. You will need half as many bottles as there are children in the group. If your group has an uneven number of children, you, the leader, should take the role of a female moth and be a child's partner. Put a small piece of cotton with a couple of drops of scent on it in each bottle so that each bottle has a different scent.

Note: With older children, hold a brief talk at the beginning of this activity about being sensitive to members of the opposite sex by not making "humorous" comments that can hurt others' feelings.

Ask the children, "How do you think moths find their mates in the darkness? What kinds of senses do you think they use?" Once they have responded, share Figure 3-4 with them as well as the information about moths and mating found in the "Discussion." Emphasize that moths detect odors with their antennae, not with a nose.

Tell the children that they are going to pretend to be moths, looking for their mates. Each male will be able to identify the correct female by recognizing her special scent. Split

the group in half, making one group the "female" moths and the other the "male" moths. There is no need to have boys play the roles of male moths and girls play the roles of the females. With older children, it is better if each of the two groups of moths contains both boys and girls. Keep the two groups separate while passing out scents so that pairs-to-be are unaware of who receives the matching scent. Give each of the "male" moths one of the small bottles containing a scent. Instruct these children to open the bottles and become familiar with the scent that they will be searching for. Generously dab the back of one of each "female" moth's hands with scent, so that each female has a different smell. When all of the scents are distributed, bring the group back together with males and females in two lines facing each other approximately 3 feet (1 meter) apart. Finally, even though you will be doing this activity in the dark (outdoors if possible), help each child to put on a blindfold to simulate that the sense of smell alone is to be used during the activity. Tell them to keep their eyes closed underneath the blindfolds.

Have the "females" hold the back of their hands up while the "males" move along the line of females, each searching for the scent that matches the one in his bottle. This simulates moths selecting potential mates. Once a male has chosen a female that he thinks has the same scent that he has, he will stand still in front of her and the female will put her hands down by her sides. When all are paired up, have the children remove their blindfolds and see who their partner is. If some males seem to have chosen the wrong mate, help them to find the partner with the correctly matching scent.

Figure 3-4. A moth's feathery antennae, which can detect odors from miles away, help it to find a mate at night. Adapted with permission from Robert T. Mitchell and Herbert S. Zim's Butterflies and Moths. *Racine, Wisconsin: Western Pub. Co., 1964, p. 81. (Original illustration by Andre Durenceau.)*

Light Up the Night

ACTIVITY: Set out different colored lights and observe which kinds attract more insects as well as which insects are attracted to particular colors of light. Look for insect eyeshine.

GOALS: Understand that insect eyes can detect certain colors of light better than others and that particular insects are sensitive to particular colors. Discover insect eyeshine and understand what causes it.

AGE: Older children

MATERIALS: Four bright flashlight beams of equal brightness (new or strong batteries would assure this); three different colored sheets of tinted transparent acetate or plastic—red, yellow and blue—that are large enough to cover the face of the flashlights with enough left to fold over the edges; three strong elastics; one sheet of paper with cardboard backing or a clipboard for each of the four groups; four pencils; newsprint and marker; "Discussion" from this chapter and from Chapter 2.

PROCEDURE: Beforehand, prepare the colored lights using four bright flashlight beams. Use red, yellow and blue transparent acetate or plastic to cover three flashlights by placing the colors over the lenses of the beams (see *"Night by Light"* in Chapter 2 for instructions). Fold the edges of the acetate down and hold in place with masking tape, or cut the acetate to the size of the flashlight lens and screw it down over or in place of the lens. Leave the fourth flashlight beam uncovered to represent white light. Make sure the flashlights have strong batteries.

Tell the children that they are going to observe how many and which kind of insects are attracted to lights of four different colors. Ask them which colors they think will attract the most insects, and the least. Do not tip them off yet as to what results they may expect during their observations. Use the "Discussion" from Chapter 2 to explain insect eyeshine, what it looks like and what causes it. Ask them to look for eyeshine during the experiment.

Divide the children into four small groups. Give one person from each group a pencil and some paper with a hard backing to write against. Set the flashlights out in an open area about 20 feet (6 meters) from one another.

Have each group sit around a flashlight. The child who is chosen as recorder in each group will write the color of the light on top of the blank page. The other children will observe how many insects are drawn to the beam as well as what kinds of insects come to visit it. When the beam is first turned on, have the children call out, generally, the kinds of insects that begin to appear: moths, beetles, bugs, etc. The important thing is not to identify each insect, but to count the numbers of different kinds that come to the light. If the children see any eyeshine, have them record the color of the eyeshine and the kinds of insects that have it. Once the flashlights have been on for five or ten minutes, have the children in all four groups, all at the same time, count and record the total number of insects that are flying around the light.

Gather the entire group together to compare results. Have the record keeper from each group call out their results and record these as a chart on newsprint. Ask the group, "Which light attracted the greatest number of different kinds of insects, the red, yellow, blue or white? Which light attracted the smallest number of different kinds? How did the other two lights rank? Which light drew in the greatest total number of insects? Which drew in the least? How did the other two rank? Did you see any eyeshine? What color was it and which insects had it?"

Shift the groups around to different lights and repeat the entire experiment. Compare results. Are they the same? If not, shift the groups around again and go one more round. Take the two results of the three periods of observation that are the most similar and have the children use these results from which to draw their final conclusions.

Now share the information from the "Discussion" in this chapter about which colors generally attract more insects. How does this information compare with the children's results? Also, describe eyeshine— how and why it forms—using the information from the "Discussion" in Chapter 2. Allow time for the children to share any other thoughts and observations they have.

The Blooming Night

ACTIVITY: Visit and smell some flowers in the dark and guess what color they are. Discuss why we cannot see colors at night. Observe the life of insects and spiders that are active on flowers at night.

GOALS: Discover the sensory world of flowers that bloom at night. Understand how the human eye perceives color. Realize that nocturnal insects and spiders are active on flowers in a way that benefits both the plants and the wildlife.

AGE: Younger children and older children.

MATERIALS: Flashlights covered with red-tinted transparent acetate or plastic for each small group (see *"Night by Light"* in Chapter 2 for instructions); one uncovered (white) flashlight; pencils; one piece of paper with cardboard backing on which to write for each group; "Discussion" from this chapter; "Discussion" from Chapter 2.

PROCEDURE: Beforehand, find an area, such as a garden, where there is a number of flowers of different colors in bloom at night. Choose a route through this environment along which you will take the children in the dark to visit flowers of various colors, including some that are red, blue and white.

Use the "Discussion" in Chapter 2 to describe to the children how our eyes are able to see colors, as well as why it is difficult for us to distinguish color when it is very dark. Ask them to predict which color flowers will attract the most nighttime insects.

Take the children to the garden and walk through to pick out which flowers appear brighter in the dark. Once the group has decided which flowers are brighter, turn the clear flashlight on those flowers (avoid shining it in anyone's eyes) and determine which color

or colors of flowers looked brighter than the rest in the dark. Now visit one kind of flower at a time in the dark. Allow the children to smell each kind of flower and try to guess what color that flower is. Once the children have guessed, use the light to reveal the flower's true color or colors. After the children have worked their way through the garden ask questions to elicit their conclusions about what they found. In the dark, flowers that are blue appear as a brighter shade of gray than flowers of other colors, although we cannot actually discern the flower's hues.

Tell the children that many animals, especially nocturnal ones, cannot see color well, if at all. Most insects see colors very well although they see ranges of color that are different than those that people can distinguish. Many insects can see colors that people cannot, including ultraviolet.

Divide the children into small groups and give each group one of the red flashlights. Lead each group over to a flower or cluster of one kind of flower. Have the children use the flashlights to observe insects and spiders on and around those flowers. They are to write down their observations, record the color or colors of their flower, the overall numbers of insects, the number of different kinds of insects that visit the flowers and any spider activity they see. After a few minutes, gather the small groups together and have each group share their findings.

Follow this activity with a question-and-answer period. Do flowers of a particular color seem to attract more insects? Are certain kinds of insects attracted to flowers of a particular color? What were the spiders doing on the flowers? How does the insect activity benefit the flowers? How do the flowers help the insects? Share the information from the "Discussion" with the children that describes some of the interrelationships among nocturnal insects, spiders and flowers.

Note: Have the children smell the same flowers during the day if the blooms are still open. Many flowers smell stronger at night.

Cricket Cacophony

ACTIVITY: Listen to crickets calling and create your own cricket chorus.

GOALS: Understand how and why crickets call in the evening and at night.

AGE: Younger children

MATERIALS: Large combs with teeth that grade from large to small, squeaky bird calls, clickers and/or other instruments of choice, Figure 3-5.

PROCEDURE: Use the information from the "Discussion" and in the introduction to *"Cricket Thermometer"* to explain to the children about the calls of the cricket. Take the children to a place where you know they can

Figure 3-5. This tree cricket is "chirping." Each wing of the cricket has a filelike ridge or vein as well as a sharp scraper. As it rubs the two wings against one another with a sideways motion, the filelike vein on one wing rubs against the scraper on the other wing to create the beautiful "chirps" that are intended to attract a mate. This cricket closely resembles the snowy tree cricket. Size: .8 inch (2.0 centimeters). (Photo by David H. Funk.)

hear crickets calling. Listen to the crickets' songs for a while. Explain that the crickets rub a scraperlike device on one wing up against a series of ridges on the other wing to make their chirps (Figure 3-5).

Now pass out combs, high-pitched bird calls or other instruments of choice and allow the children to play a tune on their "cricket callers" by rubbing their thumbnails down the teeth of the combs, twisting the bird calls or playing other instruments. Combs with teeth that grade from large to small make an interesting sound moving up and/or down the scale. Have the children "call" randomly at first, then try to have them coordinate to call in unison.

Note: Try other variations on this activity. 1) Pass out pairs of matching noise-makers in such a way that the children do not know who has the noise-maker that matches theirs. Now lead the group into a field or other open area in the dark. Have the "crickets" call and try to find their mates by listening for the noise-maker that matches their own. 2) Divide the children into two groups and have the groups stand about 20 feet (6 meters) from each other. Have one group begin by making a call in unison, then have the other group answer in unison, and so on.

Follow this activity with *"Cricket Thermometer."*

Cricket Thermometer

ACTIVITY: Listen to the number of calls made by the field cricket in fifteen seconds and use a formula to calculate the approximate temperature in degrees Fahrenheit. Convert this temperature into Celsius. Compare this estimate with the temperature recorded on a thermometer. Discuss how and why crickets make their calls.

GOALS: Discover that the level of activity of crickets and other insects is directly related to the temperature of their surroundings. Understand how crickets make their calls and how to distinguish these calls from those of grasshoppers. Understand why crickets call.

AGE: Younger children and older children

MATERIALS: Wristwatch or stopwatch with seconds indicator; pencil; paper; clipboard or cardboard backing; a few outdoor thermometers; "Discussion."

PROCEDURE: *Note:* This activity works well in autumn when studying how insects prepare for surviving the winter.

During the late summer or autumn take the children to a field, hedgerow, schoolyard, ballpark, vacant lot, park or other habitat where field crickets are calling from amid the grasses. Field crickets produce low, brief musical chirps. Cricket calls are trill-like and have a musical quality to them and you can sing or hum a note to match that pitch. Grasshoppers make a mechanical sound that you cannot hum along with. Locate a cricket calling and share the section of the "Discussion" that describes how and why crickets call. While you are doing this, have the children set the outdoor thermometers down in the grass near where the crickets are calling.

Pick out a field cricket's calls and have the children focus their ears upon it. Explain that in colder weather crickets call more slowly, and that the calling gets faster as the temperature climbs higher and the insect's metabolism increases.

Now call out the beginning of a fifteen-second period of time and have the children count the number of chirps that the cricket makes before you yell "stop" when the interval is over. You can also have the children work in pairs with one child timing the fifteen seconds while the other counts chirps. Repeat this procedure at least two more times for different field crickets and calculate the average number of chirps per fifteen seconds. Add forty to this number and you will have a rough estimate of the

current temperature in degrees Fahrenheit. For example, two chirps per second indicates a temperature of 70°F (21.1°C), and one chirp per second means the temperature is about 55°F (12.8°C).

CRICKET THERMOMETER FORMULA

_____(number of chirps in fifteen seconds)

$+\ \ 40$

$=$ _____ °F

The formula to convert Fahrenheit to Celsius is:

$$(°F - 32) \times \frac{5}{9} = \_\_\_\_ °C$$

Now compare this estimated temperature with an average of the readings on the thermometers to see how accurate the "cricket thermometers" are.

Note: The calls of the snowy tree cricket can also be used to estimate temperature using a slightly different formula in which the number thirty-seven is added to the number of chirps in fifteen seconds. See *"Cricket Thermometer"* in Chapter 8 of *Keepers of the Animals.*

Firefly Flashers

ACTIVITY: Discuss how and why fireflies create and flash their lights. Observe fireflies displaying, if possible. Play a game during which children identify their mate by recognizing a particular flash pattern of lights.

GOALS: Understand the process by which fireflies create light from chemical reactions. Realize that each species of firefly has a distinct pattern of light flashes by which mates find one another.

AGE: Younger children and older children

MATERIALS: Index cards; pen; safe dark field or other area; one flashlight for each child; "Discussion."

PROCEDURE: Beforehand, create two matching sets of index cards with coded signals of dots and dashes marked on them indicating a series of light flashes of a certain pattern. For example, ". ___ ____ . . . ____ ." Each card will have an exact match in the other set but no two cards within any set will be the same. Scout out a *dark* field or other open area as free as possible of obstacles or holes which the children could bump into or trip over. Also, locate a field or other habitat where fireflies are displaying if it is the appropriate time of year (early summer to midsummer).

Ask the children, "Have you ever seen a firefly or lightning bug? What kind of insect do you think they are? How do they make light and why do they do that?" Tell the children that fireflies are really beetles. Use the information from the "Discussion" to explain how fireflies create light. Describe how different species use light for attracting and finding their mates. Visit and observe fireflies displaying if possible.

Point out any obstacles or pitfalls in the playing area before you begin, such as woodchuck burrows or ground squirrel holes. Divide the children into two groups of equal size. A leader will need to participate to even off the numbers if there is an odd number of children. Pass out one set of cards to each group. Make certain that each child holds a card that matches a card held by a child in the other group.

Now pass out the flashlights and have the children learn to use them. Call out instructions such as "short long short" so the chidren can practice. Have the groups stand across the open field or other dark place facing each other. Each child will flash a flashlight with a series of short and long signals as marked on his or her card while searching for her or his mate across the way. After they have flashed for a few minutes, tell the children to walk across the field toward one another to find the person they think is their mate. Have them compare their cards and check to see if they chose the correct partner. Have those who chose the wrong partner go back and repeat the flashing until everyone has the correct mate.

The Spider and the Firefly

ACTIVITY: Imagine yourself as a firefly caught in a spider's web, then as the spider, and live out a drama in the world of night. Use a red light to observe a spider in action on its web at night.

GOALS: Discover that nocturnal animals face life and death struggles as predator and prey.

AGE: Younger children and older children

MATERIALS: Copy of *"The Spider and the Firefly"*; paper, pencils, chalk and chalkboard or newsprint and felt-tipped marker; flashlights, one sheet of transparent red acetate or red plastic for each flashlight; masking tape; "Discussion"; Figure 3-6.

PROCEDURE: Beforehand, scout out a habitat nearby where there are lots of active spider webs. Become familiar with a route you wish to lead children along to observe these spider webs. Prepare the red flashlights (see instructions in *"Night by Light"* in Chapter 2).

Use the "Discussion" to explain or review how fireflies make their light and what part of their bodies beam the light.

Ask the children, "What do you think it would be like to get caught in a spider's web? Do you think you could escape? What would it be like to be the spider with its prey struggling to get free from your web?"

Prepare the children for a guided fantasy as described in Chapter 1. Ask them to clear their minds and prepare to enter the worlds of the stalker and the prey. Read the following story.

The Spider and the Firefly

You are a firefly winging through the cool, damp night air over a field of grass and flowers. As you fly you signal for a mate by flashing a series of green lights. Some are short blinks, others are long flashes, but you always make the lights in the exact same pattern each time. All around you are the lights of other fireflies blinking on and off. The field is alive with the glow of flickering green lights.

There, on the ground, you see a firefly answering with a light signal just like yours. You fly down and land nearby in the grass. As you start walking over to your new-found mate, one of your legs gets caught on something. You pull to get the leg free, but another leg gets caught on the sticky silk of the spider's web. You struggle to get away by pulling on the grass with your four free legs. The harder you tug on the sticky spider's silk, the more the web shakes. A big spider with hairy legs is slowly moving down the web toward you. There, one leg is free but the other is still stuck fast to the web. The spider is standing over you now, just about to strike.

Suddenly you begin to change. Now you are a big hairy spider with eight eyes and eight long, strong legs. Your big, round body is covered all over with short, bristly hairs. You are very hungry because you have not eaten in a long time.

There in front of you is a firefly with one leg caught on the sticky silk of your web. The whole web is shaking as you hold on with eight feet to those strands of silk that are not sticky. You are almost thrown off the shaking web as you stand ready to strike at your struggling prey. But just as you begin to reach down with your front legs to grab the firefly it uses all of the strength in its five free legs and pulls hard on the grass to escape. Your front legs dart out in a flash to grab the firefly and then …

Stop the story and have the children keep their eyes closed for a few more minutes while they imagine how the story ends. Have them share their endings with the rest of the group. Later, have each child write and/or illustrate

Figure 3-6. The discovery of a spider's web captures a child's imagination. (Photo by David H. Funk.)

the entire story from either the firefly's or spider's point of view, whichever they choose.

As they share their stories, ask them to explain why they chose to be that character. Record a list of answers to these questions too: How did it feel to be the firefly/spider? How did it feel to be eaten by the spider/to eat the firefly? How did it feel to escape the spider and live/to miss your prey and go hungry? Would you rather be a predator or prey in the night world? Why?

Ask the children what they know about spiders and their webs, how they live and catch their prey (Figure 3-6). Share the brief information on spiders in the "Discussion."

Divide the group into pairs and give each pair a flashlight with red covering. Demonstrate an owl call or some other night sound by which you will call the children back together. Emphasize to the children that they are only to observe the spiders, and in no way are they to disturb the spiders or their webs. Take the group outdoors to observe spiders active in their webs. Lead them along the route you planned earlier and leave one pair of children at each active spider web. Call the children in after about five minutes of spider watching. Hold a time for them to share their experiences, ask questions and lead the entire group over to see any exciting discoveries the children may have made.

Poetry to Your Ears

ACTIVITY: Create poems from words describing the sounds of the night.
GOALS: Realize that every kind of environment has unique sounds that bring the night alive. Discover that sounds can inspire creative writing.
AGE: Older children
MATERIALS: Paper; pencils; cardboard backing or clipboards; one flashlight for each small group; battery-operated tape recorder (optional).

PROCEDURE: *Note:* Although this activity is described here for a woodland as one example, it can be modified and conducted in any kind of environment, from city to seashore and from desert to grassland. For instance, children can listen to sounds along the seashore and create poetry from words describing those sounds—waves crashing along the shore, wind through the dune grass and the resonance heard when a seashell is placed up to the ear.

Beforehand, scout out the environment you intend to bring the children to visit. Plan a route to walk to the various sites you want to include. For example, a good park or forested area for this activity is one in which individual trees, or stands of different kinds of trees are growing fairly close together. Include a number of broad-leaved trees as well as some pines, spruces and other conifers.

This activity needs to be conducted on a breezy night. Decide whether you will tape record the sounds the different trees make.

Tell the children they are going out to listen to the night voices of the trees. Ask them to be absolutely quiet during the activity so that they can better listen to the trees.

Bring the children to the group of trees. Tell them that "every kind of tree has a different voice when the wind blows through its crown. Some sound soft and gentle, others deep and powerful. Listen for a few minutes to the wind through the branches and leaves of the trees we are standing under." After some time has passed, ask the children to share some words to describe the sounds they are hearing. This is what each small group will do at their own kind of tree when they get there. You may want to help younger children by having them describe sounds using words that are onomatopoetic, such as "buzz" and "hum."

Divide the large group into a number of smaller groups so that each group will be listening to a particular kind of tree. Situate each small group beneath one of the various kinds of trees. Tell them to listen in the dark, to think of some words that describe the voice of the wind through those trees and to *remember* those descriptive words. During this time you might tape record the tree sounds. *No flashlights are to be used at this time.* After a few minutes have passed, gather the groups together. Have the small groups work by flashlight to write down the descriptive words they have remembered and fashion them into a poem. This poem can take any form. It may rhyme or not, may tell a story or simply describe, may be written in a column or in the shape of their tree. Have the children start with one of their descriptive words and create a poem by connecting that word to the others they have thought of. Encourage them to use their imaginations.

Once the poems are completed, have the small groups take turns leading the entire group to their trees. At each spot, the whole group will listen for a time to the trees, then each small group will read the poem they wrote describing the voice of the wind through their particular tree.

At a later date you might play the tape recordings and once again try to match poems and trees.

EXTENDING THE EXPERIENCE

• *Darkness Detectives*. Visit a natural area at night and find clues of nocturnal life to prove that insects and spiders live in the area, such as chewed leaves, cocoons and spider webs.
• While walking the woodlands at night, keep your eyes open for the pale greenish light of the glowing fungus called foxfire and the green-glowing gills of the jack-o'-lantern mushroom.
• Attract insects to the home or learning center grounds with a special concoction. Late in the day, thoroughly blend together in a bowl some molasses, dark beer and an overripe banana. Soak some strips of absorbent cloth, such as pieces of an old towel, in this mixture and hang these from the branches of a nearby tree or some other accessible location. As night falls, moths and other insects will come in to feed on this sweet aromatic brew, providing a convenient variety to observe. You may even be lucky enough to see a bat or two swoop down in pursuit of an insect meal.
• Make a rope walk by stringing a rope from tree-to-tree or post-to-post. Tie knots along its length to mark stations where there are activities or special things to sense. String the rope about waist height. Make sure the ground is even and safe and that there are no dangerous branches present that might poke someone's eye.
• Try drawing pictures at night while sitting quietly and observing the natural world.
• Discourage the use of "bug lights." These devices have a "black light" that acts as a magnet to draw in everything from harmless moths to Junebugs and even the bats that are pursuing these insect prey. They are indiscriminate killers of all sorts of insects and other night life and they teach disrespect for other living things. Besides, most mosquitoes, which these lights are designed to kill, are not attracted to a black light! Mosquitoes home in on their prey by sensing and flying toward the high concentration of carbon dioxide in the animal's breath.
• Conduct *"Night by Light"* from Chapter 2 for insects and spiders.
• Use Chapter 3 from *Keepers of the Animals* for stories, information and activities on spiders.
• Use Chapter 8 from *Keepers of the Animals* for a story, information and activities on insects.

NOTES

1. Lorus J. Milne and Margery J. Milne. *The World of Night*. New York: Harper & Bros., 1956, p. 235.
2. Ibid., p. 27.
3. Adapted with permission from an activity in *Hands-On Nature: Information and Activities for Exploring the Environment with Children* by Jenepher Lingelbach and the Vermont Institute of Natural Science (Woodstock, Vt.: Vermont Institute of Natural Science, 1986).

*One of the mothers called out to her son, the smallest of the eight boys.
He looked back, and as soon as he did so, he turned into a shooting
star and fell from the night sky.*

CHAPTER 4

Oot-Kwah-Tah,
The Seven Star Dancers
(Onondaga—Eastern Woodland)

Long ago, a group of Onondagas traveled to the north to fish and hunt by the shores of Kan-ya-ti-yo, the great and beautiful lake. The waters were full of many trout and sturgeon and the woods teemed with deer. The people gave thanks to Ha-wen-ne-yu, the Creator, for helping them find such a good place. Then, deciding they would spend the winter there, they built lodges.

While the men hunted and the women worked about the village, the children had plenty of time to play games. One group of eight boys found a quiet place by the shores of the lake and started to go there regularly to meet in the evenings.

"Let us form our own Medicine Society, just as the men do," said one of the boys. The other boys agreed, for the boy who suggested it was their leader. They talked it over and decided they would do everything their elders did.

"I know where there is an old water drum with a broken head," the boy who was the leader said. "I will get it and fix it and then we can dance. Wait here for me."

The other seven boys did as their leader said. They waited for him by the lake and when he returned with the drum and fixed it, they began to sing and dance around their fire, imitating the medicine songs of their elders.

They had not been dancing long when a strange thing happened. An old man with long white hair, wearing white buckskins appeared on the shore of the lake near the dancing boys. They stopped drumming and dancing as he approached.

"Listen to me," the old man said, "you must stop this dancing. If you do not stop, something bad may happen." Then he was gone.

Some of the boys were frightened, but their leader spoke up. "Brothers," he said, "that old man is just trying to frighten us. Let us pay no attention to his tricks."

So the eight boys continued to meet in their secret place near the beautiful lake. But, because the old man had, indeed, frightened them, for a while they did not drum or dance.

One day, though, the leader of the boys had a new idea. "Let us have a feast, just as our elders do when they do the ceremonies. Each of us will go to our parents and get food for the feast so that we can do it right."

All of the others agreed. That night, each of the boys asked for food to take to their secret place to have a great ceremony.

But their parents laughed at them. "You are too young to do ceremonies," the parents said. "Why do you need to take good food into the woods? You are fed enough at home."

When the boys met the next evening in their place by the lake they were all angry and sad.

"Let us dance," said the leader of the boys. "Our parents cannot stop us from doing our medicine dance!" Then he began to beat very hard on the water drum and sing.

> Ji-ji-ya, ji-hiya
> ji-hi-ya, ji-ji-ya

The other seven boys joined in the song. They followed him as he danced around and around in a circle around the fire. Their anger made their voices stronger as they sang and dust rose around them as they stamped their feet. Their song grew louder and louder until it could be heard all the way back in the village.

"Who is singing that powerful song?" said the parents of the boys. The strange music worried them and they followed the sound of it down to the hidden place by the lake.

There they saw a strange thing. The eight boys were dancing in a circle around their fire, but their feet were no longer touching the ground. As they danced, each step took them higher and higher, up into the sky. They were already above the heads of the parents, far out of reach. One of the mothers called out to her son, the smallest of the eight boys. He looked back, and as soon as he did so he turned into a shooting star and fell from the night sky.

But the other seven boys continued to dance. They went higher and higher until they reached the very top of the sky and became seven stars. They remain there to this day. The Onondaga people call them Oot-Kwah-Tah, The Dancers, though some others know them as The Pleiades.

To this day, you can see those dancing stars as they move across the heavens, circling just as dancers circle. When the winter nights are cold and clear, their flickering makes them seem to be moving to the beat of a distant drum. And though their parents did not listen to those boys long ago, today the people pay close attention to them. Each year, when the dancing boys reach the very top of the sky, around the time of January or February, it is the signal for the Onondaga Ceremony of Midwinter to begin.

KANIE TAKE RON

Then East Wind blew as hard as he could to help lift Moon into the sky. But he blew so hard that the feathers of the fan blew into Moon's face. He could not see where he was going.

The Creation of the Moon

(Diné—Southwest)

After First Man and First Woman arrived in the Fifth World, they decided to make this world brighter than the lower worlds had been. They thought and talked for a long time. At last they decided. They would make a sun and a moon.

First they made the sun. They took a piece of rock crystal and made it round and flat. They fastened turquoise around it and around the turquoise they placed rays of red rain. They placed bars of lightning beyond the red rain. They fastened onto it feathers from the flicker, the lark, the cardinal and the eagle.

Then they made the moon. They took mica and they made it round and flat, as they had made the sun although they did not make it as large. Around it they placed white shells and then sheet lightning and then water from the four directions.

After they had done this, they began to talk again.

"Where shall we have the sun and the moon rise and set?" First Man asked.

Then East Wind spoke up. "Have sun brought to my direction," East Wind said. "Let it begin its journey there each day."

So it was decided.

Now they needed to give life to sun and moon. They needed someone to carry them across the sky. The young man who had planted the reed which carried the people up into the Fifth World was chosen to carry the sun. The old man who had brought the earth in which the reed was planted was chosen to carry the moon. They were pleased.

First Man and First Woman gave them new names.

"You who will carry the sun," they said, "your name will now be Johannaa'ei, The One Who Governs the Day."

Then they turned to the old gray-haired man. "You who carry the moon," they said, "your name will now be Tle'ehoonaa'ei, The One Who Governs the Night."

Now it was time to set the two of them on their paths. First Man decided how they would find their way. He gave them each a fan made of twelve feathers from the eagle's tail, for those are the feathers the great bird uses to guide itself across the sky.

Sun began his journey first. Johannaa'ei climbed up into the sky, guided by the eagle feathers and passed safely across the heavens until he came at last to the west.

Now it was the turn of Moon. Tle'ehoonaa'ei, The One Who Governs the Night, began to climb up into the sky. But because he was an old man, it was harder for him to do this. East Wind saw how hard it was for Moon.

"I will help," East Wind said.

Then East Wind blew as hard as he could to help lift Moon into the sky. But he blew so hard that the feathers of the fan blew into Moon's face. He could not see where he was going. So it is, that to this day, although Sun always follows the twelve paths across the sky, Moon takes a wandering way. Sometimes Moon even becomes lost, turning his face away from Earth as he tries to see his way. If you look carefully at Moon on the nights when his face is fully turned toward Earth you may see those feathers on his face.

DISCUSSION

Stories that tell how the constellations came to be are among the oldest of all. There are many versions, from Greek mythology to Native North American tales. This Onondaga story ends with the seven stars called *Oot-Kwah-Tah,* "The Dancers," rising into the sky. The Dancers are also known as the Pleiades, a cluster of stars within the larger constellation of Taurus, the Bull. In the northern hemisphere the Dancers are a winter cluster that flickers in the cold skies (Figure 4-1).

The moon gives off its own cool light overhead. According to this *Diné* (Navajo) story about "The Creation of the Moon," this light comes from a moon made of mica, white shells, sheet lightning and water from the four directions. Old man, who had brought Earth, is chosen to carry the moon across the sky. His name becomes *Tle'ehoonaa'ei,* "The One Who Governs the Night." Because the twelve eagle feathers he is given to guide him are blown into his eyes as East Wind helps to lift Moon into the sky, Moon gets lost and wanders while the sun takes a direct path to the west. It is said that when Moon's full face looks directly at Earth we can still see those feathers.

Stars and Other Celestial Bodies

The Seven Star Dancers or Pleiades are well known among the *constellations*, which are associated groups of stars that cover certain areas in the sky. Among traditional Native North American cultures star stories are more than interesting tales. Observations of changes in the sky are the basis for calendars around which life is organized. Pictographs and petroglyphs made by Native North Americans in the Great Basin, which are both carved into and painted onto rocks, show detailed arrangements of star patterns—constellations—as seen from that region (Figure 4-2).[1] Many Diné star paintings are found in Canyon de Chelly, Arizona. Diné rattles that are used during healing ceremonies depict the star pattern now commonly known as the Pleiades. Some Native North Americans use the stars of the Pleiades as an "eye test" for youth. Those with exceptional vision can see more than seven stars in the cluster. Most people can discern six stars.

Even though stars appear to create images as we view them overhead, they are often very distant from one another. The stars of the Pleiades are an exception, all being about four

Figure 4-1. As many as nine stars in the Pleiades star cluster, the Seven Star Dancers, can be seen with the naked eye, depending on the acuity of the observer's vision. Some Native North American cultures use this cluster as a kind of eye test. The Pleiades cluster is about 410 light-years from Earth, contains roughly 400 stars and is approximately 50 light-years in diameter. Alcyone is the brightest star in the Pleiades; it is 500 times brighter than our sun and ten times the sun's diameter. The hazy patches in this photograph are remnants of a nebula: a vast cloud of gas and dust that formed the Pleiades star cluster 20 million years ago. (Photo used with permission from the Lick Observatory, © University of California Regents, Santa Cruz.)

hundred *light-years* away.[2] There are eighty-eight constellations and forty-one of them can be seen from the northern hemisphere. Some constellations, like the Big Dipper, Little Dipper, Cassiopeia, Cepheus and Draco, are *circumpolar:* They are located close to the North Star and are visible all year long (Figure 4-8). The Big Dipper is only a portion of the constellation of the Great Bear, Ursa Major, while the seven stars of the Little Dipper outline the entire constellation called the Little Bear, Ursa Minor. Other constellations are more prominent at different seasons. Some major constellations of the Northern Hemisphere and the times of year they are visible are shown in the chart on the following page.

When the Major Constellations Are Visible

Spring	Summer	Fall	Winter
	northern skies:	*northern skies:*	
Leo	Aquila	Pegasus	Taurus
Bootes	Cygnus	Andromeda	Canis Major
Virgo	Lyra	Perseus	Canis Minor
Corvus		Triangulum	Gemini
Crater			Orion
Cancer	*southern skies:*	*southern skies:*	Auriga
	Sagittarius	Pisces	
	Libra	Aries	
	Scorpius	Aquarius	
		Capricornus	
	near the zenith:		
	Hercules		
	Corona Borealis		
	Sagitta		
	Delphinus		
	Ophiucus		

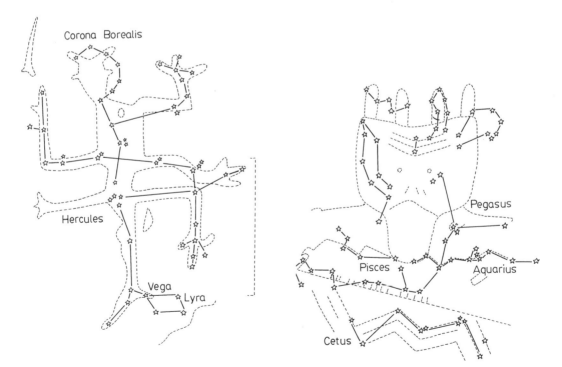

Figure 4-2. The Native North American constellations outlined by the dashed lines in this illustration are depicted in petroglyphs (rock carvings and drawings) created by prehistoric cultures of the Great Basin. The associated constellations from Greek and Roman mythology (solid lines) are shown for reference. (Adapted with permission from Anthony F. Aveni's (ed.) Archeoastronomy in Pre-Columbian America. © 1975, *University of Texas Press, Austin, Texas.)*

A portion of our galaxy, the *Milky Way*, is seen as a pale band of stars in the night sky. There are more than 100 billion stars in the Milky Way, along with planets and other heavenly bodies. Our *solar system* consists of the sun, nine major planets and their moons and all other satellites of the sun such as comets and asteroids. Some stars are much brighter than others and are said to have a greater *magnitude*. Higher numbers denote dimmer stars. A star of magnitude 1 is 2.5 times brighter than a star of magnitude 2, and so on. Extremely bright objects, such as the moon (magnitude -12.5) are given negative numbers.

Our own *sun* is a star 850,000 miles (1,367,948 kilometers) in diameter and 93,000,000 miles (149,669,550 kilometers) away from Earth. The sun is a fiery ball—a continuous nuclear reaction in which heat and light are released as a result of hydrogen being converted into helium. The sun's light travels through space for eight minutes and twenty seconds before it reaches Earth. Our nearest home star is 107 times larger in diameter than Earth, and its surface temperature is 10,000°F (5,538°C). Still, it is not a very big star. If a red giant, like Antares in the constellation Scorpius, were brought close to Earth, it would more than fill up the space between Earth and sun. The next closest star to Earth is very far off. Alpha Centauri (which is not visible in the northern hemisphere) is four light-years away. The light being created by Alpha Centauri as you read this sentence will not reach Earth until four years from now.

Planets can be distinguished from stars because they move in relation to the stars and each other. *Planet* is Greek for "a wanderer." Planets also shine more steadily and twinkle less than stars. Through a telescope a planet shows as a disk while stars are just points.

Take your group outside on a starry night and the *zenith*, the highest point in the sky directly overhead, makes a good reference point, as do the stars of the Big Dipper. The *meridian* is the imaginary line that runs from the northernmost point on the horizon through the zenith and down to the southernmost point on the horizon. The *ecliptic*, another common reference, is the path of the sun through the constellations during the year as a result of Earth's motion around the sun. On its journey along the ecliptic, the sun passes through the band of twelve constellations known as the *zodiac*.

You can refer to stars by using a powerful flashlight as a pointer, but discourage children from bringing flashlights because it takes the eyes about forty-five minutes to fully readjust to the dark once exposed for a time to the glare of a flashlight. Watch for *meteors,* which are often called "shooting stars" or "falling stars." Meteors are solid particles or objects from space that are pulled downward by Earth's gravity. They appear as tracks of light across the sky that leave a brief, glowing streak when they burn up upon encountering the friction of Earth's atmosphere.

Moon

The moon was sent up into the sky to watch the people and regulate everything, and all goes according to the moon. Especially is this so in regard to women who have their menses, but men are also affected by it, and become strong or weak as the moon waxes and wanes.[3]
—The Religion of the Luiseño, Southern California

Native North American beliefs and practices toward the *moon* reveal a deep understanding of its power and influence over our lives. The Maliseet, one of the eastern Abenaki peoples of northern Maine and the Maritime Provinces, call the moon *Paguas,* which means "he who borrows or begs light from the sun." Many of the calendars followed by Native North Americans who live in the middle and southern latitudes correlate the number of moons we have each year with the thirteen large scales on Turtle's back. Each moon has a name. Since there are twelve lunar cycles plus an extra eleven or so days in every solar year, a thirteenth moon comes around every few years as marked by the sun. The *Santee Dakota* (Sioux) moons are, starting with early spring:[4]

Ish-tah´-wee-chah´-ya-zan-wee—Moon of Sore Eyes

Mah-gah´-o-kah´-dah-wee—Moon of Ducks' Eggs

Wah-to´-pah-wee—Canoeing Moon

Wee´-pah-zoo-kah-wee—June-Berry Moon

Wah-shoon´-pah-wee—Moon of Moulting Feathers

Chan-pah-sap´-ah-wee—Moon of Black Cherries

Psin-ah´-tee-wee—Wild Rice Gathering Moon

Wah-soo´-ton-wee´—Moon of Green Corn

Wok´-sah-pee-wee´—Moon of Corn Harvest

Tah-kee´-yoo-hah´-wee´—Moon of Mating Deer

Tah-hay´-chap-shoon´-wee—Moon of Dropping Deer-horns

Wee-tay´-ghee—Moon of Severe Cold

We-chah´-tah-wee—Raccoon's Moon

In the northern extremes of North America, for several months each summer, the sun never drops below the horizon line. The moon is obscured during these sunny months. As a result, many northern cultures recognize a smaller number of moons. The Inuit of the region near what is now called Point Barrow, Alaska, recognize only nine moons.

What is the moon like? If you could experience the moon it would be strange, beautiful and deadly. There is no air pressure on the moon and its gravity is so weak it cannot hold an atmosphere in place. There is no air to transmit sound waves. If someone sneaked up behind you and yelled, you would not hear a thing! In the heat of a lunar day, the temperature can rise to above the boiling point of water at sea level (212°F or 100°C). At night the thermometer would plummet to below –200°F (–128.9°C). No sign of life or water has ever been found on the moon.

The moon's diameter is about 2,160 miles (3,476 kilometers), compared to Earth's diameter of 7,913 miles (12,735 kilometers) and the sun's diameter of 850,000 miles (1,367,948 kilometers). Mercury, the smallest planet in our solar system, has a diameter that is only about 1,000 miles (1,609 kilometers) larger than the moon's. Earth has a volume forty-nine times as large as that of the moon and, on the average, Earth is about 238,856 miles (384,403 kilometers) from the moon. Gravity on the moon is only one-sixth that found on Earth. It takes the moon twenty-seven and one-third days to revolve around Earth, but since Earth has moved ahead in its orbit while the moon revolved around it, the moon needs a few days to catch up. The moon, therefore, reaches the same place in our night sky every twenty-nine and one-half days or so. A twelve-month lunar year, then, is 354.4 days long.

At first, it may seem a puzzle that, since the sun is about four hundred times the size of the moon, the sun and moon appear roughly the same size when viewed from Earth. It is also true that sunrise and sunset—the time it takes for the entire sphere of the sun to appear or disappear, edge to edge, above or below the horizon—is the same duration as moonrise and moonset: about two minutes. The explanation is that, while the moon is about four hundred times smaller than the sun, this size difference is offset by the fact that the moon is nearly four hundred times closer to Earth than the sun.

Some scientists theorize that the moon formed separately from Earth, while others think it formed from a piece of Earth that broke away. The moon's surface is thought to have changed little since it formed 4.6 billion years ago (Figure 4-3). In fact, some of the rock pieces and lunar dust brought back from the Sea of Tranquility by the Apollo 11 moon walk on July 20, 1969, were found to be 4.6 billion years old, which is as old as the solar

Figure 4-3. The full moon as seen from Earth. (Photo used with permission from the Lick Observatory, © University of California Regents, Santa Cruz.)

system itself. The oldest known rocks on Earth are around 3.6 billion years old.

The lunar rocks form a dramatic surface covered with large flat plains called *maria,* circular *craters* up to 160 miles (257 kilometers) across (Clavius crater) and up to 5 or 6 miles (8.0 or 9.7 kilometers) deep (Newton Crater); *mountains* over 3 miles (4.8 kilometers) high and riverlike *rilles* that snake over its surface. The moon is covered with rocks and dust. Many of the moon's craters formed from meteor collisions, and they have lasted billions of years because there is no water or air on the moon to cause erosion. The moon lacks the protective atmosphere we have on Earth, so meteors crash into it and form new craters. The large, dark maria or seas (which are actually dry) are thought to have been caused by lava filling in where meteors blasted craters. The lava created flat surfaces much as water fills in lakes and oceans on Earth.

In the sky, the moon appears to change from being "full" to "new" and then to full again, with all of the crescent stages or quarter phases in between. Actually what we are seeing are varying portions of the light and dark sides of the moon, half of which is always illuminated by sunlight and the other half of which is always in shadow. Each full *lunar cycle* lasts twenty-nine and one-half days.

During the partial phases of the moon, we can often see a very faint image of the part of the moon that is in the shadow, which is actually illuminated by sunlight that reflects off Earth on to the moon. This light is called *earthshine*.

The movement and interplay of gravitational forces from both the sun and moon have dramatic effects on Earth. *Tides* are the result of the pull exerted on the oceans by the gravity of the sun and moon. Since the moon is so close to Earth, its gravitational pull is over twice that of the sun. As ocean water is drawn toward the sun and moon it builds in places, rising along the shore to form *high tide*. *Low tide* results when the seas subside. When the sun, Earth and moon are in a line, during the new and full moons, the pull on the oceans is greatest, which causes our most extreme high and low tides, called *spring tides*. Between these periods, when the moon is in its quarter phases, the pull of the sun and moon are at angles and working partially against one another. This is when we have the lower *neap tides*.

For thousands of years Native North Americans have predicted and anticipated

eclipses. Traditional ceremonies are held on the occasion of an eclipse. When Earth periodically passes directly between the sun and moon, casting a shadow onto the moon's surface, we experience a *lunar eclipse*. A *solar eclipse* occurs when the moon passes directly between the sun and Earth, casting its shadow onto Earth. Figure 4-4 demonstrates a lunar and a solar eclipse.

Caution: Do not look directly at a solar eclipse! Severe eye burns and blindness can result during certain phases of the eclipse. (See the explanation following the *"Slip the Eclipse"* activity.)

Aurora Borealis

Those who live in the northern latitudes and are hardy enough to venture outdoors on a cold winter night may witness a spectacular display of the aurora borealis, or northern lights (Figure 4-5). The sky is streaked with glowing lavenders, pinks, reds, greens and grays. There are some well-accepted theories among scientists as to what causes the auroras.

The sun's hot outer layers emit a steady stream of charged atomic particles into the solar system. This cloud of charged particles moving outward from the sun is called the *solar wind*. The sun's activity, and thus the strength of the solar wind, is highly variable. *Sunspots* are magnetic storms on the surface of the sun. At the height of the sunspot cycle there is a corresponding increase in the number of *solar flares,* violent events on the sun that send charged particles far out into space. Sometimes, in about three or four days, these particles reach Earth's atmosphere.

As the charged particles approach, Earth's magnetic field draws them toward the north and south magnetic poles. Here, the gases of Earth's atmosphere and the highly charged solar particles react, giving birth to the *aurora borealis* or *northern lights* in the northern

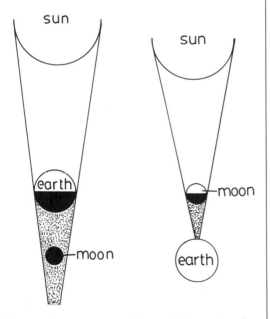

Figure 4-4. Lunar eclipse (left) and solar eclipse (right).

Figure 4-5. Opposite. The aurora borealis (northern lights) illuminates a winter sky.

hemisphere and the *aurora australis* or *southern lights* in the southern hemisphere. The auroras are more frequent and intense when the sun is most active—when there is an unusually large number of sunspots and solar flares. Sunspot activity peaks on a fairly regular cycle every eleven years. The last peak was in 1990.

How do the auroras glow? A rough analogy can be made using fluorescent light bulbs and neon signs. In these cases, certain gases fill a glass tube devoid of air and electrical energy causes the gas particles to glow. Each kind of gas emits colors. This is what happens with the northern lights, as atmospheric gases are charged by the energy of the solar wind.

Auroras can move as luminescent vertical waves of changing colors across the sky—a celestial tapestry. A greenish-yellow hue may appear with red fringe along the bottom. They can take the form of arching lights and ribbons that are often violet, blue, red-orange, gray, green or white. Excited, glowing molecules of oxygen in the upper atmosphere turn red and greenish-white, while nitrogen molecules glow red and blue-green.

Knowing how auroras form does not detract from their beauty shimmering in the winter sky. To witness one of these ethereal displays is to see nature in all its splendor.

Lightning and Thunder

While the auroras create a colorful display overhead in the northern regions, *lightning* is more common in warmer climates to the south. In some Native North American traditions, a great Thunderbird shoots lightning bolts from its eyes and claps its wings to make thunder. Powerful, explosive and, at times, deadly, lightning demands our full attention as it streaks across the night sky. When thunder and lightning approach suddenly, drop all fishing rods, umbrellas, kites and other metal objects, get out of the water if you are fishing or swimming and seek shelter in a house or car. Stay out of the water, away from fields and other open areas and

clear of tall objects such as trees, especially those that stand alone out in the open. Do not use a telescope or binoculars.

During a lightning storm opposite electrical charges build up in the atmosphere. If these charges grow strong enough an amazingly powerful electrical current—lightning—flashes between them. Lightning can move between clouds or between the ground and a cloud. One bolt of lightning can generate as much electrical current as an electrical power plant—up to 100 million volts. At first, a small *leader stroke* comes down from the cloud and makes a circuit between the cloud and a high point on the ground. Then, the powerful *lightning bolt* itself shoots back up the same path taken by the leader stroke. Although the lightning bolt appears to shoot downward, it actually travels up from the ground. Because it takes the lightning bolt only about one millionth of a second to reach from ground to cloud, your eyes cannot perceive the real direction of travel. As bright as the flash is, the actual lightning bolt is only about an inch (a few centimeters) wide.

The bolt of lightning heats the air around it to 54,000°F (30,000°C)—five times the temperature at the sun's surface. As the air heats up and expands it makes the booming sound of *thunder*. You hear the clap of thunder a few seconds after the lightning bolt flashes because sound travels roughly 1 million times slower than the speed of light. If you count the number of seconds that pass between the lightning strike and the clap of thunder that follows, then divide this number by five, you can estimate how far away from you in miles the lightning was. The distance in kilometers can be calculated by dividing the number of seconds by three.

Night and Day—Hot and Cold

Although some desert peoples are active at night to escape the hot drying sun, most of us are unaware of what occurs in nature during the yearly average of twelve hours of darkness in each twenty-four-hour cycle. In the two minutes it takes the sun to fully disappear beneath the horizon, we enter the brief gray of twilight. From when the darkness slowly rises out of the valley shadows to when the last rays of sunlight flicker and fade on the tallest hilltop, day and night mingle, then dusk turns to darkness.

The *cycle of night and day,* which affects all life, results from Earth's rotation on its axis. A complete day/night cycle occurs every twenty-four hours. Every time Earth rotates once around, someone standing at the equator travels through space the full 25,000 miles (40,234 kilometers) of its circumference. This same person also travels 1,600,000 miles (2,600,000 kilometers)—the distance Earth moves along its orbit around the sun each day. As Earth turns, sunset moves westward along the equator at the speed of 1,040 miles (1,674 kilometers) every hour or about 17 miles (27.4 kilometers) per minute! This is why time zones are about 1,040 miles (1,674 kilometers) wide at the equator. Roughly 40 percent of Earth's surface is in darkness at any given time.

Without Earth's rotation on its axis, one side would bake in endless day, and the other freeze in eternal night. This rotation results in the relatively even distribution of heat on Earth's surface. The drama of the *seasons,* however, is created by Earth's tilt on its axis of 23.5 degrees to the plane of its orbit and its revolution around the sun (Figure 4-6). This tilt causes the north pole to be angled closest to the sun during the *summer solstice* on June 21, and farthest away during the *winter solstice* on December 21. On June 21 the sun's rays strike Earth's surface more directly in the northern hemisphere than any other time of year, causing the summer heating north of the equator. The winter solstice finds the sun's rays meeting Earth at small angles. This spreads the sun's energy out over a larger surface area of ground and is the source of winter's strength. This sequence of events is further complicated because Earth's orbit around the sun is elliptical: We are closest to the sun (*perihelion*) on January 2 or 3 and farthest away (*aphelion*) on July 4. As a result, the seasons are unequal in

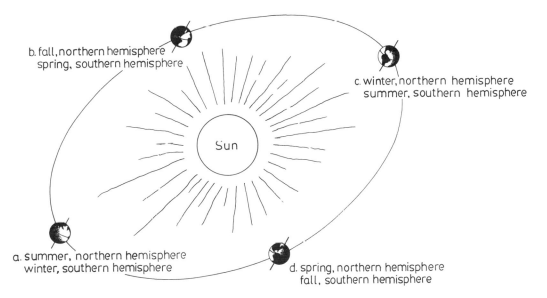

Figure 4-6. Earth's revolution around the sun and Earth's tilt on its axis result in seasons and changing day length. When day at the north pole is 24 hours long (a), night at the south pole is also 24 hours long. When Earth is at positions (b) and (d), every place has a 12–hour day and a 12–hour night. (Adapted with permission from Helen Ross Russell, Ten Minute Field Trips: A Teacher's Guide to Using the School Grounds for Environmental Studies. *Washington, D.C.: National Science Teachers Association, 1990, p. 131.)*

length, with summer being longest, followed by spring, fall and winter. Summer is more than four days longer than winter in the northern hemisphere.

Earth's tilt also causes the unequal length of night and day at different times of year north and south of the equator. Near the equator the length of tropical days and nights is remarkably similar all year. During the *vernal equinox* (March 21) and *autumnal equinox* (September 23), when the sun is directly above the equator, day and night are of equal length worldwide. The farther away from the equator one travels, however, the greater the variation of the length of night and day at times other than the equinox. The light of polar days lasts twenty-four hours during the height of summer as the sun remains above the horizon. In Alaska and northern Canada, down to about Labrador's southern boundary, and in much of northwestern Canada, summer twilight lasts all night. Conversely, when the long winters arrive in the polar regions, the sun never rises and the moon never sets. In the northern hemisphere during the summer solstice, in a region that is about 700 miles (1,127 kilometers) north of another region (for example, Minneapolis versus Memphis or Boston versus Myrtle Beach, South Carolina) day length is about one hour longer.

Overall, when day is longer than night, heat builds up and we have warm seasons. At these times of year more heat is absorbed by Earth during the day than is radiated back into space at night. During the winter, when night is longer than day, more heat is being lost in the dark than is being gained by daylight. The nighttime climate of an area is also determined by latitude and the infinite variety of hills, plains, mountains, valleys and bodies of water.

The uneven heating and cooling of air on Earth's irregular surface causes differences in air pressure. *Wind* is created when air moves from places of higher air pressure to places of lower air pressure. Warm air is lighter than cold air so it rises. For instance, in mountainous and hilly areas, air in the valley warms during the day and rises, causing an upslope

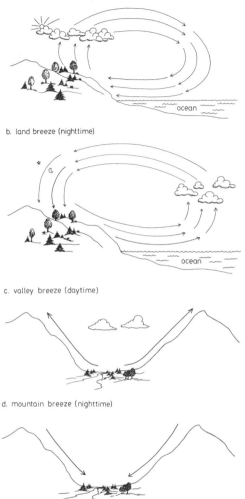

a. sea or lake breeze (daytime)

b. land breeze (nighttime)

c. valley breeze (daytime)

d. mountain breeze (nighttime)

Figure 4-7. Day and night wind patterns. a) Sea breeze or lake breeze (daytime). Warm air over the land rises. Cooler offshore air rushes inland beneath this rising warm air. Clouds often form inland. b) Land breeze (nighttime). Warm air over the water rises. Cooler air from land rushes out to replace this rising warm air. Clouds often form over water. c) Valley breeze (daytime). Valley air warms and rises upslope. d) Mountain breeze (nighttime). Air cools and sinks downslope.

valley breeze. As the air cools and sinks at night, a *mountain breeze* blows downslope (Figure 4-7). During the day along the coastline, the land heats up faster than the water and this warmer air rises. The heavier cool air from the sea rushes in beneath the rising warm air on land and a *sea breeze* or *lake breeze* forms. At night the land cools faster than the water, and the warmer air over the water rises and is replaced by cooler air blowing in from the land, forming a *land breeze* (Figure 4-7).

Clouds form when a rising warm air mass meets a cold air mass at a temperature below the *dew point* of the warm air—the temperature at which water vapor condenses into liquid and forms visible droplets. The warm air cools and can no longer hold as much moisture. *Fog,* which is like a cloud just above the ground, is made up of visible water droplets that form when the air temperature cools at night. Cool, still places, like valleys, and humid pockets near and above wet habitats are likely places for fog to form. *Sea fog,* which is common in Newfoundland and San Francisco, forms over land when air blows ashore after passing over cold ocean currents. *Dew* forms as water vapor condenses out of the cooling air onto leaves, spider webs and other surfaces, creating reflective early morning sculptures. On humid nights the leaves of some plants, such as jewelweed and wild strawberry, actually exude water in the form of tiny jewel-like beads along the leaf edges. This *guttated water* is not dew; it comes from inside the plants. When the nighttime temperature reaches below freezing *frost* forms instead of dew. Few sights in nature are as delicate and varied as the white crystal geometry of frost patterns. These sunlit starry sparkles remind us that much happens in the world of darkness that is waiting to be explored during the time we normally roam the land of dreams.

QUESTIONS

1. In "Oot-Kwah-Tah, The Seven Star Dancers," why do the boys go to the lakeshore to dance?

2. There are eight dancing boys that rise into the sky, but only seven become stars. What happens to the eighth boy?

3. What lessons do you learn by listening to the story of The Seven Star Dancers? What is another name for this constellation?

4. Why do First Man and First Woman decide to bring the sun and moon into the Fifth World in the Diné story "The Creation of the Moon?" What do they make the moon out of? How do you believe the moon was created?

5. Who is chosen to carry the moon across the sky? What is he named because of this honor?

6. In this Diné story, why is it that, to this day, Moon wanders in the sky? According to the story, why does Moon sometimes face toward Earth and sometimes away?

7. What is a constellation? How many are there? How many constellations can we see from the northern hemisphere?

8. The five constellations we can see year-round are close to the north star. What are these five called? Name three constellations that can be seen for each of the four seasons. Find them on a star map.

9. What is a star? A galaxy? Which galaxy is our solar system found in?

10. How many stars do you think there are in our solar system?

11. How far away is our star, the sun? What is the sun made of?

12. What is the zenith? The meridian? The ecliptic? The zodiac?

13. What really is a "shooting star"? What is a meteor? What is a meteorite?

14. Why do Native North Americans use the moon for their calendars? Do you ever keep track of the passing of time using the moon? How does the moon change during each lunar cycle?

15. What does the surface of the moon look like? Is it hot or cold there? Wet or dry? Does anything live there?

16. How big is the moon and how far away is it? When you look up in the sky, why does the moon look like it is the same size as the sun even though the sun is so much larger?

17. Why does the moon seem to change its shape when we see it at different times? How many days does it take for the moon to experience a complete cycle from full moon to new moon and back again to full moon?

18. How old do you think the moon is? How old *is* the moon?

19. What affect do the moon and sun have on tides? How do the moon and sun cause the tides?

20. What is a lunar eclipse? What is a solar eclipse? Why is it dangerous to look directly at a solar eclipse? What can happen if you do?

21. What causes lightning? How does thunder form? Where is it safe to be during a lightning storm? What places should you avoid and what kinds of things are unsafe to do when lightning is striking?

22. What is the aurora borealis or northern lights? What causes the northern lights?

23. Have you ever seen the northern lights? What do they look like? What kinds of colors and patterns are created by the northern lights?

24. What causes night and day? How long is each day? Why does day length change during the year? How does day length vary in different parts of North America, north and south?

25. What causes the seasons?

26. How do clouds and winds form? How do they change from day to night? What is dew and how does it form? Where and how does fog form?

ACTIVITIES
Stargazing

ACTIVITY: Look at some constellations, learn how to find them in the sky and listen to some related myths and legends. Look for meteors (shooting stars) and learn what they are.

GOALS: Understand how to locate the major constellations in the seasonal skies. Know the difference between a star and a planet, the origin of meteors (shooting stars) and how to

spot a satellite. Have fun with starry myths and legends.

AGE: Younger children and older children

MATERIALS: "Discussion" section from this chapter; pencils; paper; crayons; flashlight; books containing stories and myths of the constellations present at that time of year; reference books; star maps; Figure 4-8; several pairs of binoculars; insect repellent (if necessary); telescope (optional).

PROCEDURE: Open this activity while the childrens' imaginations are still fresh: Have children look for their *own* patterns of stars in the night sky. Then, have them illustrate some images—such as plants, animals and people—that *they* think the patterns resemble and create their own "myths" to go with them.

To begin the formal part of the *"Stargazing"* activity, familiarize yourself with the constellations that are visible at that time of year, the terms and pointers given in the "Discussion" section of this chapter and some stories about these constellations.

You may want to take the group out before dark and lead some of the activities described elsewhere in this chapter, such as *"Moon Walker"* and *"From the Milky Way to the Zodiac."* Once you are outside and the stars are beginning to show clearly, begin with the story of "How Grizzly Bear Climbed the Mountain" (Chapter 6) which describes how Grizzly Bear becomes the constellation we now call the Great Bear. Point out the Big Dipper, which is really a portion of the constellation of the Great Bear or Ursa Major (Figure 4-8). This constellation will be a reference point. Using your flashlight beam, describe and point out the zenith and the stars of the Big Dipper. These will help in locating other things for the group. Then, using the pointer stars of the Big Dipper as a reference, point out the North Star and outline the stars of the Little Dipper, which is also known as the Little Bear, Ursa Minor. Another good reference is the meridian. Trace this in the sky from the northernmost point on the horizon,

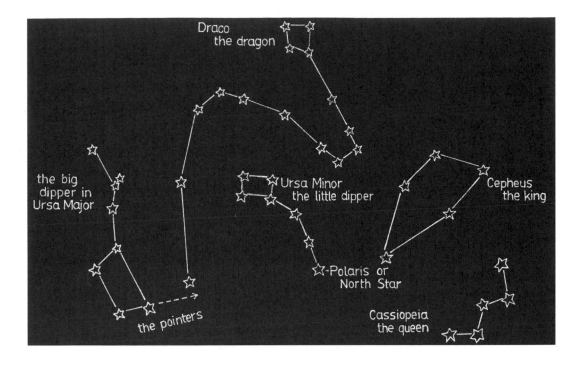

*Figure 4-8. a) (Top) The circumpolar constellations are located close to the north star.
(Bottom) b) The images of the circumpolar constellations as they are imagined in the night sky.*

through the zenith and across to the southernmost point on the horizon. Continue alternating between discussions of the constellations and stories. The binoculars can be passed around as you point out some major features of the moon if it is out. However, a moonless night, or one where a crescent phase of the moon is present, is best for stargazing because a bright moon obscures the stars. If you have access to a telescope, focus it on particular stars and planets one at a time. Have the children take turns viewing these objects. At certain times Saturn's rings and the red spot on Jupiter are clearly visible.

With binoculars you will be able to see much more detail among the stars. Although, for many people, only six stars are visible to the naked eye in the constellation of the Pleiades, the Seven Star Dancers, many more can be seen through binoculars. When viewing the constellation of Cancer in the springtime you should be able to pick out a cluster of stars called the Beehive, as well as some double and triple stars. Look for Jupiter's moons and, with high-powered binoculars, you may even be able to see Saturn's rings.

Tell the group to watch for meteors or "shooting stars," which will appear suddenly as streaks of light in the sky. The answers to many of the questions you will encounter about meteors and other subjects are found in the "Discussion." You may also see a faint, planetlike light moving steadily across the sky and taking no more than six minutes to travel from horizon to horizon. This is a satellite that is visible because it reflects sunlight.

Creating Constellations

ACTIVITY: Make a map of the circumpolar constellations by gluing "stars" (dried beans and grains) onto a cardboard "sky."
GOALS: Understand how the stars within each of the five circumpolar constellations are arranged, and how these constellations are situated relative to each other. Understand what a circumpolar constellation is.
AGE: Younger children
MATERIALS: Marker and newsprint or chalkboard and chalk; tacks; tape; rice; four different kinds of dried peas, beans or cereal grains; glue; black construction paper; cardboard; pencils; map of the circumpolar constellations (Big Dipper, Little Dipper, Cassiopeia, Cepheus, Draco) (Figure 4-8).

PROCEDURE: Transpose the star map in Figure 4-8 onto a large piece of paper or a chalkboard and post it where it is clearly visible. Discuss the definition of a circumpolar constellation. Introduce the five circumpolar constellations and tell the story about how Grizzly Bear becomes the constellation of the Great Bear (Chapter 6). Point out that the Big Dipper is only a part of the constellation of the Great Bear, Ursa Major. Have the children glue the black paper onto the cardboard and draw in the stars for the Big Dipper. (With very young children you may need to pre-mark the star locations.) These stars can be represented by gluing rice where each star is marked. The children will later use a different kind of dried pea, bean or cereal grain for each constellation, with all of the stars in any specific constellation being marked with the same kind of pea, bean or grain. When they have completed the Big Dipper, tell a story about one of the other four constellations and have them glue on another kind of dried object for those stars. Do this until all five of the constellations are on their cardboard "skies." When you discuss the Little Dipper, mention that it is also known as the Little Bear or Ursa Minor.

Since these constellations are visible year round, they are a great place for the children to start learning the stars. Make sure the children understand that the sky is really three-dimensional: The distance from Earth to the various stars in any given constellation varies greatly.

From the Milky Way to the Zodiac

ACTIVITY: Listen to a discussion about the solar system, Milky Way galaxy, circumpolar constellations and the major reference points to use when viewing the stars and other heavenly bodies and locating constellations. Make a model of the relationship between the sun, Earth and constellations to demonstrate the zodiac.

GOALS: Understand that our sun is a star. Understand the common and important terms and reference points used in stargazing, such as zodiac, meridian and circumpolar constellations. Visualize how Earth's location and movement cause us to see different stars and constellations during the year. Understand that Earth is part of our solar system, and that the solar system is part of the Milky Way galaxy.

AGE: Older children

MATERIALS: Information from the "Discussion" section of this chapter; reference books; something to mark the ground with such as chalk, string or a stick to scratch a mark in the dirt; measuring tape; Figure 4-9.

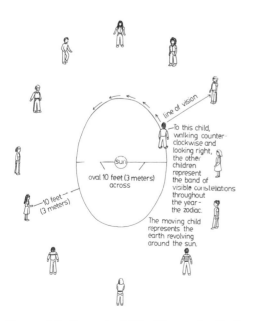

Figure 4-9. From the Milky Way to the Zodiac.

PROCEDURE: Using the information from the "Discussion" and appropriate pictures and illustrations from reference books, explain that Earth and moon are revolving around the sun in our solar system, along with nine other planets, their moons and all other satellites of the sun such as comets and asteroids. Our solar system is part of the Milky Way galaxy. Discuss the composition of our sun, its properties and the concept of magnitude among stars.

Now explain that five constellations are circumpolar and can be seen year-round, while others are best looked for during certain seasons as Earth revolves around the sun. Use the list of constellations provided in the "Discussion." The *ecliptic* is the path the sun takes among the stars as a result of our motion around the sun. The *zodiac* is the band of twelve constellations that the sun passes through as it moves along the ecliptic.

Take the children outside to demonstrate the zodiac. Mark a large oval or ellipse on the ground about 10 feet (3 meters) in diameter and stand someone in the center to represent the sun. This ellipse represents Earth's path as it revolves around the sun. Now space twelve objects (or children if you have a large group) around the ellipse about 10 feet (3 meters) out from its edge as shown in Figure 4-9.

These objects (children) represent stars and constellations. Have a child become Earth and walk counterclockwise around the inner ellipse while looking over her or his right shoulder at the "constellations" on the outside. On the way, as Earth revolves around the sun, certain constellations become visible during each season. The band of constellations she or he sees represents the zodiac. The band is broken up into twelve sections of distinctive constellations called the *signs of the zodiac.*

Reading the Moon

ACTIVITY: Observe and learn some of the major surface features of the moon by studying maps and by viewing the moon at night through a telescope or binoculars. Watch for shooting stars and learn what they really are.

GOALS: Recognize some of the large surface features of the moon and understand how they formed. Understand the true nature of meteors or "shooting stars."

AGE: Younger children and older children

MATERIALS: Binoculars and/or telescope; flashlight; map of the moon; photos of the moon (Figure 4-3). Materials for the follow-up to this activity: pictures of the lunar surface, balloons, wheat paste, water, newspaper strips, tempera paints, paintbrushes, construction paper, stapler, pencils, crayons, scissors, tape, glue.

PROCEDURE: *This activity is best when conducted on a night when the moon is in clear view and at least two-thirds full.*

Take the children out on a clear, moonlit night and view the moon through binoculars and/or a telescope. Using a flashlight, a map of the moon and photographs of the moon's surface such as Figure 4-3, point out some of the features on the moon, such as the craters and maria. Find some lunar mountain ranges and look for the riverlike rilles. (Use the "Discussion" earlier in this chapter describing the physical appearance and origin of the features of the lunar landscape.)

Watch for meteors in the night sky, which can be seen by a patient eye on almost any clear night. *Meteors* are solid particles or objects from space that enter Earth's atmosphere. The surface of Earth is protected by the atmosphere, which causes meteors to burn up from friction as they are pulled down to Earth by gravity, thus causing a streak of light that lingers briefly across the night sky. This is where the terms "falling star" and "shooting star" come from. A meteor that survives its journey through Earth's atmosphere and crashes to the ground is called a *meteorite.*

Note: As a follow-up to this activity, have younger children make a moon with detailed surface features by looking at pictures of the moon and, from these images, creating their own moon by building up papier-mâché around a balloon and painting it when it is dry. Have older children create a mural showing profiles of the different lunar formations.

Moon Walker

ACTIVITY: Watch a demonstration that shows the relative sizes of Earth and the moon, the distance between them and the causes of the phases of the moon.

GOALS: Understand the relative sizes of Earth and moon and the distance between

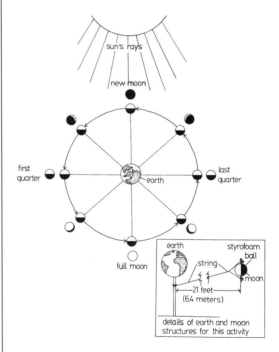

Figure 4-10. Phases of the moon and directions for assembling the props for "Moon Walker." The inner circle of moons shows the position of the moon during the various crescent stages and quarter phases of the lunar cycle. The outer circle of moons shows the corresponding appearance of the moon at each of these times as seen from Earth. (Adapted with permission from Anthony Smith, The Seasons. *London: Weidenfeld and Nicolson Pub. Co., Ltd, 1970, p. 54.)*

them. Visualize that the backside of the moon is always in a shadow and that the side facing the sun is always illuminated. Understand that the angle at which we view the light and dark sides of the moon causes it to appear "full" sometimes, "new" at others and the various phases in between.

AGE: Older children

MATERIALS: Styrofoam ball 2.3 inches (5.8 centimeters) in diameter which is painted white on one side and black on the other; tempera paints; brushes; water; drill and bit; large, round, blue balloon blown up to 8.4 inches (21.3 centimeters) in diameter with the continents drawn on in green; green felt-tipped marker; heavy string 21 feet (6.4 meters) long, plus an extra 1-foot (.3-meter) piece; pencil; large yellow ball or round piece of yellow paper to represent the sun; open area of at least 50 feet (15.2 meters) in diameter; round wooden stake 3 feet (.9 meter) long, such as a piece of broom handle; masking tape, Figure 4-10.

PROCEDURE: Make a hole from top to bottom through the styrofoam ball along the edge of the black and white zones. Do this carefully and gradually by pushing the sharp end of the pencil through the ball using a firm, twisting motion (Figure 4-10). Be sure the ball turns freely on the pencil. This ball represents the moon. Drive the wooden stake into the ground in the center of the open area, then tape "Earth" (blue balloon) on top of it. Tie one end of the long string loosely around the stake so it will turn on the stake without winding onto it. Use the short string to tie the other end of the long piece onto the two ends of the pencil sticking through the moon as shown in the diagram (Figure 4-10).

Explain that the size of the moon and Earth are accurate compared to one another, but that they are scaled down to 1 inch = 945 miles (1 centimeter = 599 kilometers). The distance between Earth and the moon, as represented at the same scale by the connecting string, is 238,856 miles (384,403 kilome-

ters). Then tell the children that at this scale, the sun would have to be 75 feet (23 meters) in diameter to represent its actual diameter of 850,000 miles (1,367,948 kilometers) and that it would be about 1.6 miles (2.6 kilometers) away in this activity! The purpose of the model of the sun you are using here is strictly to show the direction from which it is shining onto Earth and the moon.

Have the children sit near Earth at the center stake. Walk the moon around Earth while keeping the light side toward the sun and the dark side (shadow) facing away from it. You will have to turn the moon on the pencil as you walk. From Earth, the children will see that the moon looks full when it is farthest from the sun, new when it is closest to the sun, and appears as the various crescent and quarter phases when it is in between these two positions.

Slip the Eclipse

ACTIVITY: Make a cardboard model that demonstrates lunar and solar eclipses.

GOALS: Understand the causes of lunar and solar eclipses.

AGE: Older children

MATERIALS: Copies of the *"Slip the Eclipse"* stencil (Figure 4-11); Figure 4-4; scissors; models of Earth, the sun and the moon from the activity *"Moon Walker"*; black marking pen; paper clasp; paper hole punch; light cardboard; glue.

PROCEDURE: Cut out the *"Slip the Eclipse"* stencils and assemble as shown in Figure 4-11. Demonstrate the relative positions of the moon, Earth and the sun during a solar and lunar eclipse using the models from the *"Moon Walker"* activity and the information from the "Discussion" in this chapter, including Figure 4-4. Explain that during a lunar eclipse, the black disk on the *"Slip the Eclipse"* model represents Earth's shadow sliding over

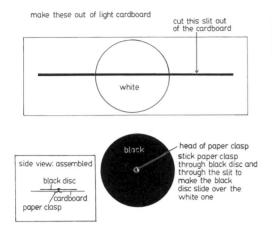

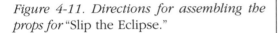

Figure 4-11. Directions for assembling the props for "Slip the Eclipse."

the moon's face (white disk), and that the sun would be shining from behind the childrens' backs as this occurred. Then explain that during a solar eclipse the black disk represents the moon moving in front of the sun and blocking it from view, as it would look standing on Earth.

Note: A variation on this activity is to simulate lunar and solar eclipses using a bright flashlight and different sized spheres at night or in a darkened room.

CAUTION: Do not look directly at a solar eclipse! Severe eye burns and blindness can result during certain phases of the eclipse. One way to view an eclipse is to remove the eyepiece from a telescope and point the telescope at the eclipse. (*Do not look through the eyepiece to position the telescope!*) Then hold a piece of white, nonreflective poster board in the focal plane near the opening where the eyepiece was. Adjust the distance of the poster board from the telescope until the image of the eclipse is in clear focus on the poster board. This same setup can be used to track sunspot movements across the face of the sun over time. Sunspots appear as dark blemishes on the face of the sun.

In addition, there are sun filters available for telescope eyepieces that allow for direct viewing of an eclipse. These filters should be used only under the direct supervision of an expert astronomer because they will not protect your eyes if used incorrectly or if they are damaged in use. *You should never look directly through the telescope eyepiece or through binoculars at an unfiltered image of the eclipse.*

Daylight—Night

ACTIVITY: Demonstrate the causes of day and night by (A) using a flashlight and globe, and (B) dividing the room in half, creating a dark and light side, and forming a circle of children that rotates through the "daytime" and "nighttime."

GOAL: Visualize how Earth's rotation on its axis brings night and day as the different regions of Earth become exposed alternately to sunlight and shadow.

AGE: Younger children and older children

MATERIALS: (A) Flashlight; a tube that is open at both ends such as an empty frozen juice can, a coffee can, a piece of cardboard rolled and taped or the center tube from a roll of paper towels or toilet paper; masking tape; globe or large beach ball; large salad bowl; lazy Susan or other rotating stand, Figure 4-12. (B) Enough blankets to divide the room in half from ceiling to floor, nails and hammer to tack up blankets or rope to hang the blankets from, desk or floor lamp with a yellow light (bulb, globe or lampshade).

PROCEDURE A: *As the World Turns.* Equip the flashlight with a tube to focus the beam

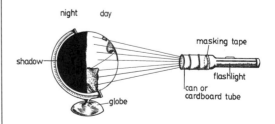

Figure 4-12. Demonstrating day and night with "As the World Turns."

(Figure 4-12). Use a narrow tube, such as a juice can, a coffee can or the center tube from a roll of toilet paper or paper towels. You may need to make your own tube out of cardboard if the flashlight beam is wide.

Mark the spot on the globe where your town or city is located. If you are using the beach ball to represent Earth, mark any place about one-third of the way down from the uppermost point. Then sit the ball in a large salad bowl and place it on a lazy Susan or other suitable rotating stand. Darken the room and focus the beam onto one side of "Earth" while someone slowly turns the globe and creates "night" and "day." Point to your location on the map and watch that spot move from light to dark and back again as the world turns.

PROCEDURE B: *The Edge of Night.* Divide the room in half by hanging blankets from ceiling to floor and leave a door-sized space at each end of the row of blankets on each side of the room. Arrange the children in a circle passing through the two openings with the curtain in the center. Light up one side of the room and keep the other side dark. Use a lamp with a yellow lightbulb or colored globe or lampshade for a sunlight effect. Tell the children that the circle represents the surface of Earth as it rotates into and out of the sunlight (day) and shadow (night). Stop the group occasionally and ask the children what time of day they are in.

Weather: Day and Night

ACTIVITY: Observe changing conditions in daytime and nighttime weather. Present a weather report on these conditions and use these weather patterns to make predictions in temperature, wind direction and humidity .
GOALS: Understand the daily/nightly cycle of heating/cooling and how this cycle affects temperature, wind direction and humidity.

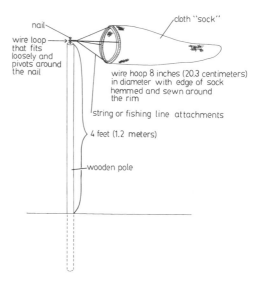

Figure 4-13. Assembly of the wind sock and support.

AGE: Older children
MATERIALS: Wind sock (see Figure 4-13 for directions and materials needed to make a wind sock); three outdoor thermometers (one for each weather station); three compasses; paper; pencils; clipboards or cardboard backing to write against; flashlights; "Discussion" and Figure 4-7; clock or wristwatch; 9 copies of Figure 4-14 *"Weather: Day and Night"* data sheet; chalkboard and chalk or newsprint and marker; three wind speed gauges (optional); a book on weather and forecasting (optional).

PROCEDURE: Beforehand, work with the children to assemble the wind sock (Figure 4-13) for indicating wind direction.

Note: Although large-scale weather systems will have an impact on the children's observations, there is still a lot to be gained by measuring local conditions. This activity is best when conducted during a stretch of settled weather when there are no significant storm fronts passing through the area.

Ask the children, "How are temperature, humidity and wind direction different during the day versus at night? Why is this so? What is dew and how does it form? What is the dew

WEATHER: DAY AND NIGHT

Date:_____

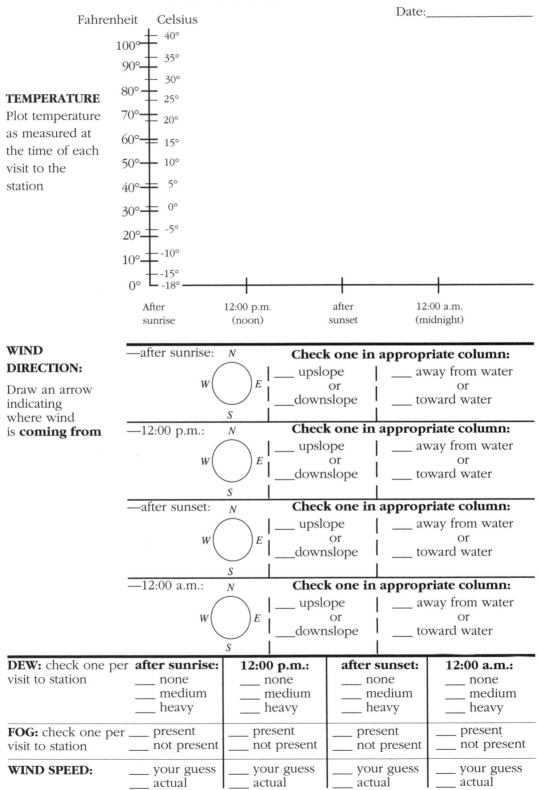

TEMPERATURE
Plot temperature
as measured at
the time of each
visit to the
station

Fahrenheit   Celsius

After sunrise   12:00 p.m. (noon)   after sunset   12:00 a.m. (midnight)

WIND DIRECTION:

Draw an arrow indicating where wind is **coming from**

—after sunrise: **Check one in appropriate column:**
___ upslope or ___downslope   ___ away from water or ___ toward water

—12:00 p.m.:   **Check one in appropriate column:**
___ upslope or ___downslope   ___ away from water or ___ toward water

—after sunset: **Check one in appropriate column:**
___ upslope or ___downslope   ___ away from water or ___ toward water

—12:00 a.m.:   **Check one in appropriate column:**
___ upslope or ___downslope   ___ away from water or ___ toward water

	after sunrise:	**12:00 p.m.:**	**after sunset:**	**12:00 a.m.:**
DEW: check one per visit to station	___ none ___ medium ___ heavy	___ none ___ medium ___ heavy	___ none ___ medium ___ heavy	___ none ___ medium ___ heavy
FOG: check one per visit to station	___ present ___ not present	___ present ___ not present	___ present ___ not present	___ present ___ not present
WIND SPEED:	___ your guess ___ actual	___ your guess ___ actual	___ your guess ___ actual	___ your guess ___ actual

Complete one copy of this worksheet per weather station each day for three days.

point? What is fog and how does it form?" Use the "Discussion" to explain to the children how the cycle of day and night/heating and cooling affects temperature, wind direction and humidity. Make sure they understand how heating and cooling create valley breezes and mountain winds in hilly areas, as well as, along the shore, sea breezes, lake breezes and land breezes (Figure 4-7). Explain what the dew point is and how temperature has an affect on the formation of dew, fog and frost.

Show the children how to orient their compasses to magnetic north by turning the compass until the magnetic north needle lines up with the mark indicating north on the face of the compass dial. Tell them that they are to line up the compass in this way each time they visit the weather station. They will use the compass and wind sock to observe *from* which direction (north, south, east, west or some degree in between) the wind is blowing. In order to simplify this part of the activity they are going to use magnetic north rather than orienting their compasses to true north.

Work with the children to set up three weather stations. This can be done in a place with a hill and valley, or on the shore of a lake, large pond or the ocean. Station A will be at the top of a hill or high on a slope away from a body of water. Locate station B somewhere along the slope between Station A and the valley or body of water. Set up station C in the valley or right next to the body of water. Have the children hang thermometers at the same height and in safe places at all three stations. They will locate the wind sock at station B.

Over the course of at least three days, have the children take readings for temperature and wind direction each morning after sunrise, at midday, in the evening after sunset and around midnight. Also have them observe humidity: fog and dew conditions. They are to use copies of the data sheet *"Weather: Day and Night"* (Figure 4-14) on which to record their findings.

Figure 4-14. Opposite. "Weather: Day and Night" *data sheet.*

Have them complete one data sheet per station for each day of observation. If you are working with small groups, have each group record the data for a particular station each day, rotating from one station to the next on each of the three days of observation.

Optional: If you have access to wind speed gauges, have the children first *guess* the wind speed, then measure and record actual wind speed.

Once the observations are completed, bring the children together and ask them to describe any day-night patterns they have found in temperature readings and wind directions. What are the patterns at each site and among the different sites? How do these patterns vary at different times of the day? Why are the times just after sunrise and just after sunset important for determining daily weather patterns? What have they discovered about humidity as observed by fog and dew? Is there any correlation between fog, dew and temperature? If children were able to measure wind speed, what were their findings? Do they notice any patterns? Did they become more accurate at guessing the wind speed over time? Are these findings what they expected given the information presented in the "Discussion"? If not, what is different and why do they think this is so?

Chart these findings on a chalkboard or large sheet of newsprint. Have the children use this information to predict temperature, wind direction, humidity (fog and dew) and wind speed (optional) at different times of day. Make more observations outdoors and see how accurate these predictions are. Branch out into weather forecasting. Two excellent books are *Weather and Forecasting* by Storm Dunlop and Francis Wilson (New York: Macmillan, 1987) and *The Audubon Society Field Guide to North American Weather* by David M. Ludlum (New York: Knopf, 1991).

EXTENDING THE EXPERIENCE
• Make a scale model of the planets, moons and sun in our solar system and hang them

from the ceiling. Calculate the relative sizes and distances for this model as a math project.

• Map or create a bulletin-board model of a part of the moon's surface. Get to know its beautiful features—the names of the maria, mountain ranges, craters and riverlike depressions called rilles.

• Share the story of "How Grizzly Bear Climbed the Mountain" in Chapter 6.

• Look up the forthcoming astronomical events for your area in the most recent edition of *The Astronomical Almanac*.[5] Share these events with the children and study the astronomical causes of these occurrences (eclipses, meteor showers, etc.).

• Look at a poster that shows Earth from space to reinforce our global connections with other peoples and environments.

• Use a telescope to observe the intricate details of the moon, Saturn's rings, the red spot on Jupiter and other secrets of the sky.

• Locate Polaris, the North Star, and use it to find your way at night. At first, follow a path to the north by walking straight toward the North Star, keeping it directly overhead in front of you. Then try walking in different directions by keeping the North Star at constant angles to the direction you are walking. Set up a treasure hunt map along which children will use the North Star and some obvious landmarks to help them locate a "treasure."

• Watch a lightning storm and listen to thunder from a safe, indoor location and use the information in the "Discussion" to calculate how far away the bolts of lightning are when they strike.

• If you live in the northern latitudes, watch for the aurora borealis or northern lights. Think of descriptive words while looking at the northern lights and write aurora poetry. (See *"Poetry to Your Ears"* in Chapter 3 for an idea of how to proceed.) Create your own stories about how the northern lights came to be.

• *Cloud Stories.* Go outside on a moonlit night when puffy cumulus clouds are blowing across the face of the moon. Lie on your back, look up at the clouds backlit by moonlight and use your imagination to see shapes and images traveling across the sky. Make up a cloud story using some of the plants, animals, people, etc., that dance before the moon.

• Grow vegetable seeds: Place some in the sunlight and some in a dark place. Watch and record their progress. Note the effects of sunlight deprivation on growing plants over several weeks.

• Use a prism to show how light can be separated into the spectral colors: red, orange, yellow, green, blue, indigo and violet. Hang a crystal prism in a sunny window and it will cast colors about the room on sunny days.

• See Chapter 4 in *Keepers of Life* for more information and activities revolving around Native North American moons and celebrations associated with lunar cycles.

• Read *Thirteen Moons on Turtle's Back* by Joseph Bruchac and Jonathan London (New York: Putnam, 1992). Create original activities to celebrate Native North American moons.

• The Aztecs, Native people of the land that is now central Mexico, see a Rabbit in the Moon. Observe the full or nearly full moon on a clear night. Look for the Rabbit in the Moon—a pattern formed by the darker moon landforms that resembles a rabbit with floppy ears. The Rabbit in the Moon is facing right; its head and ears are on the right side of the moon pointing down. Create and illustrate a story about how there came to be a Rabbit in the Moon.

• Share other sky stories from the *Keepers* books. From *Keepers of the Earth:* "How Grandmother Spider Stole the Sun" (Chapter 7), "The Hero Twins and the Swallower of Clouds" (Chapter 10), "How Coyote Was the Moon" (Chapter 13) and "How Fisher Went to the Skyland: The Origin of the Big Dipper" (Chapter 14). From *Keepers of Life:* "The Sky Tree" (Chapter 3), "Fallen Star's Ears" (Chapter 6) and "How Fox Brought the Forests From the Sky" (Chapter 13).

• See Chapter 9, *Keepers of the Earth,* for a story, discussion and activities on wind and weather.

NOTES

1. Peggy V. Beck, Anna Lee Walters and Nia Francisco. *The Sacred: Ways of Knowledge, Sources of Life.* Tsaile, Ariz.: Navajo Community College Press, 1992, p. 87.

2. Light travels 186,000 miles (299,339 kilometers) each second, or nearly 6 trillion (6,000,000,000,000) miles (nearly 9.5 trillion kilometers) in one year. This distance is called a light-year.

3. Cora Dubois. "The Religion of the Luiseño Indians of Southern California." In *University of California Publications in Archaeology and Ethnology,* vol. 8, no. 3. Berkeley: University of California, 1908, pp. 69–186, pl. 16–19. Quoted in Beck, p. 219.

4. Charles Alexander Eastman (Ohiyesa), *Indian Scout Craft and Lore* (New York: Dover Publications, 1974, pp. 162–163.

5. To order *The Astronomical Almanac* write: Superintendent of Documents, U.S. Government Printing Office, P.O. Box 371954, Pittsburgh, PA 15250-7954. Published annually.

All three of the Owl Sisters began to weep. They could not stop weep-
ing. They wept and wept and they turned into owls like the owls of
today.

Chapter 5

Chipmunk and the Owl Sisters

(Okanagan [Colville]—Plateau)

Chipmunk lived with her grandmother in a lodge near the woods. Her grandmother was old and weak and could not gather food for herself. So she sent Chipmunk to pick berries.

"Grandchild," she said, "go into the forest and pick twelve berries. That will be just enough for us. Do not eat any until we have thanked the Creator for giving us our food. And do not stay too long among the berry bushes. When night comes, the Owl Sisters hunt near there. If they catch you they will eat you."

"I will do as you say, Grandmother," Chipmunk said and she went into the forest with her berry basket. Soon she reached the berry bushes. She climbed up into them and began to pick. Before long she had picked eleven berries. But just as she picked the twelfth berry, she dropped it. When she reached down to pick it up, she brushed against some berries which were so ripe that the sweet juice covered her arm.

"Ah," Chipmunk said, "I must clean myself off." She licked off the berry juice. It was so sweet! "This is good," Chipmunk said. "I must have more." Then she put down her basket and climbed higher into the berry bushes and began to eat berries. She ate and she ate and the sun moved further toward the west. Now it was dark and the forest was filled with shadows, but still Chipmunk did not stop eating.

Suddenly Chipmunk heard a sound. She stopped eating and listened. For the first time she realized how dark it was in the forest and she was afraid. The sound grew louder. It was the sound of leaves rustling and twigs breaking. Someone was walking toward her and the footsteps were coming closer. Then the sound stopped. Chipmunk looked down and what she saw was so frightening that she almost screamed. There was the oldest of the Owl Sisters right below her.

"Little One," the Owl Sister said, "come down to me." She lifted her arms up toward Chipmunk. There were long sharp claws on the Owl Sister's hands and on her back was a basket full of the little ones she had caught. She was taking them home to eat them with her sisters. She wanted to put Chipmunk in her basket, too, but Chipmunk was too high up in the bushes for Owl to reach her. Chipmunk did not move.

"Come down," Owl said. "Your mother wants you to come home."

Chipmunk was not fooled. "My mother has been dead for many winters," she said and did not move.

Owl thought for a moment. "Come down," she said again. "Your father wants you to come home."

Again Chipmunk was not fooled. "My father has been dead for many winters," she said and did not move.

Owl thought again. "Come down," she said. "Your grandfather wants you to come home."

Chipmunk shook her head. "My grandfather has been dead for many winters," she said and did not move.

Owl thought for a long time. Then she tried once more. "Come down," she said. "Your grandmother wants you to come home."

Now Chipmunk did not know what to do. Perhaps her grandmother had called her. "I will come down," she said to Owl, "but you must cover your eyes."

"I will cover my eyes," Owl said and raised her arms over her face, but she peeked between her fingers.

Chipmunk did not climb down, though. Instead she took a great leap, right over Owl's head! Owl grabbed at her as she went by and scraped Chipmunk's back with three of her long claws. Ever since then, all Chipmunks bear those scars on their backs. But Chipmunk got away and ran home to her grandmother's lodge.

"Hide me," she said. "Owl is after me."

Grandmother looked for a place to hide her grandchild. Up in the pine tree, Meadowlark sang.

"Put her in the basket, put her in the basket."

Grandmother put Chipmunk in the basket and sat down on top of it. Then she took her white necklace and threw it to Meadowlark as a present.

Soon Owl arrived at Grandmother's lodge. "Where is the little one?" she said. She began to look, but she could not find Chipmunk. She was about to give up when Meadowlark began to sing.

"If you pay me, I will tell you. If you pay me, I will tell you."

Owl took off her white breastplate and threw it to Meadowlark. Meadowlark put it on along with the white necklace Grandmother gave him. Ever since then, all Meadowlarks have worn that necklace and breastplate. Then Meadowlark sang again.

"In the basket, in the basket, you will find her in the basket."

Owl pushed Grandmother aside, grabbed Chipmunk and put her into her pack basket with the other little ones. She left the lodge to look for her sisters. They would have a feast that night.

Grandmother sat alone in her lodge for a time. Then she began to sing.

"Coyote, Coyote, come and help the little ones.
Coyote, Coyote, come and help the little ones."

Owl was walking along when she met Coyote.

"Let us walk together," Coyote said. "Then we can make a campfire and feast together on those little ones. Why should we share them with your sisters?"

Owl was pleased to walk with Coyote. His idea sounded good to her. They walked along until they came to a good place to make a fire.

"Let the little ones out of your pack. They cannot escape us. We will have them gather the wood for the fire," Coyote said.

Owl agreed. It was a good idea. Then Coyote began to tell the little ones what to do in a harsh voice. But when he leaned close to Chipmunk he whispered, "Do as I tell you. Gather wood with a lot of pitch in it to make the fire. I will help you and the others escape."

Before long, a great fire was burning.

"Let us cook the little ones now," Owl said.

"No," said Coyote. "We must let the fire burn down to coals. Let us have the little ones gather roasting sticks."

Owl agreed. Coyote leaned close to Chipmunk again and whispered, "Be ready for my signal."

Then Coyote turned to Owl. "Let us dance while we are waiting. This will be a special feast, so you should make yourself look as fine as possible. You should decorate yourself with this charcoal and put a lot of pitch on your face and on your arms so the charcoal will stick."

Owl thought that was a good idea. She put pitch on her arms and face and decorated herself with the charcoal. Then she and Coyote began to dance. They danced for a long time and Owl grew tired.

"Keep dancing," Coyote said. "You are such a fine dancer! I like to watch you dance."

Owl danced and danced. She was so tired she began to stagger. Coyote pushed her, as if in fun.

"Keep dancing," he said and pushed her again.

Owl kept on dancing. Coyote pushed her again and now she was close to the fire. "Keep dancing," he said, and pushed her a third time. Owl danced right at the edge of the fire. Then Coyote pushed her hard. She fell right into the fire.

"Now," Coyote said to Chipmunk and the other little ones, "run to your homes. Her sisters will soon be here. They are following her tracks."

Coyote hid and watched. Soon Owl's three sisters came along.

"Our older sister has been here," one of them said. "Here are her tracks."

The youngest sister poked the fire. "Look," she said. "Our sister has left something for us to eat."

The three Owl Sisters began to eat. They ate and ate. Then one of them held up a claw. Her eyes became very wide.

"Hooooo!" she said. "Hoooo! We have done something very wrong. This is our older sister's finger! We have eaten our sister!"

All three of the Owl Sisters began to weep. They could not stop weeping. They wept and wept and they turned into owls like the owls of today. Their arms became wings and their eyes grew large and they flew off in shame. That is why the owls no longer come out in the daytime. It is only in the night that they hunt for the little ones now because they are ashamed to be seen during the day. That is how it happened, long ago.

The Great LaCrosse Game

(Menominee—Eastern Woodland)

Long ago, the birds and animals had a dispute. No one remembers for sure what their argument was about, but it went on for a long time. At last it was agreed that they would play a game of lacrosse to decide it. The first to score a goal would win.

They set up a great playing field with the animals on one side and the birds on the other. The center of that field was the Place Where the Sun is Marked on the Rock, Kesosasit on the great inland sea called Michigami. Today those waters are called Lake Michigan. One goal was placed at the south end of Michigami. Today, that is where the city of Chicago stands. The other goal was far to the north, near the place where the city of Green Bay is today.

It seemed that everything was set. All of the birds, those with wings, were on one side. All of the animals, those with fur, were on the other. But, just as they were about to begin, a small voice was heard.

"Which side will I be on?" it said.

There, on the ground was a small brown creature, no larger than a mouse. It had fur, yet it did not look quite like an animal. It had wings, yet those wings were not like those of a bird.

"You have wings, you cannot be on our side," said the animals. "Not only that, you are the smallest of all."

"You have no feathers. You cannot join us," the birds said. "And how can one so little be of any help?"

Then Otter spoke up for the little creature. "Let us not leave anyone out," Otter said. "Even if this little one cannot help much, it can still encourage our better players."

So a tiny lacrosse stick was fashioned for the little brown creature, and it was allowed to join the side of the animals.

Then the two sides lined up to face each other, with the best players in front. On the north side were the animals. The bear and the deer, the wolf and the fox, the rabbit and woodchuck, the otter and beaver, the snakes and lizards and all the other creatures who walked on Earth, even those who spent much of their time in the water, were there. On the south side were the birds. The eagle and the hawk, the owl and duck, the gull

The little brown creature spread out its legs and unfolded leathery wings. It flew up into the darkening sky and grabbed the ball away from the birds with its little stick.

and the stork, the crow and the jay, the hummingbird and kingfisher and all of the others who flew in the sky were there.

As soon as the ball was put into play, the deer scooped it up and began to run swiftly toward the southern goal. But before Deer went far, Stork hooked him with his stick and the ball fell free. Wolf scooped it up and passed it toward Beaver. But Red-tail Hawk swooped down and intercepted the ball. Up, up, into the sky Red-tail Hawk flew. The animals tried to jump up to reach him, but none could leap that high. The other birds flew up and began passing the ball back and forth over the heads of the animals. As they headed toward the northern goal, the sun was beginning to set and the animals below them were falling farther and farther behind.

Suddenly, the little brown creature, which had been riding on the back of Otter, leaped up into the air. It spread out its legs and unfolded leathery wings. It flew up into the darkening sky and grabbed the ball away from the birds with its little stick. The birds tried to get the ball back, but the little brown creature darted and dodged among them. It was so quick that no bird could catch it and even the owl could not move as well in the growing darkness as that little brown creature. It flew and flew toward the southern goal, carrying the ball over the line to score. The animals had won!

"What is your name?" the animals asked the little brown creature.

"I am Bat."

"You are the best lacrosse player of all," said the animals. Then the animals talked about what could be done to reward Bat for helping. It was decided that Bat would be allowed to sleep all during the day, when many other animals were awake. Then, when Bat came out at night, there would be plenty for Bat to eat as insects filled the night sky.

So it is to this day. And the story of how Bat helped the animals win the great lacrosse game is still told to remind people never to overlook anyone, even if they are the smallest of all.

DISCUSSION

A shrill cry rends the cloak of darkness that surrounds the campfire. One wide-eyed child turns and asks, "Mother, what kind of animal made that terrible sound? I'm frightened."

"Do not worry," she replies. "The screech owls are friends of The People. They will not harm us. You are wise to be mindful of noises when you do not know who makes them. Let me tell you a story about what happened a long time ago at night when someone heard a strange noise."

So begins a story, one of the most important aspects of life among Native North Americans. A story may, at first telling, seem to be no more than a form of entertainment. But, as the *Okanagan* (Colville) story of "Chipmunk and the Owl Sisters" demonstrates, stories are much, much more. Chipmunk does not heed her grandmother's advice to pick the berries without eating any and to come home before nightfall. She is caught by one of the Owl Sisters who intends to eat her. Grandmother asks Coyote to help and he saves Chipmunk by tricking the older Owl Sister. During the course of the story Chipmunk learns the importance of listening to what your elders say, following directions and of giving thanks to the Creator before eating. The story also explains how Meadowlark gets her white necklace and breastplate, how owls get their wings and large eyes and why they only come out at night to hunt.

Storytelling is a form of traditional education through which important lessons are revealed. *Stories* say how the world came to be and how it is to be cared for if we are to live in balance with Earth and other human beings. The wisdom and practices of a people are handed down through stories. Stories are an essential part of songs, ceremonies, dances, games and thanksgivings. Cultural continuity and stability are maintained by stories because they provide a common view; a way of relating to the world.

With the exception of some pictographs with which stories are recorded in symbols, stories were not traditionally written down. They were carried from generation to generation in the memories of the storytellers (Figure 5-1). Stories are a way of preserving not only the memories of a people, but the use of memory itself. Children often listened to a story by the fire on one night and were asked to retell it the next. "A child's first memories and first learning experiences probably took place around a fire."[1]

Traditional Native North American games are also presented in this chapter. This Menominee story tells of *lacrosse,* one of the many games that are indigenous to Native North America. Lacrosse has always been popular among Native people, yet it is more than a game. Among some Native North American cultures lacrosse was done as a ceremony to help cure a person who was ill. The ball stood for the sun, which gives us life, and each toss of the ball from stick to stick symbolized the passage of a single day. Although lacrosse games today are limited to only a few players on each side, in old times it was common for everyone in one town to play a game against everyone in another town, and lacrosse was sometimes used to settle disputes in place of fighting. The game was hard played and broken bones were common as hundreds of players fought to take the ball from one goal in their village to the goal in another village which might be miles away. It was said that everything in nature loved lacrosse and that even the Thunderbirds up in the sky played with a ball made of thunder that rumbled from horizon to horizon.

The Campfire

A drum is traditionally used to call people together for a ceremony, council, dance, storytelling or other gathering. Among the Haudenosaunee, it is a tradition to stop nearby and make a fire when approaching to visit a village of people from a different culture or nation. The smoke signals a desire for a meeting. This would lead to a peaceful gathering. Fire is also used to celebrate the many thanksgivings throughout the year.

Campsites are usually located on a dry, flat place near a river or lake in the dry season or higher up during the time of rain and floods and when mosquitoes and other biting insects are abundant. Lodges and lean-tos are usually arranged in a circle with a cooking fire in the center of each family's dwelling and a communal fire in the middle of the village.

When the fire is out away from the village, in an encampment, finding the way there is the

Figure 5-1. Opposite. In the glow of the campfire the circle of the story comes to life.

beginning of the experience. The first step is to remember where you started from and where your route has taken you. Native children are encouraged to use all their senses while traveling at night: particularly sight, hearing, smell and touch. Hills, large old trees, distinctly shaped rocks, streams and lakes are excellent landmarks. In addition, stars and constellations reveal directions. The North Star is always in the north. *In the early evening,* the tail of the Great Bear (the handle of the Big Dipper) points east in spring and west in autumn. Relative to bark on the south side of a tree growing out in the open, bark on the north side tends to feel more damp, may have moss growing on it and frequently appears darker. Bark on the south side is often dryer, lighter in color and lacks moss.

At night, when shadows are long and darkness obscures the sight, your *sixth sense* becomes heightened. This is the sense that tells you what the other five senses cannot. You sense that there is a deer grazing at the edge of a field, so you approach with particular caution from downwind. Perhaps your sixth sense tells you that some person, or animal, is behind you and staring at you. You may also sense that danger is nearby long before there are any signs of it.

BUILDING A FIRE: *Fire-making* is one human ability that distinguishes us from other forms of life. Summer is a time for building small fires while larger fires are welcome during the winter months. Fires are often built on rocks, if possible, allowing rain and wind to clear away the ashes that remain behind.

Each traditional fire-making technique is designed to create sparks that ignite tinder. Good sources of *tinder* include thin strips of birch bark gathered from trees that have fallen, shredded milkweed, the thin outer strips of cedar bark and other plant fibers. One method is to strike flint against a stone to make sparks. Another technique involves pressing a rapidly turning spindle down into a notch in a piece of wood. This is done by the use of a bow drill. (See *"The Campfire"* activity.)

Activities Around the Campfire

STORYTELLING. Stories are traditionally told around a fire in the evening, usually during the winter. Some cultures tell stories at other times of year as well. (See Chapter 1 for a more detailed discussion of stories and storytelling.) If you decide to tell stories at a time of year when they are not traditionally told, discuss this with the children so that they understand the traditions.

The stories and other traditional fireside activities are meant to teach children to strive for the height of their physical, intellectual and emotional potentials. Some highly held *values* among Native North American cultures include sharing, loyalty, thinking of others, faithfulness, initiative, a sense of duty, creative ingenuity and a sense of humor. Politeness, reverence and a sense of order are emphasized. Individuality and self-reliance are encouraged in balance with friendship and concern for others.[2]

Children are encouraged to listen and learn from experience and context, to speak only as part of an activity and to not ask every question that pops into mind. In this way, children learn from experience and context without interrupting with a question, which has the effect of separating knowledge from experience.[3] A question, once answered, tends to be dropped, but learning through discovery is a lifelong process.

NATIVE NAMES. Children of Native North American families are given different names as they grow older and reach important times of passage in their lives. In many cultures the *birth name* traditionally refers to a child's order of birth. Among the Santee Dakota, for example, a child may be called *Chaskáy* (first-born son) or *Wenónah* (first-born daughter).[4]

Among the Dakotas, *honor* or *public names* are usually given by the clan leader once the child can walk. This is an occasion for a great feast and celebration around a communal fire. At this ceremony the parents provide food and drink for villagers who are in need. These acts teach the child to be generous and of good will. An honor name often describes the strong character and well-known accomplishments of a child's ancestors. The child is expected to honor and live up to this name, or risk losing it. A child who becomes distinguished in an honorable way later in life—because of a feat of endurance, strength, courage or compassion—may be awarded a *deed name* after a bird or other animal or even one of the elements.

Nicknames, which are usually not flattering, often refer to something unusual or humorous about the child. Native North Americans frequently tease as a way of gently bringing attention to some strong aspect of a person's character that that individual would do well to pay close attention to.

FOODS AND COOKING. The fire is also a place of gathering for a meal. Each meal begins with a thanks to the Creator and the plant and animal people who have offered themselves to The People. Corn, beans and squash—the *Three Sisters*—are grown and eaten from the northeast to the southwest in North America. Berries, nuts and other natural snacks like maple sugar are eaten. *Baking* often consists of wrapping and tying the food (such as fish, corn or shellfish) in clean wet leaves or corn husks, placing it in hot ashes, mounding a bit of clay or soil over the ashes and allowing the food to cook for about 30 minutes or until done. The leaves protect the food from burning and emit steam to aid in the cooking. Along the east coast the *Wampanoag,* "People of the Dawn," have a ceremonial feast known as the *Appanaug,* which means "seafood cooking" or "clambake."[5] For the clambake, the Wampanoags gather clams and lobsters which, along with corn, potatoes and onions, are steamed on top of rockweed (a kind of seaweed) and hot rocks layered in a pit. The food is then covered with rockweed and allowed to cook. Another form of food preparation, *roasting,* is done on a spit—a stick suspended over the fire between two forked branches stuck in the ground on either side of the fire pit (Figure 5-2). Corn, wild rice, duck potato (arrowhead),

Figure 5-2. Roasting on a spit.

Indian potato (groundnut) and other foods are often *boiled* in a clay pot, bark bucket or in a bag kettle.

The bag kettle is hung from four stakes and suspended over the fire (Figure 5-3). Only the water-bearing part of the hide contacts the intense heat and flames. When fire strikes a water-filled bark or hide container the material will not burn where the container is in contact with the water inside. This is why water can even be boiled in a paper cup: Only the paper above the water line will burn off. Traditional foods are often stored in a bark-lined hole in the ground which is hidden under a cover of available materials such as stones, leaves or sand.

DANCES. Like storytelling, Native North American *dances* are part of life and a reflection of the life all around. Dances are performed for many observances and ceremonies: to honor particular plants or animals, to celebrate certain seasons and natural events like the solstice and harvest, to symbolize and to help restore balance in the relationship between nature and human beings, to offer

Figure 5-3. A hide bag kettle. Use a small fire and be certain that heat and flames only touch the hide where the upper surface is in contact with water or the hide will burn.

thanks for the gifts of nature from the Creator and to strengthen the connections within a community of human beings.

The *"Circle Dance"* in *Keepers of the Animals* symbolizes the circles of life and cycles of nature that we are all part of, the interconnectedness of life on Earth, the equality of everyone in the circle, the circle of giving and receiving and the community of people in the circle. Many related concepts are symbolized in the Narragansett *"Round Dance of Unity and Thanksgiving"* in *Keepers of Life,* including the unity of all living and inanimate parts of Earth, the importance of honoring the circles and cycles of nature, the value of keeping the circle of giving and receiving strong in order to live in balance and the interconnectedness of local communities to peoples throughout the world.

GAMES. *Games* are far more than a time of play in Native North American cultures. They symbolize the chase, the harvest and other fertility events in nature, important ceremonies, events in the agricultural cycle, war remembrances and preparations and the discovery of the probable outcomes of human efforts.[6]

A variety of games is found throughout Native North America. Although these games vary in the particular methods, rules and materials used throughout the continent, most Native cultures play many of the games discussed below. These games can be divided into two general types: *games of chance* and *games of dexterity.* Games of chance include those in which bones or other objects are thrown much like dice, as well as guessing games during which someone tries to guess where an object has been hidden, such as under a moccasin or in a particular hand.

An astounding number of contemporary games and sports share a kinship with traditional Native North American games, including

- archery
- lacrosse
- field hockey
- foot races
- shooting at a moving target
- wrestling

- soccer
- kayaking
- canoeing
- hidden ball in hand game
- dicelike games using pebbles, sticks, etc.
- hidden ball and cup game (moccasin game)

Children's traditional games include many that are still played today:

- tops
- cat's cradle
- ball tossing
- sledding
- juggling
- bull roarer
- ring and pin
- shuttlecock (like badminton)

Some traditional Native games are similar to those that were imported from other continents. *Quoits,* for instance, is similar to the game of horseshoes. An Inuit version of the game, called *Kaganagab,* consists of placing two sealskins set at about 8 to 10 feet (2.4 to 3 meters) apart. On each sealskin is placed a bone disk about the size of a dollar coin. Players divide into two teams that stand at one sealskin and take turns tossing small wooden disks toward the other sealskin. The object is to cover all or part of the bone disk with the wooden disks. Other variations on this game include one known as *Haeyo* from the Pima of Arizona. Two holes are dug about 50 feet (15.2 meters) apart. The object of the game for the two teams (two on a team) is to throw medium-sized stones into one hole while standing at the other hole. If one person gets a stone into the opposite hole, both members of that person's team have to be carried over to that hole on the backs of the other team. If both members of one team throw their stones into the opposite hole, the other team has to carry them down to that hole and back while galloping like horses.[7]

❖ ❖ ❖

Games and the other activities are some of the many ways that traditional Native North Americans enjoy and celebrate the magical time of the campfire. Flames leap and dance along with the excitement of the circle of people throughout the evening. Finally the fire dies down and energy wanes. The time of storytelling ebbs as eyelids grow heavy with sleep. It is said that, if the stories have been strong and the time shared in other ways around the fire enjoyable, children will have good thoughts as they slide into the land of dreams.

QUESTIONS

1. What does Grandmother tell Chipmunk to do when she goes out to pick berries? Why does she tell Chipmunk to come home before night comes, and not to eat any berries until she has thanked the Creator?

2. Does Chipmunk listen to her grandmother? What happens to Chipmunk because she does not do what her grandmother asks? Who ends up saving Chipmunk?

3. What kinds of lessons does this story teach Chipmunk? How can you use these lessons in your life? What other things do you learn from this story?

4. Why do the animals and birds decide to play lacrosse in the Menominee story of "The Great Lacrosse Game"? Why do people play lacrosse today?

5. Where does the game of lacrosse come from? How is it played? Have you played lacrosse?

6. What does the "little brown creature" in the story look like? How does this creature win the game? What kind of animal does it turn out to be?

7. What is a story? How is your life a kind of story?

8. Why are stories so important in Native North American cultures? How are stories used for teaching children?

9. What do Native North Americans pass down to the children through their stories? How are stories passed on to, and learned by, the next generation? When are stories usually told?

10. What is so important about the things that happen around the fire in Native North American gatherings? Why do you think fires are so special to these cultures?

11. What do Native North Americans use fire for? Where are the fires located?

12. What is the shape of the fire? Why is the shape of the circle so important? Of what is the circle a symbol?

13. Do you like sitting around a campfire? What kinds of experiences have you had outdoors around a fire?

14. What kinds of traditional activities do Native North Americans conduct around the fire?

15. Have you ever started a campfire without matches? What are some of the traditional ways that Native North Americans start fires? How difficult do you think it is to start a fire using these methods?

16. What is our sixth sense? Why do we have it? How do we use our sixth sense?

17. What kinds of names are Native children given? How do the children's parents and elders decide what to name them? Why do Native children have more than one name?

18. Do you know any Native North American names? What do these names mean?

19. What kinds of foods do Native North Americans cook over the fire? How do they bake, roast and boil their food?

20. Why do Native North Americans dance? What do the dances mean to Native peoples?

21. How is a dance like a story? Do you know any Native dances?

22. Do Native North Americans play games just to have fun? Why else do they play games?

23. What are some Native North American games? Which of the games and sports people play today are a gift from Native cultures? Do you play any of these games?

ACTIVITIES
The Campfire

ACTIVITY: Choose a site for a campfire. Set up and start the fire using a bow drill.
GOALS: Realize the important things to consider when choosing a site for a campfire. Understand how to gather materials for a fire

and what kinds of materials to gather. Understand how to build a basic fire and start a campfire using a bow drill.

AGE: Younger children and older children

MATERIALS: (A) Rake; shovel; axe; bow saw; hatchet; whittling knife; enough medium-sized stones for building a fire ring; small stones or gravel for lining the fire pit; tinder of birch bark, grass, etc.; two armfuls of kindling such as twigs and small branches; plenty of dry, well-burning logs for fuel wood such as oak, ash, maple or beech; Figure 5-4. (B) Whittling knife; bow saw; flashlight; board (willow, poplar [aspen], cottonwood, basswood, cedar, white pine, tamarack [larch], sycamore or sassafras) measuring 2 feet (60 centimeters) by 4 inches (10 centimeters) by 1.5 inches (4 centimeters) for the block; round piece of similar wood measuring 7.5 inches (20 centimeters) long and .75 inches (2 centimeters) in diameter for the drill; piece of hardwood 4 by 3 inches (10 by 8 centimeters) by .75 inches (2 centimeters) thick for the socket; sturdy bow that is 2-feet (60 centimeters) long and .5 inches (1.3 centimeters) thick made of ash, oak, hickory, dogwood or young elm; leather thong or other fray-resistant cord about 3 feet (1 meter) long; tinder bundle of cattail down, shredded milkweed fibers or the fluff from mature milkweed pods, strips of loose outer bark of a cedar tree, etc.; Figure 5-5, Figure 5-6, two buckets of sand or soil and two large buckets of water as well as a few old blankets (for safety); book or box of *dry* matches.

PROCEDURE A: *Building the Fire. Note:* Use of the knife, hatchet and axe should be done by the leader if you are working with younger children. Older children should only be allowed to use these tools if they are well trained in the use of tools and closely supervised.

Beforehand, we recommend that children gather the materials for lighting and fueling the fire and store them in a dry place. Few things are as frustrating as having a smoky, steaming fire that never really lights because the wood is wet.

Ask the children to think of what they need to consider when choosing a site for a campfire. Generate a list of those points to consider, including a site:

• that is sheltered, not too windy and reasonably flat;

• that has clear sky overhead so as not to risk lighting overhanging branches on fire;

• that can easily be cleared of all wood, leaves and other flammable material, or a site on which the fire will not spread, such as bare rock or along a sandy or rocky riverbed;

• that is easily accessible in the dark, away from any dangerous dropoffs, holes and other hazards that could pose a danger in low visibility conditions; and

• that is wide enough, at least 30 to 40 feet (9.1 to 12.2 meters) to fit everyone into the fire circle and allows room for games, plays, etc.

Scrape a shallow depression or *fire ring* about 4 feet (1.2 meters) across in the center of the campfire site. Clear away any leaves, branches, old nut shells and other flammable material on the ground for a distance of roughly 6 feet (1.8 meters) from the edge of the fire ring. If you are building the fire where there is a lot of leaf litter and duff on the forest floor, scrape away this top layer down to mineral soil. Fire can spread underground through this organic layer and re-appear several feet away. Also, organic material that looks like it has been put out can flare up quite a while later. Line the bottom of the fire ring depression with small, *dry* stones or gravel to prevent root fires and increase ventilation under the fire. Do not use stones from riverbeds and other wet places because they may explode when the water in them turns to steam and expands. Build a ring of stones about 6 inches (15 centimeters) high around the edge of the fire ring. Establish the circle around which children will sit facing the fire.

Set the fire up in preparation for lighting it. There are three kinds of materials to consider. *Tinder* consists of shredded birch bark, grass leaves and other fine dry material. Place several large handfuls of tinder in the center of the fire ring. If it has rained recently you may need to gather tinder from the dry inner bark of a fallen tree or the inner wood of an old stump.

Gather, preferably from the ground or from the dead attached lower branches of nearby conifers in case the ground is wet, several armfuls of branches ranging from very small twigs to those that are 1 inch (2.5 centimeters) or so in diameter. Do not remove live green branches from trees or shrubs. Break this dry *kindling* into pieces that are about 1 foot (30.5 centimeters) long. Beginning with the smallest pieces of kindling, and gradually working up to the larger pieces, build a conical, tepeelike structure over the tinder in the fire ring (Figure 5-4). Leave plenty of space for air to circulate between the pieces of kindling and through the tinder. The kindling should lean against itself so it will not mat down the tinder beneath it.

Gather from the ground some dead, dry logs that range from about 3 to 6 inches (8 to 15 centimeters) in diameter. Cut these logs to lengths of around 1.5 to 2 feet (50 to 60 centimeters) as the *fuel* for the fire. Lean four or five pieces of this firewood in a self-supporting tepee shape over the rest of the fire set. Allow plenty of air circulation to lower layers. Pile the store of kindling and fuelwood at least 6 feet (2 meters) from the fire ring and cover to keep dry.

An alternative to the tepee configuration is the fire set called the "log cabin" (Figure 5-4). This arrangement is more stable than the tepee form. Start by building a small version of the tepee fire in the center of the fire ring as a starter for the log cabin fire, then build the "log cabin" formation around it. Make the base logs of the log cabin fire set about 2 feet (60 centimeters) long and roughly 5 inches (13 centimeters) in diameter. Gradually decrease the length and diameter of the logs as you layer and angle them up toward the top. Build the log cabin fire set up to about 2 feet (60 centimeters) high.

Generally the softer the wood the faster and hotter it burns. Softwoods, such as pine, cedar, hemlock, tamarack and other conifers work well to start a fire and on those occasions when a quick, hot fire is desired, but they will not sustain a fire with a long-lasting steady heat. Hardwoods of medium hardness, such as willow, sage, alder, poplar, red (swamp) maple and cottonwood burn more slowly than softwoods. Ash, hickory, sugar (hard) maple, oak, walnut, beech and other hardwoods burn long

Figure 5-4. Tepee fire set (left) and log cabin fire set (right). Note the small tepee fire set built inside the log cabin set to start the fire.

and steady. These even-burning woods are especially good fuels for cooking fires.

While watching the dancing, lapping flames, it is easy to understand how fire is like a living thing that needs to be nurtured with energy and oxygen. As the fuel on the fire is consumed, carefully add more wood of a size that the existing fire will be able to ignite. The hotter the fire and coals beneath, the larger the diameter of the pieces of wood that can be added. Be certain that this new wood is spaced to allow plenty of circulation underneath so the fire can breathe: Do not smother the fire while feeding it.

PROCEDURE B: *Starting the Fire. Safety first!* If all flammable material is cleared away from the fire ring as described under "Building the Fire" there should be no problem with the fire spreading. Just in case, and in the unlikely event that someone should light part of their clothing on fire, keep the blankets handy to smother any flames. Once the fire circle is completed for the night, pour some water on the fire and stir to put out all flames and coals. Repeat this procedure until the fire is out completely. Finally, cover the fire with a layer of soil. In addition, all work with the knife, hatchet and axe should be done by the leader if you are working with younger children, and only by older children if they are well-trained and supervised in the use of these tools.

Note: Work with the children for several hours during the day and practice starting the fire with the bow drill. If you and your group master this procedure, use the bow drill to start the evening campfire. If, however, you and the group are still learning how to use the bow drill, simply light the fire with the matches and have a good time. Light a match, shelter it from the wind and use the flame to ignite the tinder at the base of the fire set you built earlier. We do not suggest trying to master the involved process of lighting the fire with the bow drill while the children wait for the campfire to begin. This can be a frustrating experience. *We highly recommend that you, the leader, learn how to light the fire with the bow drill beforehand so that you can share that expertise with the children.*

To begin, make the pieces of the bow drill as shown in Figure 5-5. The basic parts consist of the block, drill, socket and bow. Gather some dry, extremely fine flammable material for use as the *tinder bundle* to start the fire: cattail down, shredded milkweed fibers, the fluff from mature milkweed pods or strips of loose outer bark from a cedar tree for instance. Rub the fibers or bark in between the palms of the hands to make a stringy mass of fibers, then form this mass into the shape of a small bird's nest.

The *block* consists of a board 2 feet (60 centimeters) long, 4 inches (10 centimeters) wide by 1.5 inches (4 centimeters) thick. Use wood of medium hardness such as willow, poplar (aspen), cottonwood, basswood, cedar, white pine, tamarack (larch), sycamore or sassafras. Sage and yucca are also acceptable. Carve a small indentation about 6 inches (15 centimeters) from one end of the board a little way through its thickness. The end of the drill will rest in this pit and burn deeper into the block as it turns. Cut a wedge-shaped notch from the edge of the board almost into the center of the pit. The edges of this notch need to be smooth and cleanly cut.

Use the same kind of wood for the *drill* as for the block. If one of these two components is made out of a softer wood it will be consumed without creating a coal. Whittle the drill about 7.5 inches (20 centimeters) long and .75 inch (2 centimeters) in diameter. Make a dull point on both ends of the drill to fit into the block on the bottom and the socket on top.

Create a *socket* with which to hold the drill steady from above as it spins. Use a piece of hardwood that measures about 4 by 3 inches (10 by 8 centimeters) by .75 inch (2 centimeters) thick. Carve an indentation into the center of the socket so that the top of the drill will be held in place. Friction and smoking can be reduced where the drill meets the socket by putting a bit of grease in the socket

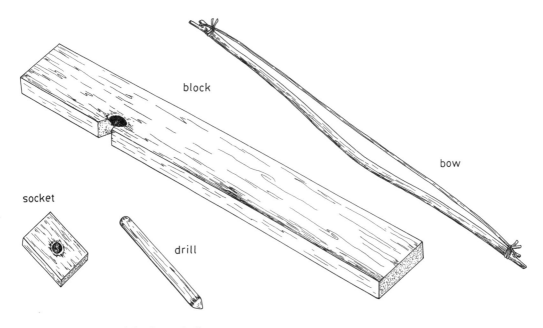

Figure 5-5. Parts of the bow drill.

pit. Natural body oils, animal fat and soap also work well. Do not use water as the wood will swell and bind.

The *bow* takes a bit of work. Use a sturdy stick that is about 2 feet (60 centimeters) long and .5 inches (1.3 centimeters) thick. Ash, oak, hickory, dogwood or young elm work well. Notch each end of the stick and tie on a cord such as a leather thong or other very strong material that will not fray or break when exposed to a lot of friction. Tie the cord so that the bow is bent in a gentle arc. The trick is to leave enough slack to be able to wrap the cord around the drill, and to have enough tension once the drill is in place to cause it to turn without slipping when the bow is drawn back and forth. You will have to adjust the tension in the bow drill until it is just right.

You are ready to begin lighting the fire. Do this very close to where the fire has been made ready to set in the fire ring. Form the tinder bundle into a loose ball about 3 to 4 inches (8 to 10 centimeters) around and push a dimple down in the center to make it into a bird's nest shape. Keep the tinder bundle close by as you work with the bow drill. Another approach is to place the tinder bundle directly beneath the notch in the block so the ember will drop into it when it forms.

Take the bow in your right hand (or your left hand if you are left-handed). Twist the drill into the cord on the bow. Set the bottom point of the drill into the pit of the block and hold the top point in place using the pit of the socket. Kneel on the long end of the block to steady the bow drill, or place one foot on either side of the drill (Figure 5-6). Use your left knee or foot to hold the block down if you are right-handed, or your right knee or foot if you are left-handed. Be certain that the drill is held straight up and down. Draw the bow back and forth using a smooth and steady stroke to twist the drill. Keep the bow level or the cord will ride up or down the spindle. Slowly and gradually build up to a moderate speed but do not stroke the bow too quickly. It is fun to get everyone involved by having the children take turns using the bow drill.

Soon some smoke will rise from the place where the drill meets the block and dark powder will form in the notch. Draw the bow faster as the smoke increases and you will be *packing a coal*. A tiny ember will eventually form in the notch. At this point draw the bow

Figure 5-6. Using the bow drill.

back and forth about a dozen more times. Quickly put the bow and drill down. Lift the block and use a knife or pointed stick to push the ember down and out of the notch so that it lands in the depression you prepared in the middle of the tinder bundle. Gently wrap the tinder bundle loosely around and enclose the ember. Lift this up and blow gently, smoothly and steadily on it until the ember ignites the tinder bundle and a flame erupts. Carefully transfer this flame to the tinder that is under the fire you set up earlier.

Do not be discouraged! It can take many attempts to master this technique, but you will succeed eventually if you persevere. Make sure to clean out the notch after each try. Some people have become so proficient at the bow drill that they can light a fire in a matter of minutes under optimal conditions. In case you are not able to start a fire after a *strong* group effort, tell the children that this is a learning experience and that you are all going to continue to try at a later time. Nothing will be gained by pushing the fire-making for a long time if it is not working.

Opening the Circle of the Fire

ACTIVITY: Share in a talk that opens the evening around the campfire in a good way and describes how to enjoy the time at the fire

while being a helpful member of a community. Share some ideas on how to learn about and share Native North American traditions respectfully.

GOALS: Understand that the time around a traditional campfire is meant to be fun, and that behavior and attitudes during this time are to support, and take place in, a community atmosphere of reverence and respect. Understand that we are all connected in the circle and everything we do affects everyone else and Earth all around us. Understand that we can learn from Native North Americans and have our lives enriched by that experience. Realize that we are not here to imitate Native Americans but to learn from and enjoy their traditions.

AGE: Younger children and older children

MATERIALS: Copy of the talk *"Opening the Circle of the Fire,"* enough dry, comfortable mats for everyone to sit on.

PROCEDURE: Have the children sit in a circle around the fire. Make sure each child has a dry mat to sit on. If the group is small enough, form the circle so that no one is sitting in front of or behind anyone else.

Be aware of the direction that the smoke is blowing and locate the group so that no one has smoke blowing toward them. Fire, however, creates its own air circulation patterns that affect how smoke moves. Smoke will often follow a person around if he or she moves and alters the air flow pattern. It works best if the storyteller is sitting down along with the rest of the group.

Practice with the children the phrase they will respond with during the talk. Whenever you say "In the Circle of the Fire," they are to respond by saying, "we are all equal." Practice a few rounds until the children are responding well and in unison. Remind them that they are to keep their eyes closed while responding.

Prepare the children as you would for a guided fantasy. During this talk they will learn of a good way to approach the campfire experience. Have them close their eyes, take a few slow deep breaths and clear their minds of thoughts so they can let the story in. They are to keep their eyes closed until you say to open them. Instruct them to listen without making any noises and to imagine that they are in the center of the Circle of the Fire.

Opening the Circle of the Fire

You are about to take a journey in the Circle. Here, where every place to sit is as good as any other, we are all equal—just as important as everyone else. You are in a community about to enter into a special time together, a time in which unexpected and even magical things can happen. All you need to do is open your imagination.

In the Circle of Fire. *(all respond: we are all equal)*

In a short while you will hear a traditional story told. You will also be asked to start on a journey of storytelling of your own. From the moment you arrived here the story of this fire began. It will never end because everything that happens will live on in your memory and become part of the story of your life and the lives of those around you. Your own story is the most important story you will ever know.

In the Circle of Fire. *(all respond: we are all equal)*

The Circle is round, it has a certain order. That is how the story of your life can be if you want it to. Many good things can fit into the order of the Circle. You are going to have fun here, too. Laugh and enjoy yourself. Let your sense of humor help you enjoy others in the circle. These are all important things that help to keep the Circle strong.

In the Circle of Fire. *(all respond: we are all equal)*

Be your best in the Circle of the Fire. It is a time to share, to think of others and keep the Circle strong with friendship. Think good thoughts, do good things

and allow your feelings to be wherever they are. You might feel scared or sad during a story. You might feel excited and happy about what is going on. Cooperate with everyone in the Circle while you have these feelings. Listen with your best listening and speak only when you have something important to say. Be respectful and polite.

In the Circle of Fire. *(all respond: we are all equal)*

Open your heart to the Circle of the Fire. The Circle reminds us of how all life is connected. It has no beginning and no end. It is a symbol of how we all fit together, each with a unique place all our own. We are all connected in the Circle. Everything we do affects everyone else and all of Earth around us. When you think of the Circle, do so with reverence. When you do something in the Circle, act wisely.

In the Circle of Fire. *(all respond: we are all equal)*

Ask the children to open their eyes and sit in silence for a moment. Invite them to ask questions or share whatever they want now that they have listened to these words about the Circle of the Fire.

Tell the children that "the Circle of the Fire is a time to experience things that come from the traditions of Native North American cultures. There are about 550 different Native cultures in what we now call North America. Each culture is unique: It has its own beliefs and ways of living. We are receiving a great gift by what we share tonight. We can give back by helping Native North Americans whenever we can. They are not a people of the past. They live here in this land with us, today. We are not trying to be 'Indians' tonight. We are simply learning from their cultures and enjoying their traditions. We will not be dressing up or painting ourselves like Native Americans, talking like them, sitting like them or mimicking them in any way. There will be no war whoops or tomahawk chops. We are going to be ourselves as we look at Native Americans in a new way. They are our neighbors who have a lot to teach us and have shared much with us, and to whom we can give much back."

Note: See "Teaching Racial Tolerance, Understanding and Appreciation" in Chapter 1 for more ideas regarding good conduct toward Native North American cultures.

Storytelling

ACTIVITY: Share different kinds of stories around the campfire. Afterward, prepare stories, skits, group theater sketches and storytelling projects to share around a campfire at another time.

GOALS: Understand how important stories are to Native North Americans and what stories mean to these cultures. Realize that there are many different kinds of stories. Understand how storytelling is of value to individuals and cultures today.

AGE: Younger children and older children

MATERIALS: Large pad of newsprint and marker; other materials as needed should you decide to become elaborate with some of these activities.

PROCEDURE: Beforehand (optional), consider inviting a guest storyteller to present to the children. Make arrangements and work out a schedule with that person.

Begin by sharing with the children one or both of the stories that open this chapter. You may also choose some other traditional Native North American stories, such as those in this and in the other *Keepers* books. Use the information and tips on storytelling from the "Discussion" and from Chapter 1 as guidelines for telling a traditional story.

An effective and dramatic approach to telling the first story is to surprise the children by having a guest storyteller—someone they do not know—come in to tell this opening story. There is a certain magic when the

children experience storytelling from a person who has come just to share stories. Every region has tellers of Native American stories available through local arts groups and informal networks.

After the storytelling has been opened, there are many different ways to actively involve the children in storytelling:

• Using the information from Chapter 1 and from the "Discussion," describe the art of storytelling among Native North American cultures. Emphasize that stories are traditionally handed down by memory from one generation to the next. Children would often be asked to retell a story after they had heard it. Tell a particular story and instruct the children to listen very closely. Now have a few children take turns retelling the story. Repeat several rounds of this "story retelling" using a different story each time.

• Following a traditional story, ask questions to reveal what the children heard in the story. "What does the (main character) in this story learn from his or her experiences? What does this story teach us? What did you think of as you were listening to the story? Does this story remind you of any stories you have heard before? Which one(s)?"

• Improvise a group story. Ask the children to come up with an idea, such as "How the Moon Came to Be in the Sky," or "Why It Is Important to Tell the Truth." Start out the story with an opening line and have the children raise their hands and take turns adding each new piece to make the story unfold.

• Have the children share some of their family stories. Many families pass stories down over dinner, at parties, holidays, weddings and at other gatherings. Open the circle for the children to share. When the circle is opened for personal or family stories children should be invited to share, but not required to do so.

Here are some further activities that the children can work on afterwards in preparation for sharing around another campfire.

- Have the children work in small groups to become familiar with a particular story. Each child will take on the role of one of the characters in the story, or some part of the background involved in the story, such as a tree, rock, etc. One child will become the narrator. When the group is ready, the narrator will read the story while the other children act out their roles. This kind of group theater storytelling can be developed over the course of several days, with children acting out and pantomiming their roles while the narrator speaks. Have an adult be the narrator when working with younger children.

- Have the children create a storytelling bag and place objects in it that remind them of stories they know. When an object is pulled from the bag by the storyteller or by someone in the audience, the story that object represents is told. Things that help us to remember are called *mnemonics*.

- Have the children create their own stories and share them around the fire.

- Create skits based on traditional stories and original stories made up by the children.

- Create a picture language and use it to tell a familiar story or a story the children have created.

- Ask each child to choose an animal, or a plant such as a kind of tree, as her or his protector during the world of night. Have the children create stories about how those plants and animals help to keep them safe during nighttime adventures.

Bear Dance [8]

ACTIVITY: Share a kind of group dance to celebrate the bear, symbol of courage.

GOALS: Enjoy performing an exercise adapted from a traditional Santee Dakota dance. Understand the meaning behind the Bear Dance.

AGE: Younger children and older children

MATERIALS: Strips of newspaper, newspaper to crumple; wheat paste; water; tempera paints; paintbrushes; scissors; dead branches for the bear's den frame; hatchet; a green or brown tarpaulin or blanket; small stones or other objects to mark off the circle; drum and striker.

PROCEDURE: Beforehand, work with the children to create a large papier-mâché mask of a bear with big holes to see and breathe through. Clearly mark off a circle near the fire that, depending on the size, age and number of the children, is big enough for them to escape a charging "bear" but small enough to give the bear a chance to catch them. Create a "den" for the bear in the form of a small lodge constructed from a few dead branches covered with a green or brown tarpaulin or blanket.

Note: Begin by sharing a bear story, such as "How Grizzly Bear Climbed the Mountain" in Chapter 6, followed by a discussion of what it means to have courage.

Share the significance of the Santee Dakota (Sioux) Bear Dance with the children. This dance is symbolic of the courage of the bear. It also acts out the need to overcome fears and to have courage—a good topic for activities done at night. Native North American dances also focus on other animals and their virtues, such as the wolf, buffalo, rabbit, deer and elk. Ask the children, "What are you afraid of at night? Why do you think courage is important?"

Assign someone to be the first bear. This person will put on the bear mask and enter the bear's den. To start with, the rest of the children will stand around the inside edge of the circle. Begin beating the drum. Play a two-part beat over and over by striking the drum alternately hard-soft, hard-soft, hard-soft, and so on. The bear will come out of the den and dance to the drumbeat around the circle as it mimics the movements of a bear. The bear will do a simple two-step, shifting from one foot to the other with each pair of drumbeats like so: right-step, left-step, right-step, left-step and so on. The other children will do a similar two-step in place around the edge of the circle. After the bear circles once, it will return to the den. The rest of the children will now stand alert inside the circle as they wait for the bear to emerge. Tell the children that, during the chase that is about to begin, they cannot go outside the circle while they are still in the game. When the bear is ready it will rush out and try to touch the children. Each child that is touched by the bear will sit around the edge of the circle on the outside and wait for the next round. The bear can go back into the den at any time, where it is safe from being touched. When a child touches the bear without being touched by it, that child becomes the bear. If the bear touches everyone before anyone is able to touch the bear first, chose another person to be the bear and begin a new round of the Bear Dance. With each new bear the cycle of the dance and chase are repeated and everyone comes back into the game.

Note: This dance is often followed by a Native meal eaten while the group sits in a circle.

Fireside Feast

ACTIVITY: Prepare simple, wholesome traditional foods and enjoy a meal around the fire.
GOALS: Discover and enjoy some of the many foods that come from Native North American cultures. Understand some traditional ways that food is prepared using the campfire.
AGE: Younger children and older children
MATERIALS: Foods chosen for the *"Fireside Feast;"* strong cooking fire with a thick bed of hot coals; water; utensils for handling and preparing food as well as pots and pans (should you decide to use nontraditional cooking methods over the fire); reuseable cups, glasses, bowls, plates and silverware for each child as needed; provisions for washing dishes; cookbooks listed at the end of the "Procedure" for this activity; materials as needed for the required traditional cooking setup such as a hatchet, whittling knife,

green branches, cord and leather bag kettle; "Discussion"; Figures 5-2 and 5-3.

PROCEDURE: Beforehand work with the children (if possible) to choose and gather together the foods you will prepare, cook and eat around the campfire. Consider these Native North American foods and dishes:

- corn: grits, popcorn, hominy, chips, bread, corn on the cob, stew, meal, succotash (a traditional Narragansett dish), tortillas, Johnnycakes (Nokehick), hush puppies, pone, syrup, nacho chips
- potato: baked, mashed, chips, french fries
- sweet potato
- tomato: sauce, salsa, juice
- squash: zucchini, pumpkin, gourds
- bean: kidney, butter, snap, string, lima, common, navy, pole, Mexico frijole
- fruit and berries (forty-seven kinds of Native berries have been identified): blueberries (twenty varieties), elderberries (four varieties), gooseberries (more than a dozen varieties), wild grapes, cranberries, ground cherries, wild currants, sour chokecherries, blackberries, raspberries, manzanitas, strawberries
- wild rice
- avocado: guacamole
- nut: peanuts, cashews, acorns, piñola (pine nuts), hickory nuts, black walnuts, butternuts, hazelnuts (filberts)
- pepper: red, green, yellow and many other varieties, including hot peppers
- sunflower seeds
- mesquite
- prickly pear cactus fruit
- banana
- amaranth
- mint
- chocolate

While some of these foods, such as chocolate and maple syrup, make tasty desserts, we *highly* recommend that any foods high in concentrated and/or refined sugar not be served around the fire. Children can easily become overenergized by sugar, losing their concentration and control, especially in large groups. Serve Native berries, fruits and nuts instead.

With younger children, it may work best to have a simple menu with groups of children helping with different tasks. The food could be prepared ahead of time and reheated with the children helping to serve.

With older children, have them help decide the menu, and work on pre-preparations of different foods such as mixing dry ingredients for corn bread or wrapping potatoes and corn on the cob for baking. Plan that the fireside preparation and cooking take no longer than forty-five minutes or so, unless you have a small group of children who work well together. Think of games or tasks that the children can do while they wait.

The fire needs to have the right fuel and be at the right stage for each kind of cooking to take place. A good, long fire that has died down to a thick bed of red-hot coals is best for baking. Roasting is most effective over a strong fire with a bed of coals beneath. Hardwoods, such as hickory, ash, maple, beech and oak, burn down to long-lasting coals and impart a nice smoky flavor to roasted foods. An intense fire and coals that cover a small area works best when boiling food using a pot or bag kettle. Softwoods, such as pine and spruce, or a soft hardwood such as aspen, burn quick and hot for boiling. See the "Discussion" and Figures 5-2 and 5-3 for details of traditional techniques for how to cook with each of these methods.

For the sake of cleanliness and convenience, especially when working with groups of children, we recommend the use of conventional cups, bowls, plates and utensils. Simply have everyone line up and wash their own place setting after the meal is over. Do not use paper plates, plastic forks, paper, plastic or Styrofoam glasses or cups or other throw-away place settings. The use of disposable gear teaches a philosophy that is contrary to that of living so as to minimize our negative impact on Earth. Take advantage of the situation by exploring and discussing, with the children, the positive reasons for using reuseable place settings instead of disposable ones.

Some excellent books to consult for ideas on recipes and food preparation are *How Indians Use Wild Plants for Food, Medicine & Crafts* by Frances Densmore (New York: Dover Publications, 1974), *Native Harvests: Recipes and Botanicals of the American Indian* by Barrie Kavasch (New York: Vintage Books, 1979), *Clambake: A Wampanoag Tradition* by Russell M. Peters (Minneapolis: Lerner Publications, 1992) and *Comida Guatemalteca: Guatemalan Food* which was written by Guatemalan women who are refugees in the United States (Seattle, Wash.: Pro Guatemalan Children, 1992). Additional books are listed in the "Notes."[9]

Native Games

ACTIVITY: Play some traditional games of Native North America.

GOALS: Understand the meaning of games to Native North American cultures. Realize that many contemporary games and sports are gifts from Native North Americans. Have fun playing some traditional games.

AGE: Younger children and older children

MATERIALS: As needed for specific games chosen, Figure 5-7. See the descriptions that follow.

PROCEDURE: Beforehand, prepare all necessary toys and accompanying materials for the particular games chosen.

Ask the children, "What kinds of games do you play that come from Native North Americans? What other kinds of games and sports that they play do you know about? Why do you think the Native peoples of North America play games? Are there more reasons than having fun? Why do you play games? Why are games important?"

Discuss with the children the ideas expressed in the "Discussion" about games. The following list provides simple instructions for preparing and playing a number of Native games.

Tossed Ball. Toss a large inflated ball into the air in the midst of the group. Players must try to keep the ball in motion up in the air without letting it fall or touch the ground. Traditionally this game was played with an inflated animal bladder. A lightweight inflatable ball, such as a beach ball, will do.

Ball Juggling. Each player keeps from two to four balls (often three) in the air by tossing from hand to hand. Clay or stone balls are used traditionally, roughly 1 to 2 inches (2.5 to 5.1 centimeters) in diameter. Small, round stones from a riverbed work well. Other lightweight rubber balls may be substituted.

Running Races. Foot races are traditionally done at the end of the day after chores have been completed. Divide the children into groups by age or size and mark off courses of appropriate length for each level. Lay out long- and short-distance races for each group. Players race from the starting point over to and around a tree, rock or other natural turning point and back again.

Cat's Cradle. This game is found among cultures throughout Native North America. The Zuni and Diné peoples of the Southwest say that cat's cradle was taught to human beings by the Spider people, powerful and wise figures in many of their stories.

Cat's cradle is played by using the hands (lips and teeth are allowed too) to manipulate string into a variety of intricate patterns. It is nearly impossible to write directions on how to play cat's cradle without filling pages with detailed steps to take. The best way is to learn how to play from someone who knows and share that knowledge with the children. There is an endless variety of forms that can be created, some of which are shown in Figure 5-7a. A good book for beginners is *Cat's Cradle, Owl's Eyes: A Book of String Games* by Camilla Gryski (New York: Beech Tree Books, 1983).

Tops. Tops are traditionally made from wood, bone, stone or clay. They may be plain or painted with designs. Some tops have holes drilled into the sides to make them whistle as they spin. *Whip tops* are spun off of a cord made of sinew or bark that is attached to a long pole. The top is whipped as it spins to keep it going. *Peg tops* are about 4 inches (10 centimeters) tall. There are many different designs, all of which involve spinning the top spindle between the thumb and index finger (Figure 5-7b).

For the sake of simplicity and safety, we recommend that the children use peg tops to play the following games.

• Sit in a circle and have someone spin their top, then quickly run around the outside of the circle and try to get back to their place before the top stops spinning.

• Spin the tops and see whose top spins the longest.

• Try to keep the top spinning within a marked circle so that it does not cross the edge.

Ring and Pin. Make the ring out of a piece of bark, a thick piece of leather, a thin flexible twig bent and tied into the shape of a circle, or some other suitable material (Figure 5-7c). Depending on how difficult the game is to be, the ring diameter should be between 1.25 inches (3.2 centimeters) to 5 inches (13 centimeters): the wider the easier. Use any strong, flexible cord to attach the ring to the stick toward one end. Hold onto the short end of the stick with the ring dangling from the cord. Swing the ring up and forward and try to thrust the far end of the stick through the hole in the ring. One point is usually awarded for each successful catch of the ring on the stick. Different designs can be made to make the game more interesting for older children. For instance, when playing with the design using two connected rings, two points are earned for catching the ring by the outer hole and four points for catching it through the inner hole.

Buzz. This game is best for older children. Make the buzz from a round section of a branch about 2 inches (5 centimeters) thick

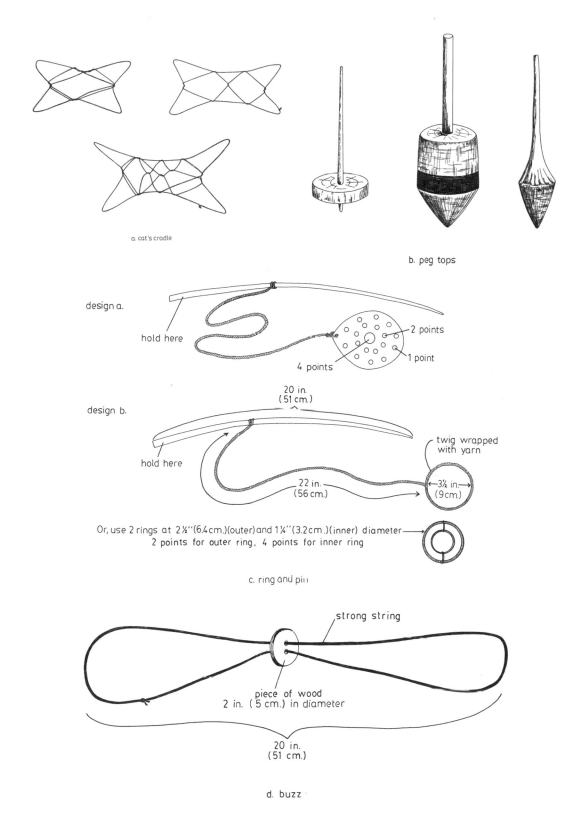

a. cat's cradle

b. peg tops

design a.

hold here

2 points

1 point

4 points

design b.

20 in.
(51 cm.)

hold here

twig wrapped
with yarn

22 in.
(56 cm.)

3½ in.
(9 cm.)

Or, use 2 rings at 2½"(6.4cm.)(outer) and 1¼"(3.2cm.)(inner) diameter
2 points for outer ring, 4 points for inner ring

c. ring and pin

strong string

piece of wood
2 in. (5 cm.) in diameter

20 in.
(51 cm.)

d. buzz

Figure 5-7. Native North American Toys. a) cat's cradle. b) peg tops. c) ring and pin.
d) buzz.

with the two holes drilled about 1/2 inch (1.3 centimeters) apart from one another. For balance, each hole must be exactly the same distance from the center. In order to be certain that no pieces will fly off of the buzz as it spins, make sure that the bark is removed from the piece of wood and that the wood is not cracked. Thread the cord or string as shown in Figure 5-7d. Slip your fingers through each end of the loop and spin the buzz around vigorously until the cord has wound up tight. Quickly pull outward on both ends at once and the buzz will spin around. Keep the buzz going by alternately pulling (each time the cord winds up tight) and relaxing (each time the cord has unwound and begins to rewind). As you relax your hold, bring your hands together a little to allow room for the string to contract as it winds up tight again. With practice, you can keep the buzz turning indefinitely by pulling and relaxing your pull in synchrony with the rhythm of the buzz. The buzz makes a distinct whizzing or "buzzing" sound when it is spinning.

EXTENDING THE EXPERIENCE

• Learn some Native North American sign language while sitting around the fire. A good book to use is *Indian Talk: Hand Signals of the North American Indians* by Iron Eyes Cody (Happy Camp, Calif.: Naturegraph Publishers, 1970).

• Read about Native North American names in the "Discussion." Choose a name for yourself based on a plant, animal or element in nature that you feel close to and which you feel fits your character.

• Set up and follow a trail to the campfire site. Mark the trail with white strips of cloth, about 6 inches (15 centimeters) long, tied to branches of trees or attached to some other objects. Set them out about 3 feet (1 meter) off the ground and space the markers about 15 feet (5 meters) apart—close enough to be followed easily in the dark. Make the trail varied, interesting and safe—away from holes, low branches, twigs that might poke an eye,

etc. Have small groups of two or three children take turns leading the group to the campfire along this trail. Turn this trail into an adventure by leaving things that will be used at the fire at each marker so children can find them.

• Practice using your sixth sense at night. First, read about the sixth sense in the "Discussion." Your sixth sense tells you what your other five senses cannot, and it is connected to empathy for people, plants, animals and the rest of nature. Clear your mind of all thoughts, fears, worries and tune in to the smells, sights, sounds and feeling of the night. Become part of the world of night and allow it to become part of you. With practice your sixth sense will grow stronger. Make up sixth sense activities of your own or see how often you react correctly during these exercises:

—Have someone hide behind a tree about 20 feet (6 meters) behind you. This person is to face away from you while standing behind the tree. Without your knowing it, the person is to come out from behind the tree, turn around and stare at you. Whenever you sense that the person has come out from behind the tree and is staring at you, turn around and face him or her. How many times do you turn around to find the person staring at you compared with how often the person is still hiding behind the tree?

—Stand with an arm outstretched and look straight ahead. Have someone stand behind you and slowly and silently reach forward to touch your arm. When you sense that your arm is just about to be touched, but before it is actually touched, quickly pull it away.

• Build a simple lean-to about 10 feet (3 meters) from the fire. Choose a sheltered, dry place. Make certain that there are no weak or rotting trees or branches overhead or nearby that may fall on the site or blow over onto you. Test the wind direction and locate the lean-to upwind from the fire ring. Choose two support trees that are about 10 feet (3 meters) apart. The support trees can be closer if the lean-to is being built for just one or two

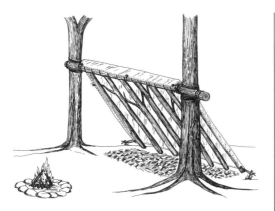

Figure 5.8—A simple lean-to.

people. Use some sound, dead branches that you have gathered and cut to length for the poles of the lean-to. Lay a sturdy ridge pole across some branches in the support trees about 4 feet (1.2 meters) off the ground. If there are no branches in the correct position, lash the pole to the trunks of the trees (Figure 5-8). Rest the tops of the roof poles on the ridge pole and angle them down to form a roof on the side away from the fire so the opening will face the heat. Lash the tops of the roof poles to the ridge pole and push the ends a bit into the ground to stabilize them. Cover the roof poles with a large green or brown waterproof tarpaulin. The sides of the lean-to can be left open or closed. A bed of soft needles or leaves, gathered from the ground, finishes this temporary shelter.

• Do the *"Circle Dance"* described in Chapter 4 of *Keepers of the Animals*.

NOTES

1. Peggy V. Beck, Anna Lee Walters and Nia Francisco, *The Sacred: Ways of Knowledge, Sources of Life.* Tsaile, Ariz.: Navajo Community College Press, 1992, pp. 58–59.

2. Charles Alexander Eastman, *Indian Scout Craft and Lore.* New York: Dover Publications, 1974, p. 188.

3. Beck et. al., pp. 48–49.

4. Eastman, pp. 112–113.

5. Russell M. Peters. *Clambake: A Wampanoag Tradition.* Minneapolis, Minn.: Lerner Publications, 1992.

6. Stewart Culin. *Games of the North American Indians.* New York: Dover Publications, 1975, p. 35.

7. Culin, pp. 722–727.

8. Adapted from Eastman, pp. 141–142. This dance is also described in *Indian Boyhood* by Charles Alexander Eastman, New York: Dover Publications, 1971, pp. 145–152. Ohiyesa (Charles A. Eastman) originally adapted this Santee Dakota Bear Dance so it could be performed by children. The dance has been adapted for this book.

9. *Comida Guatemalteca: Guatemalan Food* is available from Pro Guatemalan Children, P.O. Box 18824, Seattle, WA 98118-0824. Additional books on Native North American foods and cookery include *American Indian Food and Lore* by Carolyn Niethammer (New York: Collier Books, 1974); *Corn Recipes From the Indians* by Frances Gwaltney (Cherokee Publications, 1988, P.O. Box 256, Cherokee, NC 28719); *Northwest Native Harvest* by Carol Batdorf (Surrey, British Columbia, and Blaine, Wash.: Hancock House Publishers, 1990); and *Wampanoag Cookery* by Helen Attaquin, Cynthia Akins, Amelia Bingham, Rachel Jeffers, Lorenzo Jeffers, Virginia Moran, Red Wing and Gladys Widdiss (American Science & Engineering, 1974, 20 Overland St., Boston, MA 02215).

Grizzly Bear did not listen. Instead he growled and reared up on his hind legs. "I shall take what I want," he said. "Leave here or fight me."

CHAPTER 6

How Grizzly Bear Climbed the Mountain

(Shoshone—Great Basin)

Long ago, Black Bear was chief of the animals. One day, as she wandered around the mountains looking for food, she found an anthill and began to dig into it. From a place higher on the mountain, Grizzly Bear looked down and saw what his chief was doing. Grizzly Bear was always hungry. He came down the hill and tried to push Black Bear aside.

"I will dig here," Grizzly Bear said.

But Black Bear would not move. "Brother," Black Bear said, "this food is mine. I was here first. Do not try to push me aside. There is enough here to share."

Grizzly Bear did not listen. Instead he growled and reared up on his hind legs. "I shall take what I want," he said. "Leave here or fight me."

Black Bear was not as large as Grizzly Bear, but now she was angry. It was not right to drive someone away from that which was theirs. It was not right to refuse even to share. Grizzly Bear swung his great paw with its long sharp claws at Black Bear, but she was too quick for him. She dodged his blows and struck back again and again. Before long, Grizzly Bear was defeated. He crouched before his chief.

"Grizzly Bear," Black Bear said, "you have broken the laws of our people. You must leave our land forever."

With his head still low to the ground, Grizzly Bear shuffled away. He was filled with sorrow for he knew he could no longer stay among his people. He had broken the law and was banished forever. He climbed higher and higher, up into the dark mountains. Now night had fallen, but he did not stop climbing. Snow was falling around him, covering his fur with white, but he paid no attention. He paused only now and then to shake the snow from his back. The snow was everywhere around him, white flakes drifting through the darkness as Grizzly Bear continued on his way. All around him it was cold and dark, except for the glittering snow, and the wind was strong, but still he climbed higher. As he climbed, he wished there were some last thing he could do which would be good for his people.

That night, the animal people looked up into the sky with wonder. There was now a long snowy trail across the sky, a trail which had never been there before. At the end of that trail was a shape made of seven stars. The animal people recognized that shape. It was the great Grizzly Bear.

"How can this be?" the animal people asked Black Bear. "How did Grizzly Bear get up into the sky land?"

"That trail across the sky," Black Bear said, "is the snow which Grizzly Bear shook from his back as he climbed. It has marked the path all of us must follow when we leave this earth to go to the hunting grounds in the sky. Though he was banished from our land, Grizzly Bear has done one last good thing for our people. He has shown us the way to the sky land and has waited there at its end so that we can know the right road to travel when we leave this life.

So it was that Grizzly Bear entered the sky land, leaving behind him the trail of the Milky Way. That is the path which the people follow to the last hunting grounds. So it was that Grizzly Bear did one last good thing for the people.

DISCUSSION

In this Shoshone story, "How Grizzly Bear Climbed the Mountain," after he is banished for not sharing food with Black Bear, who is chief of the animals, Grizzly Bear walks up to the sky land to do one good thing for his people. He is transformed; he leaves a snowy trail, the Milky Way, stretching across the night sky to show them the way to reach the last hunting grounds. Grizzly Bear remains visible as seven stars—the Big Dipper or Great Bear—so his people will know where to go when they leave this world.

Native North Americans have long considered bears as kin to human beings. Perhaps it was the strong familial bond between a mother bear and her cubs, as well as the many other humanlike attributes of bears, that prompted some Native peoples to be-lieve that grizzlies were the first human ancestors. The mother bear is often held up as an example of how parents should care for their children.

To many Native North American cultures animal families are to be learned from. Cranes, geese and many other animals mate for life. Certain animals, such as bears, coyotes, wolves, cranes, foxes and others, have highly organized social structures and family units. Often these animals demonstrate genuine affection and warmth for members of the family, such as licking and kissing, tail wagging, playing and all kinds of enthusiastic greetings. Among coyotes, some unattached females act as aunts or baby-sitters while the pups' real mothers go out to gather food. Up to four adult coyotes—the two real parents and both a male and female helper—have been seen raising one litter together. The stepparents even bring food back to the den, where they regurgitate it and offer it to the pups.

Traditional Native North American Families

In Native North American traditions the *family* is the center of the community, the meeting place of all of a person's relationships. The band of family, friends and elders is home, school and provider for children, offering different role models and much affection and love. In many traditions the woman's name is used in a family, and women have great power. Ownership of provisions is held in common and all share the same fate during times of abundance and scarcity. Living well means sharing: striking a balance between self-fulfillment and meeting the demands of relationships with other people and all of creation. Moral virtues—the ethical conduct for relationships—are derived from the laws of nature and strengthened by discipline of the body, mind and spirit.[1] Ideally children are treated kindly and are seen as a source of wisdom, not just as young ones needing to be taught. Adults lead by the example of good character, providing the basis for social harmony in the tribe. When children go astray, they are led back by the use of an appropriate lesson story, teasing and gentle persuasion. Physical punishment is not used traditionally; striking a child, it is believed, will break the child's spirit. Mistakes are considered part of the learning process.

Bears

Native North Americans from throughout North America see wisdom, strength, courage and decisiveness in the bear, which holds a prominent place in Native stories, songs and dances (Figure 6-1). Bears were called, by some, "the beast that walks like a person," because they can rise up on two feet, and because the bone structure in their feet and their footprints are very similar to those of human beings. Bears have been called by many names that show great respect, such as "four-legged human," "chief's son," "old man,"

Figure 6-1. Tsimshian ceremonial headdress mask representing a bear. From British Columbia, Canada. (Photo courtesy the National Museum of the American Indian, Smithsonian Institution.)

"grandmother" or "grandfather." The Abenaki of the East would often say "these are our cousin's tracks" upon seeing the prints of a black bear.[2] An Abenaki elder once said that "a bear is wiser than a man, because a man does not know how to live all winter without eating anything."[3] Bear dances, songs and ceremonies are common.

Bears are the largest carnivores that live on land in North America. The three species of bear on the continent are the black bear, grizzly bear and polar bear. Bears are famous for their habit of holing up in a state of dormancy or winter sleep during the cold months, in dens ranging from hollow logs, caves and holes dug beneath the roots of trees to piles of brush and, in the case of polar bears, snowbanks. Winter dens are sometimes lined with bark, leaves, grass or moss. **BLACK BEAR.** With a combined head and body length of 5 to 6 feet (1.5 to 1.8 meters), a shoulder height of up to 3 feet (.9 meters) and a weight of up to nearly 600 pounds (272 kilograms), the *black bear* is the smallest of the three bears. The color of an adult's fur ranges from dark or brownish black with a tan muzzle, to brown, blue or cinnamon. Often there is a small patch of white on the throat. Black bears frequent wild swamps and forests of mixed softwoods and hardwoods. They are sometimes seen foraging in shrubby growth near streams, lakes, ponds and other wetlands. Opportunistic feeders, black bears have a liberal diet, including nuts, berries and other fruits, leaves from hardwoods, honey, fish, reptiles, insects, frogs and garbage. Although they have been extirpated from most of the central and north central United States, they once ranged throughout North America and are still found in many areas from coast to coast and from Mexico and Florida to northern Canada.

Female black bears breed and bear a litter every other year. Healthy, mature females usually give birth to two cubs in the winter den in January or February. The tiny, 6- to 12-ounce (170- to 340-gram) cubs are born blind, with eyes closed and covered with a fine mottled gray fur. Their eyes open in about one month, and they can walk after two months. They leave the den in their third month and are weaned in late summer but remain with their mother until their second summer (Figure 6-2). The young bears first mate when they are three and one-half years old. Black bears can live to be twenty-five years old.

People are more likely to encounter signs of black bears than the bears themselves. *Bear trees*, on which bears have scratched marks high up using claws and teeth, are a common sight in bear country. Except for people and dogs, black bears have few predators. They can, however, run up to 32 miles per hour (51.5 kilometers per hour) and are excellent tree climbers, where they can sometimes be found eating or taking a nap. Their repertoire of grunts, growls, snorts and bellows is another sign of their presence. Bears are commonly heard without being seen.

GRIZZLY BEAR. Because of their tremendous size, willingness to confront people and historic range from coast to coast, *grizzly bears* are the only modern North American animal that really challenged human beings for territory. Some biologists distinguish a separate species called the Alaskan brown bear, while others classify them all as grizzly bears. Their yellowish to dark brown fur often has a whitish frost to it, giving them their *grizzled* or gray appearance. Considered by many to be the most

---

Figure 6-2. Opposite. A black bear mother and her two cubs quench their thirst along the shore of a lake. The cubs may one day weigh nearly 600 pounds (272.2 kilograms) and can live as long as thirty years or more. Although it originally ranged throughout North America, the black bear has largely been eliminated from much of the central and north-central United States. Size: adult reaches a combined head and body length of 5 to 6 feet (1.5 to 1.8 meters) and a weight of 200 to 475+ pounds (91 to 215+ kilograms).

powerful carnivore that walks Earth, grizzlies, the largest bears, can weigh up to 1,500 pounds (680 kilograms), can charge up to 30 miles per hour (48.3 kilometers per hour) and, when standing on their hind feet, reach over 9 feet (2.7 meters) tall. They eat mostly carrion, salmon in season and a wide variety of other foods similar to what the black bear eats. Their wintering and breeding habits are like those of the black bear, except that the young are nearly hairless and females give birth in alternate years or every third year.

Grizzlies have survived in North America since the Pleistocene days of mastodons and saber-tooth tigers, when grizzlies stood over 12 feet (3.7 meters) on their hind legs! Since the arrival of European cultures, however, grizzlies have been poisoned, trapped and shot whenever they stood in the way of development or threatened livestock or people. While only a few people are hurt or killed by grizzlies each year, 84 percent of all grizzly deaths are caused by people. As a result of this slaughter, grizzly bears are now listed as a threatened species in the lower forty-eight United States and as endangered in Mexico. While there are healthy populations in Canada and Alaska, there are only about six hundred left in the northwestern Montana Rockies, about three hundred in Yellowstone National Park and a few in the Idaho panhandle.

POLAR BEAR. Barren rocky shores, islands and ice floes of the stark, frigid Arctic are the realm of the *polar bear*. Polar bears can weigh over 1,100 pounds (499 kilograms). Their fur may be white or a pale yellowish-white and the hollow hairs make remarkably efficient insulation. They are primarily carnivorous and feed mostly on seals but will also eat birds and fish. Polar bears have been known to hunt and eat human beings as well. Other foods include carrion and eggs. During the summer they will come ashore and supplement their diet with mosses, lichens, seaweed and other kinds of vegetation. They sometimes store food on the frozen ground or under the snow. Quite a bit of time is spent stalking basking seals along the shore and waiting by a breathing hole in the ice for a seal to come up for what may turn out to be its last breath.

Pregnant females overwinter in a den dug under a deep snowbank. Here, two cubs are born to the dormant mother. Males may also den up for shorter periods. The young remain with their mother until they are about two years old; females breed every other year. Polar bears spend a considerable amount of the year on and near the ice floes, and, with their webbed paws, they are excellent swimmers. Sometimes the young hold onto their mother's short tail in the water.

The Healing Vision

Bears are considered to be a source of power and invulnerability. They are believed to have great healing abilities. Many traditional Native North American healers are born into the bear clan. The image of a bear is frequently incorporated into healing ceremonies. Bears, which are remarkably free of disease in the wild, are admired for their wisdom as a sort of doctor. If one watches what a bear does when it is sick—what plants it eats, where it goes—one may find that those same plants and those same actions can be just as helpful for a human suffering from a similar illness. A strong tradition among many Native North American healers is that of finding the cure to any illness among the plants that grow in one's own homeland. If a bear is wounded, it knows enough to go to a place where there is mud that will help cover the wound and help it to heal faster. The motion picture *The Bear* depicts this with great accuracy.

The healing, heavenly bear that many now call the Big Dipper, the Great Bear, watches over and inspires us to walk our own good road and to discover how to live in a healing way with all our relations. Black Elk emphasizes the importance of first enacting a vision of how we can make a good change, in order to help our vision to become reality in this world. In preparation for acting out his vision Black Elk painted images from his vision to the four directions on the sides of a tepee made of bison hides. In "How Grizzly Bear Climbed the Mountain," Grizzly Bear is so selfish at first that he is told to leave his land forever. On his journey he creates a starry trail to the sky land that shows others how to make their way to the final hunting grounds. Grizzly Bear still rests among the stars for all to see as a symbol of transformation, of choosing to walk a good road.

QUESTIONS

1. What does Grizzly Bear do wrong in the story "How Grizzly Bear Climbed the Mountain"? What happens to him as a result?

2. What good deed does Grizzly Bear do to make amends as a gift to the other animals? Where can we see Grizzly Bear today?

3. Do bears and other animals have families? What can bears teach us about families?

4. What kinds of other animal families are you familiar with? How are these families similar and different than human families?

5. Why are families important to Native North Americans? What are their traditions that keep a family strong?

6. How are children treated in traditional Native North American families?

7. What kinds of animals have strong families?

8. Why do you think bears are seen as such close relatives to people in Native North American traditions? In what ways is a bear like a human being?

9. What are the three species of bears in North America? Are any of them a threatened or an endangered species? Which one(s)?

10. How big is a grizzly bear? What else do you know about grizzlies?

11. What do you know about black bears and polar bears? What do they eat? Where do they live?

12. Do any bears live near you? Have you ever seen a bear?

13. Are bears dangerous to people? Are people dangerous to bears?

14. What can bears teach us about healing? How do bears heal themselves when they get sick?

15. How can Grizzly Bear inspire us to heal our relationship with plants, animals and the rest of Earth, including other people?

ACTIVITIES
Journey to the Star Bear

ACTIVITY: Take a fantasy journey to the great, healing bear among the stars. Look down at Earth and see the home of our great family from on high. Return to Earth and see the bear for the first time as a guardian, healer and inspiration.

GOALS: Experience seeing our Earth home from the perspective of the sky to better understand how finite and fragile it really is. Understand that we are part of a family of all living things on Earth, and that we are all related. See the Great Bear among the stars as a guardian, healer and inspiration to guide us on our road to taking care of the plants and animals.

AGE: Younger children and older children

MATERIALS: Room that can be darkened; color picture or poster of Earth from space; Figure 4-8; enlarged copy of Figure 6-3; black construction paper or posterboard; white chalk or white tempera paint; small paintbrush, water and containers for paint; darkened room; sheets or other material for covers; tacks; bright flashlight or flashlight lantern; copy of *"Journey to the Star Bear";* and overhead projector and screen or sheet to project onto (optional).

PROCEDURE: *Note:* This activity can be conducted indoors as described below. If the night sky and the Big Dipper are visible, you can modify the activity to be conducted outdoors.

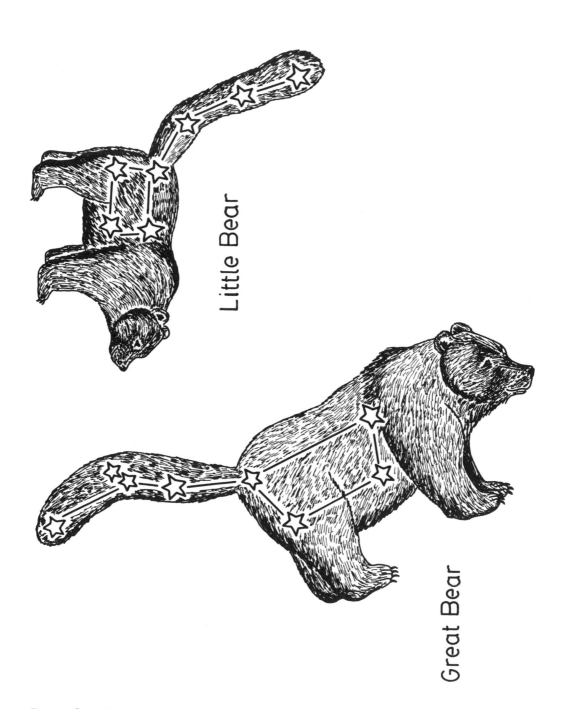

Figure 6-3. The images of the constellations of the Great Bear and Little Bear as they are imagined in the night sky. The Big Dipper is only a portion of the constellation called the Great Bear (Ursa Major), while the seven stars of the Little Dipper outline the entire constellation of the Little Bear (Ursa Minor).(Rotate this illustration clockwise 1/4 turn for the correct perspective.)

Beforehand, obtain a copy of a color picture or poster of Earth from space that is large enough to have all the children view it at once. A beautiful photograph or a color poster is best.[4] Look at Figure 4-8 for a map of the stars showing the circumpolar constellations (the North Star and constellations that revolve around it and so are always visible in the northern hemisphere). Share Figure 4-8 with the children. Show them Polaris, the North Star; the Little Bear (Ursa Minor), the Little Dipper; the Big Dipper in the Great Bear (Ursa Major); and the pointer stars showing the way from the Big Dipper to the North Star.

Create a large version of the image of the Great Bear among the stars from Figure 6-3 using black construction paper or posterboard and white dabs of paint for stars. White chalk can also be used but the stars will not be as bright. Set up the room for this activity so that the Earth image and bear image are hidden under covers that can be removed quickly during the fantasy. Use a room that is very dark, and focus a light on the Earth image and star bear to spotlight them one at a time, respectively, in the dark during the fantasy. A flashlight could be used.

Another option is to use an overhead projector to beam an enlarged image of a photograph of Earth and of Great Bear toward a screen, white sheet or light-colored wall at the appropriate time during the fantasy journey.

Now darken the space, shut off all lights and prepare the children for a guided fantasy journey to sky land (see Chapter 1). Be sure they are calm and quiet before beginning. Read the following journey. Note that the directions for you, the leader, are enclosed in parentheses and set in italics.

Journey to the Star Bear

You are going to take a great journey to a strange land that is far, far away. You begin one starry night as you are walking around. The sky is beautiful overhead. Bright stars and dim stars spangle the dark sky. As you look up you imagine them forming the shapes of many different animals. There, like a pale white path reaching across the night, is the band of stars in the Milky Way. There, too, are the seven stars of the Grizzly, Great Bear, the Big Dipper.

You are overtaken by an irresistible urge to follow that path of stars into the dark of night up toward Grizzly Bear. As you walk and wonder how this would feel, you notice your body begins to feel lighter and lighter. Now you're light as a feather, now as light as a speck of dust.

Gently and carefully you take a first step up into the sky, climbing toward the Milky Way. To your surprise, your feet bear your weight in thin air, and you are on your way to sky land. Soon you reach the Milky Way and walk toward Grizzly Bear, your feet stepping along tiny points of starlight.

Now you reach the stars of Grizzly. From there you look back at Earth.

(Uncover the photograph of Earth, shine the beam onto it and ask the children to open their eyes to look at Earth.)

It is a beautiful circle floating in space. The blue of its waters, the green of its forests and the white of its clouds make it appear like a shimmering jewel against the darkness. You realize that Earth is your home, and the home of all plants, animals, people and other forms of life. Many Native North Americans say "all our relations" when greeting plants, animals and people, addressing them like brothers and sisters.

You are suddenly aware of the size of Earth and that it will never be any bigger than it is now. Grizzly tells you that it is up to you and all of humankind to take care of Earth, our home.

(Shut off the beam and ask the children to close their eyes again.)

You begin to feel homesick and want to get your feet back on the ground.

Start walking back down along the Milky Way. The carpet of stars shimmers and glistens all around you, like sunlight reflecting off the water in little sparkles of light. Lower and lower you go until, finally, your feet touch Earth.

You turn and look back up at Great Bear in the sky.

(*Uncover the image of Great Bear among the stars. Ask the children to open their eyes and look at Great Bear as you highlight the image with the beam of light.*)

Bear looks down on us and reminds us of a mother bear and her cubs. She protects them, nurtures them, loves them and makes sure they have everything they need to live. Great Bear asks us to do the same for all our relations here on Earth because she is a great healer to Native North Americans. Now Great Bear reminds us that people need to treat Earth well, that the plants and animals need us to care for them, love them, share with them and heal our relationships with them—to act as friends and family to them. Great Bear will always be right above us in the stars to watch over us, guide us and inspire us to treat all our relations on Earth like members of our own families.

Wait in silence for a few moments before you turn on the lights. Allow time for the children to share their experiences and any thoughts and feelings they have. Can they think of any particular wild plant or animal that they want to have join their families? Ask them to share these plants and animals and write them down so they are not forgotten.

Follow this activity with *"The Healing Circles."*

The Healing Circles

ACTIVITY: (A) Choose a wild plant or animal that you want to bring into your family and into whose family you would want to be included. During a nighttime fire circle activity, bring that plant or animal into your family, ask to be brought into the plant's or animal's family and make a commitment to do all you can to love and care for that plant or animal. (B) Create your own vision of how you will care for that plant or animal in the future by writing a story, a play, a puppet show or a song, or by drawing a series of illustrations or whatever form of expression you choose.

GOALS: Appreciate our interrelatedness as one family on Earth: an ecological community of all things. Understand the nature of making a commitment to a wild plant or animal member of our family, to transform and heal our relationship with that plant or animal for the better, and following through to honor that commitment. Practice creating a reinforcing vision to empower a positive outcome for the plant's or animal's future. Understand that love, caring and sharing, as well as knowledge, action and commitment are essential to healing our relations with Earth and all plants and animals as symbolized by the plant or animal you have brought into your family. Understand the healing nature of bears.

AGE: Younger children and older children

MATERIALS: (A) *Needed to prepare for* "The Healing Circle": index cards; pencils; cut-out photographs and illustrations from magazines and newspapers—one of each plant or animal the children have chosen; scissors; paper; construction paper; posterboard; crayons; tempera paints; paintbrushes; water containers for paint. *Needed for* "The Healing Circle": matches; fire ring or fireplace; index cards with appropriate words written on them (both your words and the children's); the completed children's illustrations; stick to stir the ashes; shovel; metal container for the ashes; large pail of water to monitor the fire; "Discussion." (B) pencils; paper; other materials as needed for specific projects the children choose to care for their plants and animals; other materials as needed for the media in which children choose to record or enact their visions of positive relationships with those plants and animals.

PROCEDURE A: *Opening Our Family Circle*.

Note: Due to the highly personal nature of this activity, you—the leader—are advised to read it over carefully and assess whether it is appropriate for your children and their particular learning environment.

Beforehand, scout out a suitable, *safe* fire ring or fireplace to use after nightfall for "The Healing Circle." (See *"The Campfire"* in Chapter 5.) Now record on some index cards the words you will need to speak to lead this activity. Prepare an index card with the words that each child will speak as he or she brings a plant or animal into the family circle. Suggested words are found in the text of this activity. (Or you can wait and have the children make up their own words once they have chosen their plant or animal.)

Have each child choose a wild plant or animal that he or she wants to bring into the family and into whose family he or she wants to be brought. Children can use the plants and animals they thought of in the previous activity, *"Journey to the Star Bear,"* or any other plant or animal they choose at this time. Their plant or animal could be an endangered species or something local and common, such as an oak tree, a flower, a robin, a deer, a seal, an elk or a butterfly (depending on where you live). Have the children research and read about their plants and animals to better understand the kind of help they need to survive. If you have very young children, you may want to conduct the research about their plants and animals and read the findings to them. Children will now choose projects they will do to take care of the plant or animal they have brought into their family and include a description of these on the index card containing the words they will speak around the fire ring.

Now help the children to find photographs or illustrations of their plants and animals in magazines or newspapers—ones that they can cut out and keep. Have them create their own illustrations of the plants and animals on white paper, construction paper or posterboard. These could be simple line drawings, crayon sketches or paintings. Make sure they do not mark up the backsides of these illustrations. Then have the children create illustrations of their own likenesses on the flip sides of their drawings of the plant and animals. Place the original (model) photographs or illustrations of the plants and animals off to the side and save them for use later.

The Healing Circle

With their illustrations in hand, have the children form a circle outdoors around a fire ring after dark. (This can be done indoors in front of a fireplace, or with the burning to be done at a later time outdoors if necessary.) Share the brief information from the "Discussion" that describes bear families and the healing nature of bears, then read this short introduction to the group.

The mother bear shows us how to love and care for the members of our family. All of the people, plants, animals and other beings are members of one great family of relationships. We are an interconnected ecological community of all our relations sharing this Earth home. The bear shows us how we can heal and change our relationships to live well with members of this family.

The circle is an important symbol for our family, Earth and how we may live well with each other. We are about to enlarge the circle of our family and practice giving a gift back to the plants and animals to complete the circle that they began by giving to us. If we live in the way of the circle, life will go round and round with no end.

Now, one at a time, have each child take the illustration of his or her plant or animal into the center of the family circle and hold it up as she or he reads these words from the index card you have prepared ahead of time (or from cards containing the child's own words to the plant or animal if he or she has composed an original speech):

"*(Plant's or animal's name)*, I am your relation and you are mine. I now bring you into my family, and I ask you to bring me into your family. I will do all that I can to be a good relation. These are the things that I will try to do: *(child fills in specific projects here)*."

Then have the child carefully place the illustration of the plant or animal (that has the illustration of the child on the back) into the fire ring and return to his or her place in the circle.

Once all of the children have done this, light the illustrations on fire as you say, "These flames are the energy that now strengthens our relations. This smoke goes up as a reminder that we all live together on our Earth home and need to take care of one another."

When the flames have died down and ashes remain, stir them together and say, "As I stir these ashes, we all become one family."

Once the ashes have cooled thoroughly, bury them in the ground as you say "Thank you, Earth, for providing our family with all of the things we need to survive."

Finally, have each child take the original photograph or illustration of her or his plant or animal (the ones you put aside earlier) and hang it in a prominent place at home as a reminder of the new family member.

PROCEDURE B: *The Giving Circle.* Use the appropriate information and activities from throughout this and the other *Keepers* books to help the children create a plan for the many ways they can care for their plants and animals.[5] This plan will consist of two parts. The first part will be a detailed list of specific projects to carry out. The second part will consist of a positive "vision" of how their relationship with that plant or animal will grow. This can take the form of a story, illustration, poem, sculpture, play, puppet show or song—any form of expression the children choose. When one has a vision of what could come to be and believes in that vision, it becomes an empowering force and helps to overcome any hardships or hurdles encountered along the way.

EXTENDING THE EXPERIENCE
• Learn stories of other animal constellations that appear overhead in the starry night sky. Make up stories to go with these constellations and perform them for others as a play or puppet show.

• Create your own entirely new plant and animal constellations and stories from patterns you see among the stars. Draw star maps of these new constellations, write out their stories and share these with others while stargazing.

• Share other stories from the *Keepers* books that are about plants, animals and families. For example, "The Coming of Corn" and "How Fisher Went to the Skyland: The Origin of the Big Dipper" from *Keepers of the Earth;* "How the People Hunted the Moose," "Eagle Boy," "Salmon Boy," "The Woman Who Married a Frog" and "The Dogs Who Saved Their Master" from *Keepers of the Animals;* and "The Bitterroot" and "Blue Dawn" from *Keepers of Life.*

• As a follow-up to *"Journey to the Star Bear,"* use a star map and a package of glow-in-the-dark, stick-on stars to create the circumpolar constellations overhead on the children's bedroom ceiling or on dark paper taped to the ceiling of the learning center. Place Polaris, the North Star, directly overhead and form the other constellations accurately around Polaris. Now there are two bears—Little Bear (the Little Dipper) and Great Bear (in which the Big Dipper is located).

• Make a list of all the plants and animals brought by the children into their families during *"The Healing Circle."* Include in this list the things that the children promised to do to care for these plants and animals. Make copies of the list for the children as suggestions for how they can expand their family as well as their commitment to take action to care for these plants and animals.

NOTES

1. Frances G. Lombardi and Gerald Scott Lombardi. *Circle Without End: A Sourcebook of American Indian Ethics.* Happy Camp, Calif.: Naturegraph Publishers, 1982, p. 20.

2. A. Irving Hollowell. *Bear Ceremonialism in the Northern Hemisphere.* Thesis. Philadelphia, Penn., 1926. In Harold McCracken, *The Beast That Walks Like Man.* Garden City, N.Y.: Hanover House, 1955, p. 38.

3. George Bird Grinnell. *When Buffalo Ran.* New Haven, Conn., 1920, p. 38. In McCracken, p. 35.

4. A spectacular full-color poster, "The Full Earth," as photographed from space by Apollo 17 en route to the moon, is available from Hansen Planetarium, Publications Department, 1845 South 300 West, #A, Salt Lake City, UT 84115.

5. See the other books in the *Keepers* series for more information and activities on stewardship of plants and animals.

Glossary and Pronunciation Key to Native North American Words, Names and Cultures

The following rules are used for the phonetic description of how each word is pronounced:

1. A line appears over long vowels. Short vowels are unmarked. For instance, "date" would appear as dāt, while "bat" would appear as bat.

2. An accent mark (´) shows which syllable in each word or name is the one emphasized.

3. Syllables are broken with a hyphen (-).

4. Syllables are spelled out as they are pronounced. For instance, "Cherokee" appears as chair-oh-key.

Where appropriate, the culture from which each word or name comes is given in brackets { }, followed by the meaning of that word or name or an explanation of its significance as it appears in the text.

WORDS

aboriginal. A word sometimes used to refer to the original Native inhabitants of the American continents. Preferred by some people, especially in Canada, to terms such as "Indian" or "Native American."

Appanaug (App´-uh-nawg). {Wampanoag} A word meaning "clambake" or "seafood cooking."

bull roarer. A bull roarer is made by tying a flat piece of wood of a certain shape to a long string and whirling it around in a circle. Bull roarers are used by people all around the world, including Africans, Native Australians and Asians, as well as by various North American Native peoples. The sound may be interpreted as the voice of a powerful being or it may simply be used as a means of calling people together.

clan. In many Native nations, people are not only related by blood but by clan. Each clan is usually connected to and named after either an animal or a plant, and a clan is inherited at birth. If your people are matrilineal, as are the Haudenosaunee, then your clan is the same as your mother's.

Among the Mohawk Nation of the Haudenosaunee today there are three clans: Turtle, Wolf and Bear. Even though someone may not be related to you by blood, if they are of your clan then you have a bond with them. Further, in many cases you are not supposed to marry someone who belongs to your own clan. This clan system creates bonds within the culture outside of your own family and also ensures that different clans will constantly be linked to each other by marriage.

da neho (dah ney-hō´). {Haudenosaunee} Means "I have spoken."

Fifth World. {Diné} According to the Diné Creation story, the world in which we live is the fifth in a series of worlds that were deserted or destroyed as a result of wrong-doing.

haeyo (hey´-ōh). {Pima} A game played by throwing stones into holes dug in the ground some distance apart. This game or Native games like it are the probable precursors of the contemporary game of horseshoes.

hageota (hah-gey-ōh´-tah). The Haudenosaunee word for "storyteller."

Ha-wen-ne-yu (Hah-wah-ney´-yu). Haudenosaunee word for the Creator, the "Holder up of the Heavens."

ji-ji-ya. Vocables—words sung in a Haudenosaunee song that have no translation, a bit like "tra-la-la" in English ballads. These are not regarded as "nonsense words," however, but as sounds that carry emotion and power.

Johannaa'ei (Jo-hah-na-ah´-ey-ēē). {Diné} The Sun. Literally "the One Who Governs the Day." Described in traditional stories as the father of the hero twins and a source of powerful things that help the people.

kaganagah (kah´-gah-nah-gah). Inuit game played with sealskins and disks of wood and bone.

Kan-ya-ti-yo (Gah´-nyō-di´-yō). Literally "it is a beautiful lake," the Onondaga word for the lake now known as Ontario.

Kesosasit (Kay-sōh-sah´-sit). {Menominee} Literally "the place where the sun is marked on the rocks," a location on the shores of Lake Michigan.

madagenilhas (mah-tah´-gey-nill-hahs). Abenaki word for bat. Literally "fur-hide bird."

Medawlinno (meh-daw´-lēē-noh). {Abenaki} "Scholar," one who is learned. A diviner. The root of the word is medawila, which means "loon." Thus, it implies that the medawlinno is one who dives down to the world of spirits to find answers.

medicine. As this word is used in contemporary Native American cultures it refers both to medicinal preparation used for curing illnesses and to things that may bring good fortune or a certain kind of power.

Medicine Man. A term used in some (but not all) contemporary Native cultures to refer to a man who uses various kinds of medicines and ceremonies for physical, mental and spiritual healing. Some Native nations, such as the Cherokee, simply prefer to refer to these people as "Indian doctors."

Medicine Society. Among some Native nations, such as the Onondaga, those people who have learned a certain kind of knowledge and then been accepted and initiated into a group devoted to a certain kind of ceremonial practice are referred to as belonging to a "Medicine Society."

métis (meh-tēē´). A word in French meaning "mixed blood." It is used to refer in Canada to a nation of people who are themselves Métis and are of Native and European ancestry. At one point in Canadian history the Métis people came very close to secession and forming their own nation.

Michgami (Mitch-ee-gah´-mēē). {Menominee} Literally "big lake." The name for Lake Michigan.

nokehick (no-kē´-hik). {Narragansett} Literally "parched cornmeal." Today, nokehick refers to a type of corn cake which is also known as johnnycake.

Oot-Kwah-Tah (Oot-gwah´-dah). {Onondaga} The Seven Star Dancers, known to Europeans as The Pleiades.

Paguas (Pah-gwas´). {Maliseet} The moon. Literally "the one who borrows light from the sun."

petroglyph. Shapes scraped or pecked into stone.

pictograph. Shapes painted onto stone.

piñola (pēē-nyo´-lah). Pine nuts. Nuts of the piñon pine.

quoits. Native American game, precursor to horseshoes.

shaman. A Siberian word used to refer to a medicine person or a diviner who calls upon the spiritual world for help in his or her work. Sometimes used by non-Natives to refer to Native medicine people.

squaw (skwaw). {Abenaki} Word originally derived from "squa," meaning "woman." In contemporary vernacular, "squaw" often refers to women in a derogatory way and its use is discouraged.

succotash. {Narragansett} A dish made of beans, squash and corn.

Tarak'ut inilgit (Tah-rahk-uht-ee´-nil-get). {Inuit} A word for a shaman or medicine person. Literally means "those who have eyes in the dark."

T'cho (T´-chō). {Yuchi} The sun.

tepee. {Lakota} Also spelled tipi. The word for house or dwelling place.

Three Sisters. The term used by the Haudenosaunee to refer to Corn, Beans and Squash, who are seen as Three Maidens who help to sustain the people by providing them with food.

Thunderbird. A powerful being in the shape of a great bird. The lightning is sometimes seen as coming from the Thunderbird's eyes, the thunder the beat of its wings. Native people of the west and the Great Plains speak of the Thunderbird. In the northeast, Native people speak of the Dew Eagle as the counterpart of the Thunderbird. Thunder is also seen as a man-shaped powerful being, a "Grandfather" by many Native nations.

Tle'ehoonaa'ei (Dleh´-ey-oo-nah-ah´-ey-ēē). {Diné} The moon. Literally "The One Who Governs the Night."

wampum. The purple and white shells of the quahog clam that were shaped into disks and strung into patterns by the Native people of the northeast. Wampum was not originally used as money but as a record of agreements between nations. The use of wampum as currency originated with European Americans.

NAMES OF INDIVIDUALS

Black Elk (1863–1950). {Oglala Lakota} Hehaka Sapa (Hey-hah-kah´ Sah´-pah) or "Black Elk" was a Lakota medicine man who first became known to readers in 1932 with the publication of John Neihardt's *Black Elk Speaks: The Life Story of an Oglala Holy Man. The Sacred Pipe,* recorded and edited by Joseph Epes Brown, contains Black Elk's account of the Seven Rites of the Oglala Sioux.

Charles Alexander Eastman (1858–1939). {Santee Dakota} Also known by his Dakota name "Ohiyesa," (Oh-hee-yey´-sah) which means "The Winner." His autobiographical book, *Indian Boyhood,* which tells of his being raised in a traditional manner among his Dakota people, was published in 1902. Eastman, a prolific writer, was a graduate of Dartmouth and Boston University, became a practicing physician and worked as a doctor among the Lakota at the time of the Wounded Knee massacre. One of the founders of the Boy Scouts of America, his many books were influential in shaping the public perception of life among his people.

Chief Irving Powless, Sr. (1905–1985). {Onondaga} Chief of the Onondaga Nation from the 1960s until he passed away at the age of 79, Irving Powles, Sr. dedicated his life to the causes of the Onondaga and the Longhouse. Fluent in the speeches and ceremonies of the Haudenosaunee, Chief Powless spent much of his time at the Longhouse working for the benefit of the People. He devoted considerable time and energy to preserving the traditions of the Onondaga and other Haudenosaunee cultures. Chief Powless was an accomplished and respected orator. His famous "Thanksgiving Speech" was presented to many important gatherings of the Six Nations Iroquois Confederacy.

Chief Luther Standing Bear (1868–1939). {Oglala Lakota} Born and raised in the period when the traditional life of the Lakota people was drastically being changed, Standing Bear was educated at Carlisle Indian School in Pennsylvania before returning to teach in the reservation schools at Rosebud and Pine Ridge. Eventually he moved to Los Angeles where he worked as an actor in the movies. In Los Angeles he wrote the four books for which he is remembered: *My People, The Sioux* (1928), *My Indian Boyhood* (1931), *Land of the Spotted Eagle* (1933) and *Stories of the Sioux* (1934).

Crowfoot (1830–1890). {Blackfoot} Crowfoot, Isapo Moxica (Ee-sah-poh Moh-shee´-kah), was one of the most famous of the leaders of the Blackfoot/ Blood peoples in the nineteenth century. The Blackfoot were the last of the Native nations of the plains to sign a treaty (in 1877) with the Canadian government. Crowfoot is known for his attempts to lead his people without bloodshed along the road of peace with the Europeans, often against great odds.

Ella Sekatau. (Seh´ -kah-taw) {Narragansett} Dr. Ella Sekatau DHL is ethno-historian and cultural education consultant for the Narragansett Indian Tribe. She is also a political activist and an accomplished artisan well known for her fine weavings and embroidery. Ella Sekatau was instrumental in the reconstruction of the seventeenth-century New England Indian village at Plimoth Plantation in Plymouth, Massachusetts. Her contribution to documenting the history of the Narragansett people helped to bring about the recognition of the Narragansett by the U.S. government in 1983.

Kanietakeron (Gah-nee-ey-da-gey´-loo). {Mohawk (Iroquois)} This traditional name for David Kanietakeron Fadden, who was born in the month of March, means "Patches of Snow." He is a member of the Wolf Clan from the Mohawk Community of Akwesasne and is Museum Educator at the Iroquois Indian Museum in Howes Cave, New York. In addition to the story illustrations for *Keepers of the Night,* his work has appeared in *Keepers of the Animals* and numerous Native American publications including *Akwesasne Notes, Indian Time* and materials from the Six Nations Indian Museum where he works to preserve Haudenosaunee traditions.

Russell M. Peters. {Wampanoag} Russell M. Peters, whose Indian name is Fast Turtle, is a former President of the Wampanoag Indian Tribal Council. He was director of the film series for public television called "People of the First Light" about the Native American cultures of New England. He is the author of two books: *The Wampanoags of Mashpee* (1987) and *Clambake: A Wampanoag Tradition* (1992).

CULTURES

Abenaki (Ab´-eh-na-kee). Means "Dawn Land People." People living at the sunrise, "People of the Dawn." A northeastern Algonquian group of the area now known as Vermont, New Hampshire, southern Quebec, northern Massachusetts and western Maine. One of the Wabanaki (Wa´-bah-na-kee) "Dawn Land" peoples who also include the Micmac, Maliseet, Passamaquoddy, Pennacook and Penobscot. These peoples once formed a loose alliance or confederacy (circa 1750–1850) that held triannual meetings at Caughnawaga, Quebec. In recent years the Abenaki, and other Wabanaki peoples, have strengthened and celebrated in common their rich cultures.

Anishinabe (Ah-nish-ih-nah´-bey). Means "First Men" or "Original Men." The Native people found in the central and northern Great Lakes areas of North America. They are the same people known as the Ojibway and the Chippewa, names applied to them in the last few centuries and used widely today by Anishinabe people themselves. *Ojibway* (O-jib´-i-weg) was a name given them by their neighbors and probably means "Those Who Make Pictographs." *Chippewa* is a variant of Ojibway. (Ojibway is also translated as "puckered up" referring to their moccasin style, puckered in front.) Currently the Anishinabe is one of the largest Native groups, with a U.S. and Canadian population of over 160,000.

Aniyunwiya (Ah-nēē-yoon´-wi-yah). The name the Cherokee use for themselves, means "The Real People." They also call themselves Tsa-la-gi (which became "Cherokee"), derived from the Choctaw *chiluk-ki,* which means "Cave Dwellers." The Cherokee, a large southeastern culture, along with the Choctaw, the Chickasaw, the Creek and the Seminole (who were themselves, a branch of the lower Creek Nation) were called the "Five Civilized Tribes" because they successfully adopted white ways. The fact that they were only called "civilized" because they had taken on certain culture traits from the European-based immigrants is an expression of the ethnocentric attitudes toward Native people held by the white culture.

Aztec (Az´-tek). A group of peoples in central Mexico who share the Nahuatl language and certain social customs. Although they referred to themselves as "Mexica," the name "Aztec" comes from Aztlan, a semi-mythical location from which the Mexica traveled before coming to the Valley of Mexico, where a great city was constructed on the islands in Lake Texcoco. The Aztecs are known today for their monumental architecture, including giant stone pyramids and their highly urbanized culture. Much of their culture was destroyed in the Spanish conquest and in the years that followed, including most of their books in picture writing which were used to record history, pharamacology, religious beliefs, taxes and censuses and many other aspects of their way of life.

Baffin Island Inuit (In´ -you-it). Once referred to as "Eskimo," a non-Inuit word meaning "fish eaters," the Native people of Baffin Island, a large island off the northeast Arctic coast of Canada, refer to themselves as the Nunatsiqmuit, "The people of the beautiful land." They are closely related in language and culture to the many other Inuit groups found in Greenland, northern Canada, Alaska and Asia. Their way of life has been traditionally dependent both upon the animals of the land, especially the caribou and the fish and large aquatic animals of the ocean. Their clothing, made from a mixture of animal skins and furs, has been described as the most efficient cold-weather gear ever invented and their skin boat, the kayak (quayak), has been adopted by the modern world as a sport craft that is unparalleled in maneuverability and durability.

Blackfoot. *See* Siksika.

Cherokee (Chair-oh-key´). *See* Aniyunwiya.

Colville (Kōl´-vill). *See* Okanagan.

Dakota (Dah-kō´-tah) *See* Sioux.

Diné (Dih-ney´). "Navajo." Diné means "The People." The most numerous of the Native nations in the United States with over 200,000 people, most of whom live on the huge Navajo Reservation. Covering 15 million acres in the Four Corners area where the states of New Mexico, Arizona, Colorado and Utah come together, the Navajo Reservation is the size of West Virginia. The Navajo, like the Apache (who called themselves *Tineh*), are close relatives of the Athabascan peoples of Alaska and the northwest and speak a similar language. They migrated from the north to the southwest more than a thousand years ago. The name *Navajo,* which means "Enemy People," was given to them by the original residents of the southwest, the Pueblo peoples, whose villages they often raided. The typical Navajo dwelling is an eight-sided, dome-shaped, single-family structure called a *hogan.* At present, the lands of the Navajo and their traditional ways of life are being seriously threatened by commercial mining interests that wish to strip much of the land for coal and uranium.

Haudenosaunee (Hō-dē-nō-show´-nē). Iroquois name for themselves which means "People of the Longhouse." The Iroquois lived in large bark longhouses, each house holding as many as sixty people and headed by a clan mother. The word *Iroquois* is a corruption of the Abenaki word *Ireokwa,* which means "Real Snakes." Their language is related to that of the Sioux and the Cherokee, and their traditions tell of a migration from the west. The Iroquois people were originally five nations—the Mohawk, the Oneida, the Onondaga, the Cayuga and the Seneca. Their traditional territory included most of present-day New York state, from the Hudson River to the Niagara. Centuries ago the Creator sent the Peacemaker to the five nations, who were engaged in constant warfare. With the aid of Hiawatha and the woman known as Jigonsaseh, the Peacemaker formed a league of peace, unity and strength symbolized by a great white pine tree with a vigilant eagle perched atop it clutching five arrows. The Iroquois League was an important influence on the formation of the U.S. system of government and on the drafting of the U.S. Constitution. The Tuscaroras were admitted to the Iroquois League in 1722 after many refugees from the Tuscarora Wars (1711–1713) in the southeast fled northward. Iroquois people today are found on thirteen reservations and reserves in New York State, Quebec, Ontario and Wisconsin.

Hopi (Hō´-pēē). Means "The Peaceful Ones." The Hopi have a long history of resolving conflicts through peaceful means. Their extremely sophisticated knowledge of dry-land farming has enabled them to survive in the arid mesa regions of what is now northern Arizona, where their multi-level, multiple-residency structures of adobe and wood have stood for centuries. Some Hopi buildings have been continuously inhabited for more than five hundred years. The Hopi's artistic traditions include weaving and pottery, both of which they say were given them by the benevolent Grandmother Spider, who is seen as one of the primary creative forces. Hopi prophecies speak of past worlds destroyed by misdeeds and of a possible future cataclysm if human beings do not follow a way of life in balance with the natural world and all its beings. Their present-day lands are completely surrounded by the huge Navajo reservation.

Inuit (In´-you-it). The name used for themselves which means "Real People." The Native peoples who are found widely across the far north, including Siberia, Alaska, Canada and Greenland.

Not regarded by themselves or "Indians" as "American Indian." The word "Inupiaq" is used in Alaska and western Canada. There are many different Inuit groups around the Arctic, who speak in varying dialects. However, they recognize their kinship and have adopted the name "Inuit" to apply to all peoples once called "Eskimo." A knowledge of the animals of ocean and land is vital for survival in the far north, as is an attitude of respect and gratitude. Distinctive Inuit practices include methods of winter travel over tundra and sea ice, hunting and fishing techniques for capturing marine and land animals, specialized tool designs, unique social customs and strong oral traditions. They are well-known for their use of skin boats, harpoons, oil lamps and spear throwers. Contemporary Inuit people survive by combining the new with the old and by making their reliance upon nature and their respect for it a central part of their new way of life.

Iroquois (Ear´-ōh-kwah). *See* Haudenosaunee.

Kwakiutl (Kwah-gyūhlt´). The name "Kawakiutl" is applied today to a group of fifteen different tribal nations of similar language and culture located on and in the area of Vancouver Island off the Pacific coast of present-day British Columbia. The name now most commonly used by these allied peoples is Kwa-kwa-ka'wakw, which means simply "Kwakwalu-Speaking People." The Kwakiutl people developed a rich culture in balance with the ocean and the land. Great boat-builders, their houses were large buildings made of cedar planks and they are still known today for their skill as wood-carvers. Without agriculture, they developed a rich way of life that affords them enough leisure time to develop one of the more intricate social and religious systems on the continent, including the potlatch give-away ceremonies which ensured that the material wealth amassed by powerful individuals would eventually be shared among the people.

Lakota (Lah-kōh´ tah). *See* Sioux.

Lenape (Len-ah´-pāy) (Delaware). The full name of this ancient confederacy of Native nations— *Lenni Lenape*—translates as "We, The People," or "The Real People." Their traditional area is the mid-Atlantic coast, between present-day Connecticut and northern Delaware, controlling much of the Hudson and Delaware River valleys, including the area of present-day New York City. Because of their location, they were called "Delawares." Another name applied to them has been "Munsee," which comes from *Minisink*, "People from the Stony Country," one of the three principal tribal bands making up their confederacy. Removed in the nineteenth century, while some Lenape remain in their original homelands, the largest communities of Lenape people today are in Ontario, Wisconsin and Oklahoma.

Luiseño (Lews-en´-yō). One of the Native nations of southern California, the name "Luiseño" comes from San Luis Rey, which was a Spanish mission placed in their traditional territories. Rather than a single unified tribal nation, the Luiseño peoples were made up of many different villages, each with its own well-defined hunting, gathering and fishing territories and each apparently calling itself by the name of its village. Thus, there is no one word in a Native language which we can easily substitute for "Luiseño." Their diverse environment, ranging from high mountains to seashore, provided a great variety of food sources, one of the most important of which was the acorn. Despite the harsh treatment they endured under Spanish rule and the Gold Rush years between 1849 and 1859, in which two-thirds (about 70,000 people) of the Native peoples of California were murdered or killed by disease, the Luiseño have survived. There are seven contemporary bands of the Luiseño, including the Twenty Nine Palms band of Mission Indians in Palm Springs and the La Jolla Band of Valley Center.

Maliseet (Mah´-lih-sēet). The Maliseet people are part of the Wabanaki nations of northern New England, northeastern neighbors to the Passamaquoddy of Maine (whose language is almost identical) and southwestern neighbors to the Micmac of New Brunswick and Quebec. The name "Maliseet" probably comes from a Micmac word that means "lazy speakers." Like the Passamaquoddy, the traditional yearly round of activities ranged from inland hunting and gathering to seashore fishing and the hunting of marine mammals. The Maliseet people of New Brunswick call themselves Walastawkwiyak, which means "People of the Beautiful River."

Menominee (Meh´-nahme-nēe). The traditional homeland of the Menominee or "Wild Rice People" is in northern Michigan and Wisconsin, where the gathering of wild rice was one of their mainstays. Like other Algonquin peoples of the northeast, they practiced some farming of squash, corn and beans, but were also expert hunters, fishers and gatherers. The Menominee have become well known in recent years for their determination in successfully fighting the federal policy of termination. In 1953 the House Concurrent Resolution 108 set forth a policy of gradually terminating all Indian Reservations, without the permission of the Native nations themselves. The Menominee of Wisconsin were the first terminated, in 1961, when their reservation became Menominee County. The Menominee community no longer could afford to keep up its hospital, its housing deteriorated and unemployment increased. They also immediately began to lose their land because of unrealistically high taxes and the pressure of non-Native developers. The Menominee, however, refused to give up and reservation status was restored to them in 1973.

Mohawk (Mō´-hawk). Abenaki word *maquak*, used to refer to the Haudenosaunee who live in the area of Mohawk Valley in New York State and call themselves *Kanienkahageh* ("People of the Flint"). Name means "Cowards." *See* Haudenosaunee.

Muskogee (Mus-kō´-jēe) (Creek). One of the "Five Civilized Tribes." The meaning of "Muskogee," the word the Creek use for themselves, is unknown. They were named "Creek" by the English, who observed that their villages were always near small streams. Their language is similar to that of the Choctaw and the Seminole, who are actually an offshoot of the Lower Creek Nation. Their original homelands stretched along the Atlantic Coast from Georgia through Alabama. They were forced to leave their lands in the southeast and migrate to the Indian Territory between 1836 and 1840 and brought many of their traditional village names and family structures with them to Oklahoma, as well as traditional religious practices, songs and Stomp Dances, which are carefully maintained to this day. One of their most important ball games was a forerunner of contemporary hockey. The Green Corn Ceremonial is the peak of their annual religious celebrations. Today the highly progressive Creek Nation is organized into nineteen towns in eastern Oklahoma, with its central offices in Okmulgee.

Narragansett (Nayr-ah-gahn´-sett). The Narragansett, the "People of the Small Bay," were one of the larger and more important tribal nations of the area now known as New England. Present-day Rhode Island approximates the traditional territory of the Narragansetts who drew on both the sea and the forests, as well as farming, for their subsistence. Their current tribal offices are located in Charlestown, Rhode Island.

Navajo (Nah´-vah-hō). *See* Diné.

Netsilik Inuit {Eskimo}. *See* Inuit.

Oglala Lakota {Sioux}. *See* Sioux.

Okanagan (Oh-kah-nah´-gun). Name for a Native people of the Pacific Northwest. The Colville are a division of Okanagan. Okanagan is usually translated as "People Who See to the Top." The traditional territory of the Okanagan people is located in present-day eastern Washington. The contemporary Colville Reservation, in Nespelem, Washington, incorporates Okanagan and nine other Native tribal nations.

Onondaga (On-un-dah´-gah). Means "The Place Among the Hills." One of the five original Haudenosaunee nations. Onondaga is the place where the Great Pine Tree, the emblem of their League of Peace, is symbolically planted. The contemporary city of Syracuse, New York, is on Onondaga land and a large part of the city is still leased from the Onondaga Nation. *See* Iroquois.

Paiute (Pie´-yoot). The Native peoples known today as the "Paiute" are made up of a number of culturally and politically different populations that shared a common language and whose traditional territories include much of Nevada, eastern Oregon and parts of northeastern California. In some areas salmon fishing was of great seasonal importance. In others fishing was of minor importance. All the various Paiute groups were efficient hunters and gatherers and although they lived in well-defined set territories, regular seasonal migrations took place to benefit from whatever sources of subsistence were available at that time. Dome-shaped or cone-shaped houses made of willow frames overlaid by woven tule mats were common throughout the region. The name "Paiute," like the name "Ute" is a loan word from another Native language, and its meaning and exact origin are uncertain. The Paiute people simply call themselves *Nimi*, which means "People."

Pima (Pēē´-mah). The Pima, along with their neighbors the Papago, call themselves *Tohono O'odham*, which means "Desert People." The name "Pima" appears to originate with a phrase used to answer the many questions the early Spanish asked them and which the Pima preferred not to answer: *Pi nyi maach*, which means "I do not know." Sophisticated and peaceful desert farmers, the Pima still live in a portion of the original ancestral lands in Arizona.

Santee Dakota (San´ -tēē Dah-kō´-tah) {Sioux}. The easternmost of the Sioux nations. In the 1700s

and 1800s their traditional lands included the area now known as Minnesota. *See* Sioux.

Shawnee (Shaw´-nēē). The name "Shawnee" comes from the Shawnee self-designation *sawanwa*, which means "person of the south." Made up of many different groups, who occupied areas throughout much of what is now known as the South and the Midwest, they have been associated at various times with the Lenape, the Muskogee and the Haudenosaunee, and they seem to have been a people frequently in movement, even before the coming of the Europeans.

Shoshone (Shōw-shōw´-nēē). The name "Shoshone," which is said to mean "Snake People," is of uncertain origin and may come from a word in another Native language. The traditional territories of the Western Shoshone people, from Death Valley in California through central Nevada and into northern Utah, were among the last to be settled by European Americans. It was not until 1935 that a large number of the Western Shoshone were settled onto the newly organized reservations and several major groups still refused to participate. The gathering of plants, especially seeds such as those of the pine nut, have been of great importance for their subsistence, although they also hunted a wide variety of game animals such as the bighorn sheep and the pronghorn antelope, especially in communal hunts or drives. Clothing was made of skins and rabbit-skin robes were often used in winter. Winter shelters were conical and covered with bark, while circular brush dwellings were common in summer. The Western Shoshone refer to themselves as *Niwi*, or "People." Today, the traditional Western Shoshone people are still engaged in a struggle to regain control of land which they say was illegally taken from them.

Siksika (Sik-sih´-ka). A people of the northern plains, especially Montana and the province of Alberta in Canada. The name Siksika means "black foot" and refers to the black-dyed moccasins that were traditionally favored. Like many other of the northern Plains peoples, the Blackfoot followed the buffalo herds and reshaped their culture around the horse after its introduction sometime in the early eighteenth century.

Sioux (Sū). Perhaps the best-known Native peoples of North America today are the people popularly known as the Sioux. (Sioux is a name that comes from the Anishinabe word *nadowe-is-iw*, a word that means "snakes," indicating the Sioux were their enemies.) They called themselves either

Dakota or Lakota, depending on whether they spoke the Eastern or the Western dialect of their languages and also referred to themselves as *Ocheti Lakowin* (Oh-che-ti Lah-ko-win), "The Seven Council Fires." The Dakota are one of the seven main "council fires" of the Sioux people. *Dakota* in the Santee Sioux dialect means "Allies" and refers to the Sioux of the eastern plains of Minnesota. The Oglala Sioux are one of the branches of the western Lakota people.

Wampanoag (Wom-pah-nō´-ag). Literally "Dawn Earth People" or "People of the East" and often translated as "People of the First Light." Their original homeland is the area now known as eastern Rhode Island, Cape Cod and coastal Massachusetts. The Pilgrims landed on Wampanoag land in 1620 and were saved from starvation by the Wampanoag. In 1675, led by Metacomet (King Philip), the Wampanoag fought an unsuccessful war to stop the English settlers who were, by then, driving out the Native peoples. Although they were scattered by the English, the Wampanoag fought to maintain their tribal identity and have survived as Native people. The largest Wampanoag communities today are found in the area of Martha's Vineyard and Nantucket.

Yuchi (Yū´-chēē). The name "Yuchi" means "Located Over Yonder." One explanation of this name is that it was a reply given to a European who asked their identity and was given their location instead. The original home of the Yuchi people was the area now known as Georgia and Carolina. The "Westo" people for whom the Savannah River was originally named are actually the Yuchi. Like the other Native peoples of the southeast, they were sophisticated farmers, and there is specula-tion that some of the great mounds and other earthworks of the southeast were Yuchi in origin. They have long been associated with the Muskogee (Creek) nation, having been brought into the great pre-Columbian Muskogee Confederacy along with a large number of other southeastern tribal nations. The Indian Removal Bill of 1830 resulted in the forced relocation of most of the Muskogee and their allied nations to Oklahoma and the Yuchi went along with them, although some chose to follow other Muskogee people (The Lower Creeks) into Florida where they became part of the Seminoles or *Isti simanole*, a Muskogee phrase meaning "those who have broken away." The Yuchi language is very different from Creek, but in large part, the Yuchi people have been associated with and even absorbed into the contemporary Creek nation. The Yuchi Tribe of Oklahoma maintains tribal offices in care of the Creek Nation in Okmulgee.

Zuni (Zoo´-nēē). A Pueblo people who call themselves *Siwi*, a name whose meaning is not known. Their traditional homeland is along the banks of the Zuni River, in the 200-square-mile area just west of the Continental Divide on the border between New Mexico and Arizona. The Zuni's present-day population of about six thousand people makes it the largest of the Pueblo nations. The Zuni are a highly philosophical and religious people, and many of their ceremonies remain closed to all outsiders. The great early winter celebration of Shalako, one of the most spectacular of all Native ceremonies, remains open to all who come. The poetic nature of their songs and stories is shown in recent translations of Zuni narratives, such as Dennis Tedlock's *Finding the Center* (Dial, 1972).

Other Versions of Native North American Stories

Joseph Bruchac

All of these stories may be found published elsewhere. The tellings I have done have been influenced not only by written versions, but also by versions I have heard told and by conversations with storytellers from these traditions. Below is a list of books containing these stories and others I recommend to those who wish to know more about these traditions.

"The Birth of Light." *Native American Legends,* compiled and edited by George E. Lankford (August House Press).

"How the Bat Came to Be." An fine version of this often-told story appears in Basil Johnston's *Tales the Elders Told* (Royal Ontario Museum).

"Moth, the Fire Dancer." *Why the North Star Stands Still and Other Indian Legends* by William R. Palmer (Zion Natural History Association).

"Oot-Kwah-Tah, The Seven Star Dancers" is one of the most widely told Native stories of the northeast. I know of more than twenty written versions. One of the best is in Arthur Parker's *Seneca Myths and Legends* (University of Nebraska Press).

"The Creation of the Moon." Again, there are many versions of this tale which is part of the Diné Creation epic. I especially recommend *Diné Bahane, The Navajo Creation Story* by Paul G. Zolbrod (University of New Mexico Press).

"Chipmunk and the Owl Sisters." Jay Silverheels tells a version of this in his tape *Indian Wisdom Stories* (Canyon). With the permission of Jeannette Armstrong, who is authorized by her Okanagan people to tell this story, I have modeled my telling after a version done by her great-aunt Mourning Dove in the book *Coyote Stories* (University of Nebraska Press).

"The Great Lacrosse Game." This story is told throughout the northeast and the southwest. I know of twelve different versions. A Cherokee version of the tale by Lloyd Arneach was published as *The Animal's Ballgame* (Children's Press). My own telling of the Creek version was published as "The Great Ball Game" (Dial).

"How Grizzly Bear Climbed the Mountain." *Indian Legends from the Northwest* by Ella Clark (University of Oklahoma Press).

Index